AUTOROUTES
TO THE SUN
GUIDE

by

Karol Libura

LE GUIDE (UK) • **London**

Published by LE GUIDE (UK), London

First published May 1986

This edition published March 1987

©Copyright 1986 M.K.Libura, London

ISBN 0 9511254 1 9

All rights reserved.

No part of this publication may be reproduced, stored in a retrieval system, or transmited, in any form or by any means, electronic, mechanical, photo-copying, recording, or otherwise, without the prior permission of the publisher.

Printed and bound in Great Britain
by
Kingprint International, Richmond, Surrey.

FOREWORD
(To the first edition)

This Guide, I consider to be a unique publication in its form and content and is primarily meant for the users of the motorway from Calais to the French Riviera, all the way to Menton – the "Pearl of France" according to the proud announcement at the motorway's exit, which welcomes you to that splendid place, right at the Italian border.

The Guide has been the consequence of my utter frustration over the years, driving to the South of France with no apparent choice of suitably compiled information on the subject and readily obtainable on the market.

So there we are, here is "The Motorway To The Sun, Guide", which hopefully presents most of the relevant information in ONE, which will make the driving to the Sun a more pleasurable experience, as the journey could be planned in detail, well before it begins, and any changes required at the last minute could be tailored again, exactly to your needs.

The hotels shown through the Guide are offering top quality services in their respective range of ratings and warm hospitality will make you a welcome guest regardless of those ratings.

Most of the information, given in this Guide, is checked personally and correct at the time, but obviously, it has to be appreciated that misinterpretation, omission or resulting consequence cannot be a subject of the Publisher's responsibility.

This is the first edition of the Publication and therefore your comments in particular, are very welcome, as by such a response the future editions, no doubt expanded and improved, will inevitably remain unique to the satisfaction of us all.

I am looking forward to hearing from you, enjoy the Guide,

BON VOYAGE.

Karol Libura
March, 1986

CONTENTS

Look no further	page 7
Introduction	9
The toll	10
Telephoning	11
Symbols indicating some of the services	13
Hotels	14
Hotel details;	
— along the Route	64
— in Paris	54
— on the Riviera and along the coast	131
Listing of hotel locations	14
At-a-glance diagrams for planning your trip	16
Check-list	22
The AA's 5-Star Service information	23
L'Arche restaurants	24
News Letter	25
Some of the expressions that you will meet along the routes	27
Some tips and further information	30
The Beaune Memorial to the Victims and Road Safety 112	
French national holidays	35
French expressions;	
— days of the week	35
— months of the year	35
— numbers	36
— how to book a room in a hotel	36
From English to French: some useful expressions	36
Parts of the car and associated vocabulary	37
Conversion tables	38
Tyre pressures	39
A vous Paris	41
Your guide to Le Guide	62

The actual routes (going South) 69

    Calais — Paris   70
    Caen — Paris   80
    Paris — Bordeaux   88
    Paris — Menton   102
    Orange — Perpignan (Spanish border)   140

The actual route (going North) 151

    Perpignan (spanish border) — Orange   152
    Menton — Calais   162
    Bordeaux — Paris   194
    Paris — Caen   206

LOOK NO FURTHER

"......... a handy little book which no one using the French Autoroute from Calais to the Riviera should be without."

The Times

And now, read the following comments upon the publication from the very users of the first edition ;-

" ... as regular visitors to the South of France for very many years we have studied your guide carefuly and we think it is excellent and we certainly recommend it."

Frank and Pamela Reade
from Liverpool,

" ... we found the information invaluable on our journey down through France, and await your next edition with interest."

B.C. Russell
from Sunbury-on-Thames,

"I must say that although we travel up and down the Autoroute yearly to either Menton or Perpignan, we did find the book most useful and very accurate."

Inga E. Muir
Stockton-on-Tees
Cleveland,

"With regard to the Motorway Guide to the Sun, I would like to say that I found this book very informative, interesting, and colourful.

The routes are clear and concise with special mention of the signs to follow en route to Paris and also through Paris which I found to be helpful especially for the first time traveller going South.

In conclusion, I would not travel to France without this book in the future, and I look forward to seeing further editions in the years to come."

> Linda Sands
> from Wemyss Bay,
> in Scotland,

"Many thanks for the Guide — it is excellent and answers all the sorts of questions we have.
Keep up the good work." Says;

> A.R.Norman
> from Oxford.

Now, try the Guide for yourself and add your opinion to those of the satisfied travellers to the South of Europe.

Will your comments match theirs? Let it be known, regardless.

Address for your correspondence:

Karol Libura
Le Guide UK,
Spencer Close,
Park Royal,
London NW10 7DU

INTRODUCTION

To reach your destination in France by car, the motorway will certainly be the best alternative despite the tolls which will be, to a certain extent, offset by the steady saving on petrol consumption. You will find that it is a pleasure to remember picnicking in the Rest Areas which provide good facilities, normally in splendid weather, thus adding to the safety of the journey. And the scenery is frequently stunning and changing all the way. For the first time comers it could be found quite exotic,and it is.Besides the motorway is many times safer than any other route.

The Guide presents its contents in a self-explanatory manner as you progress your journey along the Motorways to the Sun. The core of the guide consists of pages diagrammatically showing the motorway and the semicircular "greens" as Rest Areas.

Petrol stations, hotels and restaurants are marked by the side of the Rest Areas at which the services are offered.The petrol stations are marked by a symbolic petrol pump, and similarly, the hotels and places of eating are indicated by a bed and a fork with a knife respectively.

Wherever it is appropriate, the hotels are cross-referenced with the page, on which the extended details are described, including a photograph and a small map, side by side.

A number in black, between the Rest Areas, shows the distance between them.(km)

The distance between petrol stations, usually offering wide range of services, is shown by a black number in a circle.

The number in red by the semi-circular 'greens" indicates the cumulative distance from the begining of your journey on the motorway.

A red number in a red circle, at the top or bottom of the page (depending on the direction of travel), shows each page's total distance covered.

Parallel to the diagrammatically shown motorway, there are rectangles on the opposite page which contain the names of the Rest Areas, symbols of the type of services offered, and a sentence or two of description relevant to the particular Area.

In this guide, all the accesible pull-ins allowing for a break in the journey, are called "REST AREAS", regardless of the type of services provided. But you may come across names like; service area, toll area or toll station.

It has to be said at this stage that almost all of the Rest Areas are attractive in their own ways, and there is always an Area within a short drive which should meet your particular needs.

Please note, that in this edition, some Rest Areas are noted as "lit at night" and some others are not. Some of the latter may well be lit.

And again, at some Rest Areas along the motorway the Info — Route service is provided but not all of them are specified in this edition.

On the small map of France with the relevant motorways marked on it, appearing at the top of every page showing the Routes, there is a RED DOT which is represented by the content of the page, and the location of the DOT indicates your position on the motorway, along which you are travelling

The red arrow shows the direction of travel.

And finally, the Guide provides you with the information regarding the motorway, the toll, telephoning in France, hotels, diagrams — allowing for efficient planning of your journey, translation of most of the French phrases appearing by the side of your motorway or elsewhere, that you would almost certainly like to understand, and some tips that you may find useful and a lot more besides.

THE TOLL

The toll is charged on the French motorway network except on sections in the immediate vicinity of towns.

At the entry to the charged sections of the motorways (Barrière de Péage) a ticket is normally obtainable from an automatic dispenser after pressing a button or it will be handed to you by an assistant. The ticket gives information regarding the toll charges for all exits, depending on the category of the vehicle and the distance travelled.

At the exit "Barrière de Péage", the toll charge is normally paid to an assistant but at some locations there is, as well, an alternative way of paying, which is by throwing into a "basket" the required amount in the right coins, about which the information is given well in advance.

A separate marked lane must be used if change is required at locations where there is an automatic service. It is almost a "must" to have sufficient local currency.

The toll prices shown throughout the Guide are for passenger cars and they may be revised slightly during the year. Higher prices are payable for cars with caravans and for other type of vehicles.

In order to get a receipt for payment at the exit "Barrière de Péage", you ask for a "Certificate de passage" or you press a button to get one when using an automatic service lane.

TELEPHONING

Since 25th October 1985, there have been changes introduced and they are as follows:-

There are now 2 telephone zones;

— PROVINCE and,
— PARIS/REGION PARISIENNE

All telephone numbers are of 8 figures.

For the PROVINCE, to the old 6 or 7 figure telephone numbers the Area Code numbers is added at the front accordingly.

For the PARIS/REGION PARISIENNE zone:

— Paris,
— Hauts-de-seine,
— Siene-Saint-Denis,
— Val-de-Marne, a figure 4 is added at the front to the existing telephone number,

— Val-d'Oise,
— Yvelines, a figure 3 is added in a similar manner, and finally:

— Essonne,
— Seine,
— Marne, a figure 6 is added at the front as above.

11

Note the following:

If the intended telephone — call receiver lives near the border of the two, previously neighbouring telephone areas, the Area Code of one or the other may be applicable.

So, if direct dialling is possible, you telephone:

To France from the UK;

1. To Paris/Region Parisienne, dial:
   010 33 1 (telephone number),

2. To the Province zone, dial:
   010 33 (telephone number).

From France to the UK, dial;

— 19,
— wait for the dialling tone, then dial:
— the Country Code (44),
— the Telephone Area Code (STD), minus the first zero,
— the telephone number.

An example to call London:
19 (wait) 44 1 961 1656

In France;

1. Within the PROVINCE ZONE;

   — dial, just the 8 figure telephone number.

2. Within PARIS/REGION PARISIENNE ZONE;

   — dial, just the 8 figure telephone number.

3. From PARIS/REGION PARISIENNE to the PROVINCE ZONE;

   — dial 16,
   — wait for dialling tone,
   — dial the telephone number.

4. From the PROVINCE ZONE to the PARIS/REGION PARISIENNE ZONE:

   — dial 16,
   — wait for dialling tone,
   — dial 1,
   — dial the telephone number.

Symbols

indicating the type of some of the services offered along the autoroutes:-

WC	—	WC, serves the purpose
🚻	—	WC with full facilities
☎	—	Telephone
♿	—	Handicapped facilities
🍴	—	Restaurant
🛏	—	Hotel
🛍	—	Shop
☕	—	Cafeteria
🍼	—	Nursery
💱	—	Currency exchange
🎠	—	Apparatus for children
ℹ	—	Information
✉	—	Post
Gend	—	Gendarmerie
SOS	—	Road side emergency telephone

THE HOTELS

The hotels appearing in this publication, offer a full range of quality accommodation and relevant services, starting from 1 to 4-star luxury hotels.

The hotels listed along the diagrams on pages 16 — 21, at the locations marked; "Aire de ….." are situated actually on the Rest Areas of the motorway, so you are not likely to be inconvenienced in any way. But to take advantage of the services provided by the other hotels mentioned along the diagrams, it is necessary to leave the motorway. However, the locations of some of these hotels are just by the side of the motorway or very close by and may well be considered as equally convenient. Please, consult the relevant location map.

As you progress the journey along the actual routes of the guide you will see that the same is marked by diagrammatical beds; bigger bed which is shown on the left hand side of the route, indicates hotel facilities at the Rest Areas, whereas the off-the-autoroute hotels are marked by the smaller bed appearing by the exit slip-roads where appropriate. With regard to the Pullman and some of the Altea hotels shown in this guide, and in order to avoid repeating the long list of the high quality services offered, you need to take note of the following, in addition to the specific details of a particular hotel;-

● Inter-hotel reservation ● fully equipped bathrooms ● automatic morning call ● mini-bar ● radio ● television ● Laundry and dry cleaning ● safes ● telex ● crrency exchange ● travel and enterteinment reservation ● children up to 12 years of age are accepted free in the parent's room.

Listing of the hotel lacations
(chronologically as you travel)

	no. of hotels	page
Calais	1	67
Ardres	1	67
Aire de **Assevillers**	1	66
Caen	1	215
Cabourg	1	80 & 81
Deauville	1	214
Rouen (Val-De-Reuil) — just by the M-way	1	208

Paris	15	54 — 58

Orleans (Olivet)		194 & 195
Aire des **Ruralies**		—
(Opens in the Autumn 1987)		
Bordeaux	1	100
Toulouse — en route to Perpignan		
(not covered by the Guide)	1	101

Aire de **Nemours**		66
Aire de **Venoy**	1	67
Dijon	1	65
Aire de **Beaune**	1	66
Mâcon	1	65
Aire de **Mâcon**	2	—
Porte de Lyon	3	64,152,161
Lyon	1	64
Orange	1	160
Aix-en-Provence	1	64
Aire de **Lançon**	1	65
Aire de **Vidauban**	1	—
(no access when driving north)		

The Riviera and beyond, along the coast (the listing begins with Menton at the Italian border, town by town towards the West End of the coast)

Menton	4	132,133
Saint — Agnes *	1	133
Roquebrune Cap-Martin	3	133,134
La Turbie	1	134
Monaco	1	135
Nice	5	135,136
Cannes	1	137
Toulon	1	137
Bandol	1	137
Marseille	2	138
Fos-sur-Mer	1	138
La Grande Motte	1	139
Montpellier	1	139

*****Sainte-Agnes**, is a small village, 3 km away from the sea and situated at the altitude of 750 m which makes it the highest village in Europe. From Menton it is very well sign-posted.

LONDON

Allow 2 hrs time to get to Dover

124

DOVER

Crossing time:
by a hovercraft — 35 min.
by a ferry — 75-90 min.

CALAIS

17

Hotel Le Relais
See page 67

Ardres

143

Mercure Hotel
See page 66

Aire de **Assevillers**

123

PARIS

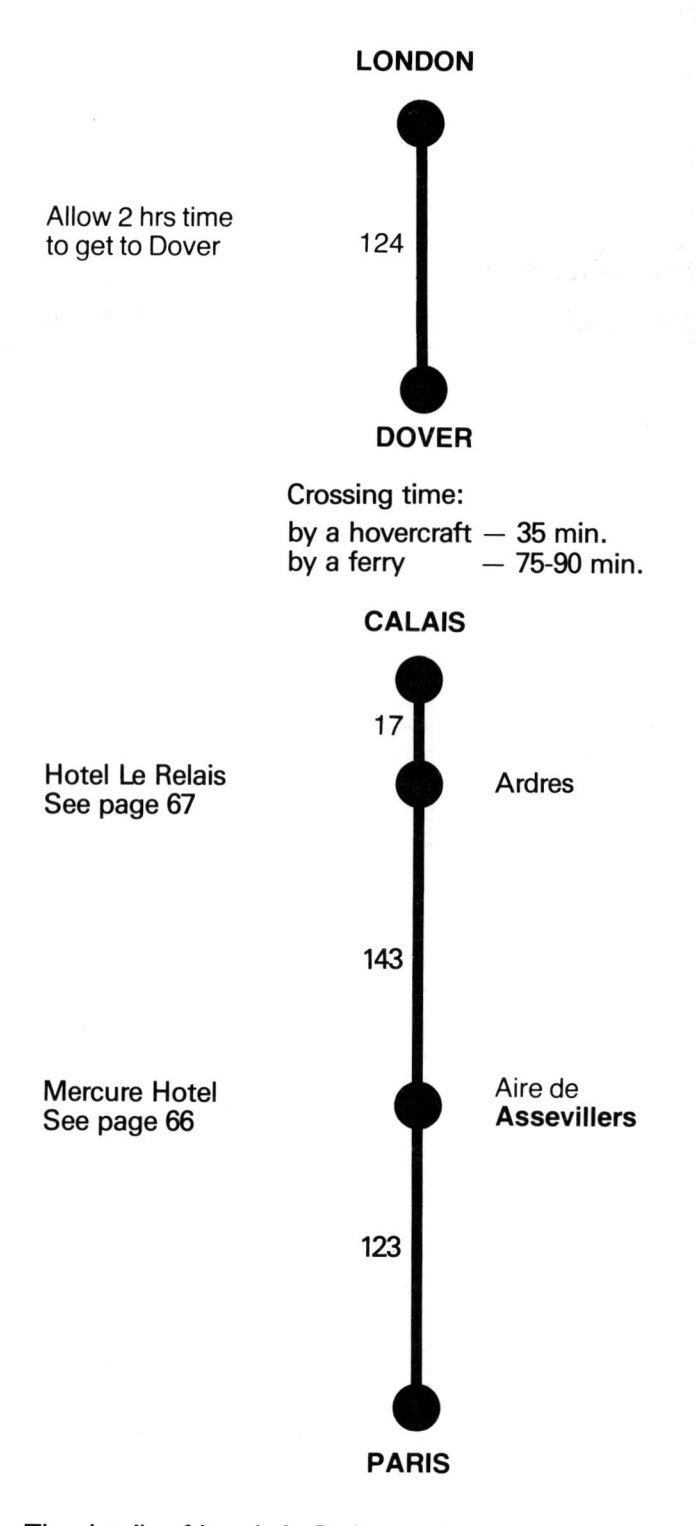

The details of hotels in Paris are shown on pages 54-58

Hotel Metropole, see page 215

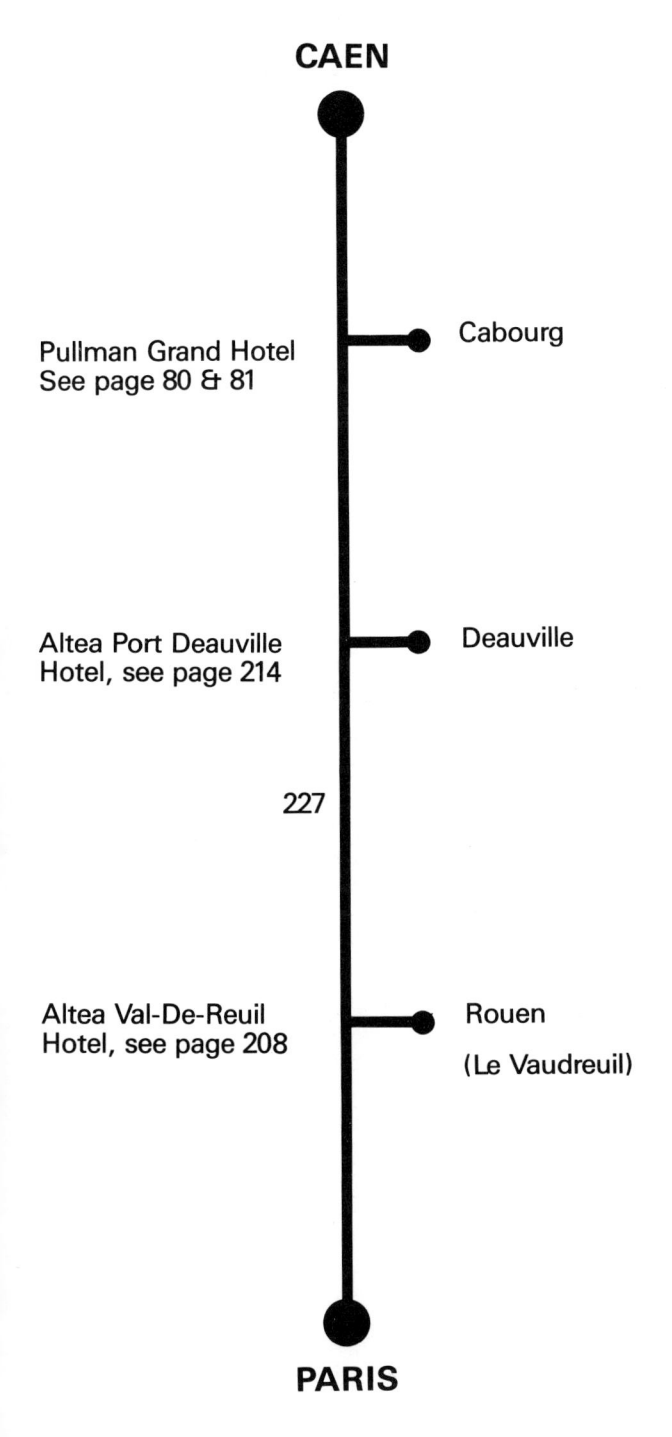

CAEN

Pullman Grand Hotel
See page 80 & 81

Cabourg

Altea Port Deauville
Hotel, see page 214

Deauville

227

Altea Val-De-Reuil
Hotel, see page 208

Rouen

(Le Vaudreuil)

PARIS

The details of hotels in Paris are shown on pages 54-58

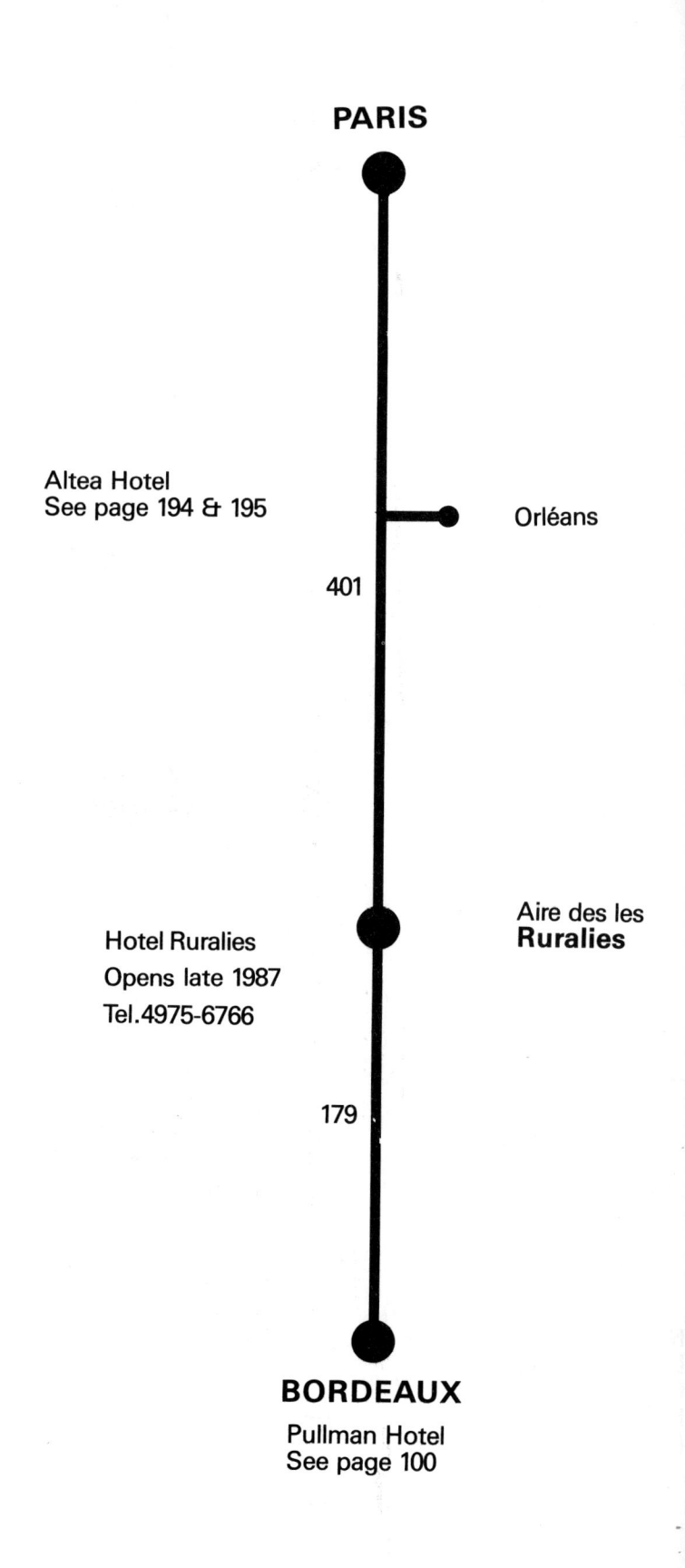

PARIS

Altea Hotel
See page 194 & 195

Orléans

401

Aire des les **Ruralies**

Hotel Ruralies
Opens late 1987
Tel. 4975-6766

179

BORDEAUX

Pullman Hotel
See page 100

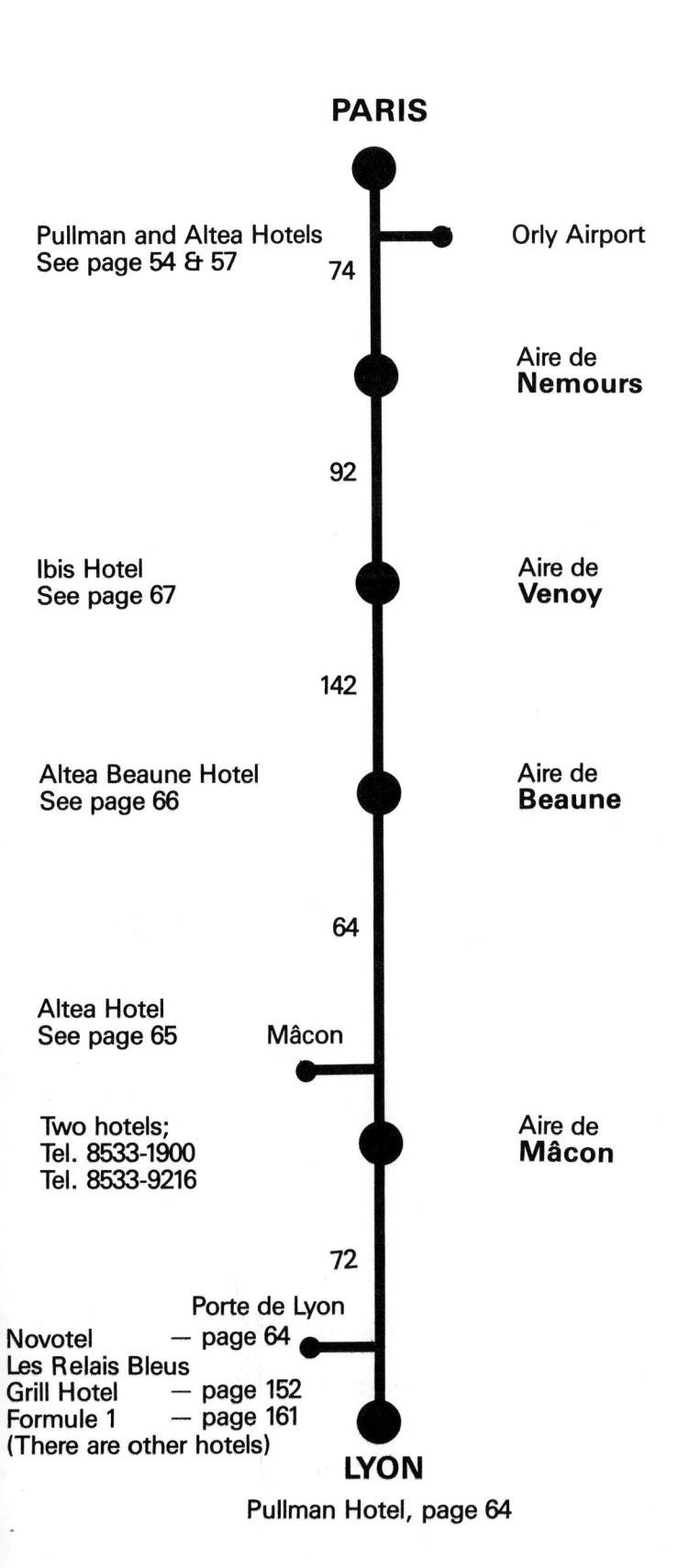

PARIS

Pullman and Altea Hotels
See page 54 & 57

74

Orly Airport

Aire de **Nemours**

92

Ibis Hotel
See page 67

Aire de **Venoy**

142

Altea Beaune Hotel
See page 66

Aire de **Beaune**

64

Altea Hotel
See page 65

Mâcon

Two hotels;
Tel. 8533-1900
Tel. 8533-9216

Aire de **Mâcon**

72

Porte de Lyon — page 64

Novotel
Les Relais Bleus
Grill Hotel — page 152
Formule 1 — page 161
(There are other hotels)

LYON

Pullman Hotel, page 64

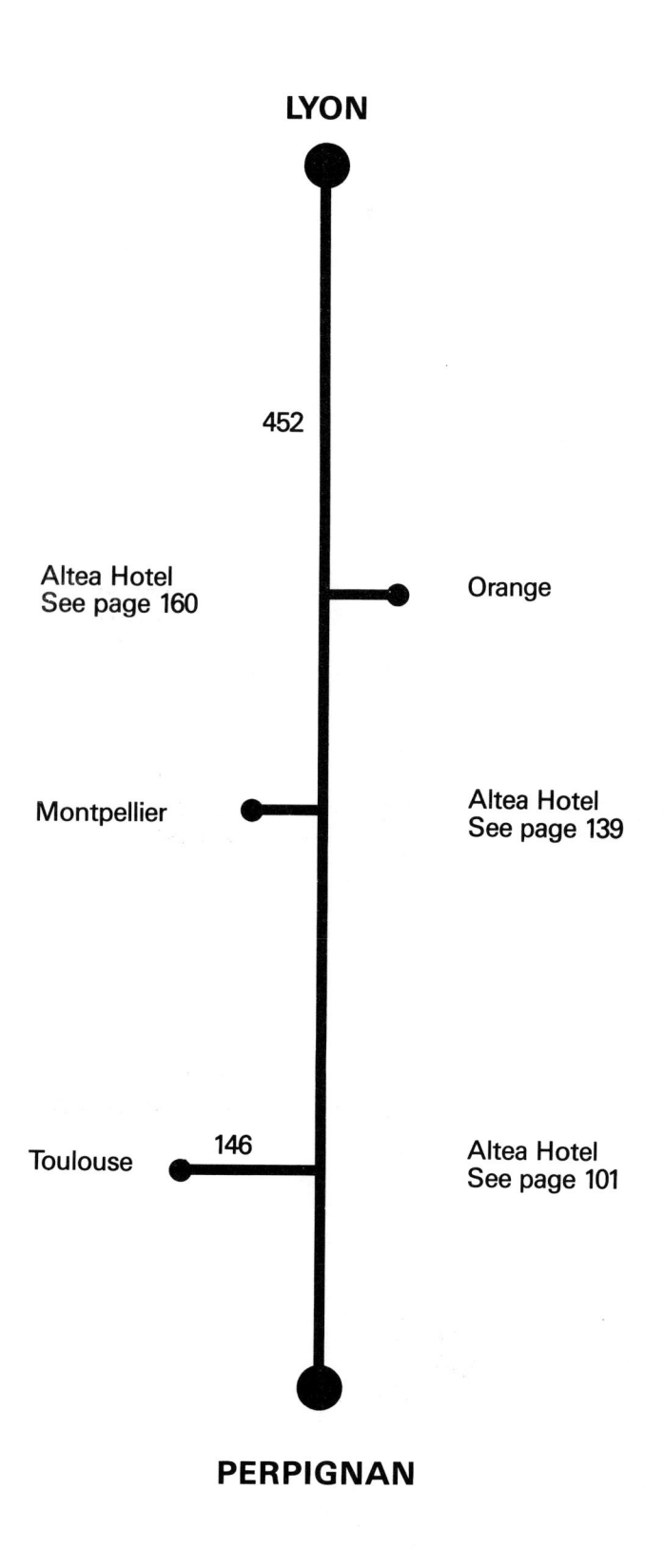

LYON

452

Altea Hotel
See page 160

Orange

Montpellier

Altea Hotel
See page 139

Toulouse

146

Altea Hotel
See page 101

PERPIGNAN

LYON

Altea Hotel
See page 160

Orange

282

Pullman Le Pigonnet
See page 64

Aix-en-Provence

Mercure Hotel
See page 65

Aire de
Lançon

112

One hotel
Tel. 9473−0221

Aire de
Vidauban-Sud

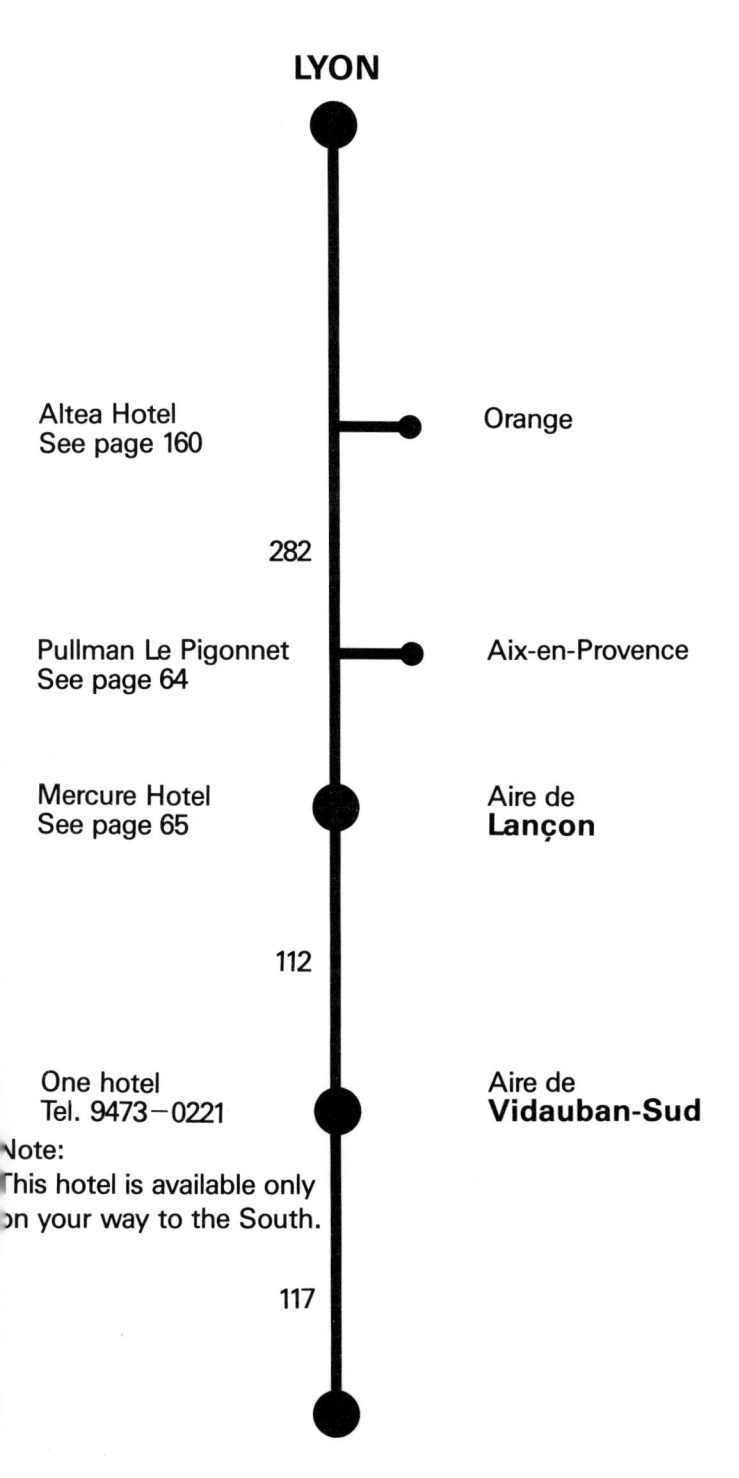

Note:
This hotel is available only
on your way to the South.

117

MENTON

For hotels of the Riviera and along the Coast,
see pages 132 − 139

Your Check — list

1. Full driving licence,
2. Car registration document and written authority for use if the car is not in your name,
3. Breakdown insurance cover, well appreciated when you do, require help — see page 9,
4. Your tickets,
5. Passport. Must be valid beyond the date of return,
6. Money, travellers cheques. Cheque book, credit cards — keep them separately,
7. Green Card — no longer compulsory in France, even with the British third party insurance, which gives you better cover than the minimum otherwise applying in France. However, a fully comprehensive insurance is advisable.
8. G B sticker — for Great Britain,
9. Red triangle. Compulsory for France if your car is not equipped with hazard warning lights. Recommended in any case.
10. Spare set of light bulbs, a "must",
11. Main beam deflector. You no longer need to have yellow tinted lenses,
12. First aid kit,
13. Fire extinguisher,
14. Petrol can (Must be empty on ferries),
15. Basic tools, including feeler gauge,
16. Spare parts; e.g. plugs, points, hoses, fan belt ...
17. Driving glasses, of course,
18. 2-pin plug adaptor for your electrical equipment,
19. Michelin Map of Paris (blue cover — 100 metres to 1 cm) a "must" if you contemplate driving into Paris.

WHY IS IT BIG ENDS ALWAYS GO IN LITTLE PLACES LIKE LE BROCQ?

On a recent family motoring holiday in France, Mr. John Attenborough's car had a breakdown. "A major breakdown," in his own words. The car's big end had gone.

It was on the border with Spain, in the foothills of the Pyrenees. The holiday could have been in ruins, had he not taken out the AA's 5-Star Service.

Mr. Attenborough made one call to the AA's Emergency Centre in Boulogne. Within hours, he was continuing his journey in a hire car paid for by the AA (his own car was brought home for him).

On his return journey, he left the hire car at St. Malo, and was met by a Hertz representative at Portsmouth with a brand new car to get him home.

AA's 5-Star Service will cover your car, your family, against sickness or illness, and your belongings.

All for the price of a family meal.

For full details of AA's 5-Star Service, send this coupon to: 5-Star Service, AA Travel Services Ltd., Fanum House, Dog Kennel Lane, Halesowen, West Midlands B63 3BT. Or see your local AA Travel Agent.

☐ Please also send me a copy of Argosy Motoring Holidays in Europe. *(tick box)*.

NAME: _____

ADDRESS: _____

You don't have to belong to the AA to get AA 5-Star Service.

Introduction to L'Arche's restaurants

L'Arche is a respected brand name for a major chain of restaurants covering the motorway network in France and offering a relaxing stopover at relevant Rest Areas, which are marked by L'Arches logo throughout this guide.

L'Arche restaurants will provide you with reasonably priced meals or snacks, all year round, from 7.00 a.m. — 10.30 p.m. (at least). The absolute cleanliness of L'Arche restaurants including the kitchens, so obviously backed by kind and courteous staff, inspires total confidence.

So do not be surprised to find perfectly kept lavatories or a telephone in good working order. C'est normal.

Further more, L'Arche offers you; a "Baby's Corner", a play ground for children, and a selected range of sweets and biscuits.

And finally, see pages 62 and 63 for an at — a — glance map showing the locations of L'Arche's restaurants in France. As you know, since L'Arche is the biggest company in the catering business, it would be desirable to hear your opinions and comments, in order that the restaurants can maintain their high standard of service.

In conclusion; kindness, courtesy and quality is exactly what L'Arche's restaurants have at their disposal, and are eager to serve you with.

(write to the address shown under "Look no further")

NEWS LETTER

It is a great pleasure for me to be able to introduce the News Letter section into the Guide.

I have received many letters from you, the users of the Guide who are genuinely interested in the success of this very new publication which has been launched into a sea of guides each produced by very able and well established participants.

I have strongly believed in the need for this type of publication and I am pleased to have been proved right.Thank you. Every letter has been supportive and many of them propose interesting inclusions of further information. It seems that the creation of LE GUIDE — the ultimate edition of the publication, has taken place.

As you may have noticed on page 6 under "Look no Further", I quote some of the comments from typical letters, expressing in a variety of ways,the same support for,and acceptance of, LE GUIDE, the quality publication for all going to the South of France or South of Europe for that matter, along the French L'Autoroute du Soleil and elsewhere.

However, there were very frequent cases of complaints regarding unsatisfactory binding of the book and all cases have been answered and replacements promptly sent.I trust this enlarged edition renders these early problems.

And now,coming back to your splendid letters I would like to confirm that many of your suggestions have been realized and some others will require further research and some time to allow for expanding the volume of Le Guide. In conclusion a lot of food for thought.

Here are some further quotes;

"...I have already promised to loan the guide next year to people who have never used the Autoroute before. However, before it can be used again I hope you will be able to forward to me new copy as upon the very first opening the book collapsed, page by page. All very frustrating and more than a little annoying."

"Further to the telephone conversation regarding the Motorway to the Sun I am writing to confirm my annoyance and disappointment with the binding of the publication. After only half an hour of using the Guide a page fell out and subsequently more and more, making it very difficult to keep the correct pages opposite one another, as it is necessary in order to use the information."

and finally on a positive note, a letter from Anthony Fyffe from Bournemouth;

"I have just spotted (& bought) a copy of your publication in W.H. Smith in Bournemouth. My interest was aroused as soon as my eyes alighted upon the title, and the second paragraph of the Foreword kindled memories of a similar nature. It was my great pleasure to watch the autoroutes being built stage by stage, and the end product of my watching was a series of route maps to the South of France detailing all that was to be found along the route.

No such maps existed at that time and none exist today; for a variety of reasons my own compilations were brought to an end in the mid-seventies. Thus I am not looking at your book in the light of competition, but as someone else who has taken on the challenge of meeting a demand.

As a map compiler of route maps (and other types) for over thirty years I never cease to be surprised at the reactions of map users to maps themselves, and the reactions to my own series ranged from, total astonishment at the complexity to absolute delight at the easiness of use...",

and another one from Linda Sands;

"...Another feature in the book which I thought was helpful was the hotels and the star ratings covering each one, certainly to suit everyone. I would like to see more of your excellent range of hotels that can be convenient as well as economical to stay at for a holiday, not just passing through and to be found not in the big resorts at the South of France, but at the smaller resorts situated along the coast, e.g. "Le Plaissence" which is to be found at a small town called "La Ciotat" not far from Marseille.

This hotel is family run and the bedrooms are clean and tidy. They also include WC and shower and restaurant which offers excellent food and service. Personally we do not go anywhere else if we visit the South of France."

With your approval, obviously, a News Letter section could be considered as a constant feature of LE GUIDE or, perhaps a self-contained supplement in which interesting letters could be discussed at length, and become a sort of a Forum for exchanging experience from holidays or business trips with all the members of LE GUIDE, so to speak.

No doubt, there are cases of unpleasant moments taking place for some, and these especially should be brought to light for the benefit of everybody.

Many of us have gained a lot of experience due to being observant during frequent journeys along the French routes or due to actually having gone through some undesired happenings resulting from unwise decisions or regardless.

Please, share what you think is worth shareing. Tell your story of your holiday; good, bad, funny or ridiculous, so to be warned, learn, laugh and have a good time. Recommend your holiday place, a good garage, place of interest, anytning and everything.

Let's be useful to each other and there will not be a better way. Unless, of course; you know different. As the famous Esther says. Tell us.

Some of the expressions that you will meet along the Route and elsewhere

Accôtement non stabilisés — *soft, hard shoulder*

Allumez vous feux — *switch on your lights*

Attention, sortie de camions — *careful, lorries turning*

Auberge de Jeunesse — *Youth hostel*

Barrière de péage — *toll barrier*

Bison Futé — *summer time operating, advisory service for motorists*

Bruit — *noise*

Cedez de passage — *give way*

Centre Ville — *town centre*

Cette cabine peut etre appelee a ce numero — *this cabin may be telephoned under this number....*

Changeur de monnaie — *money exchange*

Chaussée déformée — *uneven, bad surface*

Danger vent — *dangerous wind*

Défense d'entrée — *entrance forbidden*

Déviation — *diversion*

Disque de stationnement — *Blue zone parking disk (obtainable in France from a Police station or Tourist office.)*

Douane — *customs*

Eau potable — *drinking water*

Essence (normale) — *2 star petrol*

Eteignez vos feux — *switch off your lights*

Fin allumage de feux — *switch off your lights*

Gravillons — *loose chippings (gravel)*

Hôtel de Ville — *Town Hall*

Halt à péage — *stop at the toll barrier*

Jeux, mis a la disposition des enfants aux risques et perils de utilisateurs — *utilisation of the apparatus should be under supervision of parents*

Ni vitesse, ni bruit — *no speed, no noise*

Nids de poules — *potholes*

Parcours sportif adultes — *exercise track for adults*

Par la passerelle — *to the footbridge*

Passage protégé — *right of way*

Peage — *toll*

Pique-nique, jeux d'enfants — *picnic area, suitable for parties with young children*

Pièce acceptée — *coins accepted (usually appears before approaching the barrier of toll)*

Pluie — *slippery (after raining)*

Poids lourds — *heavy vehicles (normally associated with a road sign, showing a route to be followed)*

Préparez votre monnaie — *have your coins ready*

Priorité à droite — *priority of the traffic coming out of the right hand side*

Propriete privee — *private property*

Rainnuarage — *road londitudinally grooved (special notice to be taken by motocyclists)*

Rappel — *reminding the last warning*

Regarde votre distance de securite — *keep safe distance to the vehicle in front*

Relentir — *slow*

Risque de verglas — *black ice, icy patches*

Roulez au pas — *dead slow*

Salle à langer — *nursery facilities*

Sans monnaie — *for those without coins (change)*

Sauf riverains — *no entry except for access of inhabitants*

Serrez à droite — *keep to the right*

Serrez à gauche — *keep to the left*

Syndicat d'Initiative — *Tourist Information Office*

Sortie, (Sortie de voiture) — *exit*

Sortie prochaine — *next exit*

Stationnement interbit — *parking prohibited*

Super — *4 star petrol*

Un train peut en cacher un autre — *one train hides another one (on level crossing)*

Toutes directions — *all traffic*

Vehicules lents, restez à votre droite — *slow vehicles, keep to the right*

Verglas — *black ice, patches of ice.*

Verifiez votre monnaie — *check your change (coins)*

Vers — *towards (Vers Lyon)*

Vitesse — *speed*

Voir à droite — *look to the right*

Vous n'avez pas la priorite — *you have no right of way*

NN (Nouvelles Normes) — *new rating system for hotels*

Police de route or Garde Mobile — *Traffic Police Patrol*

Some tips and further information

— Important, make sure that the braking system of your car is in order. Have it bled and the fluid changed if necessary.

Remember, high altitude driving in hot weather may affect the efficiency of the braking system of your car.

— Have the tyres pressure right, check frequently.

— It is a good idea to begin your journey with the petrol tank full.

— Drive on the right side of the road which happens on the Continent to be the right hand side.

— **Be aware of the priority of traffic coming out from the right hand side.**

— "Passage protegé" — right of way. Ignore it, it can be disastrous. Just drive with care.

— Keep your own pace and safe distance from the vehicle in front.

— Do not drive between two heavy vehicles, do enjoy a good view all round. Besides, at the extremes you will not get sandwiched.

— On the main road be very careful. Some road users appearing at speed from your right hand side, may give you a bad headache.

— On the motorway, closer to the italian border, there are sections of contra-flow traffic. Be careful, as in one case I found, (perhaps due to tiredness) your lane seems to disappear as if it was an exit slip road and you may be tempted, in confusion to drive straight on, against the oncoming traffic.

— At certain mountainous sections of the motorway, there is no "hard shoulder", but frequent SOS bays are provided instead.

— Seat belt rule, as in the UK. On the whole of the French road network, including the towns, it is obligatory to wear seat belts, otherwise, at best, you risk £25 to £60 fine.

   Children under 10 years of age must not sit at the front.

— First aid basic items, useful to have. The same applies to basic tools and spare parts.

— You may feel unhappy with some manners of driving if you are not used to it. The "priorite a droite" rule is exercised with a religious conviction, regardless of the situation, so do not try to apply logic of your own. If the unexpected takes place, just keep cool.

— If you break down always ask for an estimate before allowing repairs.

— Display the warning triangle in cases of emergency and, or have the hazard lights on.

— Free emergency telephones are sited at about 2km intervals along the autoroutes. Very often you will find them just in front of the Service Areas and most of them are marked in this guide. Once the emergency telephone is answered the Police will arrange road side assistance and medical service in case of an accident.

— Always check/compare your bill or credit card slip with the petrol pump indicator to agree both, before you pay or sign. Take the reading from the pump immediatly after delivery.

— Two grades of petrol are available: super — equivalent to 4-star, and normale (essence) — 2-star equivalent.

— At petrol stations additional services may be available if requested.

— On the Boulevard Peripherique keep in lane, at least second from the right hand side. The extreme right hand side lane driving can lead to some frustration as the in-coming traffic joins the Boulevard in a manner as if there was nobody else driving. But the "Priorite a droite" rule, explains everything. Note, that on roundabouts you may experience the same, although now, the traffic on the roudabouts is governed by the same rules as in the UK. However, be watchful when approaching rounabouts. There are signed roundabouts bearing the words; "Vous n'avez pas la priorite" (you do not have the right of way) which simply means that the traffic on such roudabouts has priority. The other possible variation of the expression you may come across is; "Cedez le passage" — give way.

— Take special care if you decide to stop at the "zebra crossing", because, if the road is wide enough, it is very likely, that a local road user behind you, will go past, thus creating a dengerous situation.

— Note, that on the Continent the pedestrian has no "right of way" as in the UK.

— No doubt on many occasions you will become a pedestrian yourself. Watch out. As a pedestrian (who is used to the "right of way" in the UK) you may occasionally want to cross the road, and quite rightly opt for the "zebra crossing". It cannot be overemphasised, that you look, listen and wait for the right moment to cross the road and be even more careful if a car stops in order to let you go first. Especially important when accompanied by children.

— If you happen to drive through the town centre of Calais on the way to Paris, you will face at a certain point a choice to turn right for Paris and Boulogne, or left for St.Omer. Take the route for St.Omer. Otherwise you will find yourself driving to Paris through Boulogne, along a secondary road.

— Always book your hotel and Channel crossing well in advance, wherever possible.

— More formal appearance is required if you consider a visit to some restaurants, theatres and casinos.

— On beaches, topless is a normal occurance and is widely accepted.

— As it is apparent from the conclusion of my research exercise in connection with this publication, that visiting the South of France is a contagious "want", you may be well advised therefore to start collecting a variety of good quality maps and relevant equipment which will prove to be a good investment.

— Be aware of the fact that driving at a speed of 80 m p h you travel 40 yards in ONE second. Do not allow therefore, your concentration to lapse; take frequent breaks at Rest Areas.

— Do not ignore speed restrictions to the limits of stupidity which happens to be a common occurance, and very often the only explanation to the cause of many serious accidents.

— Always stop at level crossings to ensure safety, regardless of whether they are manned or not, or automatic.

— Beware of instances, where people approach you and ask for money for a variety of reasons. They would be well dressed, speak your language and tell you a story of how they were robbed or that their car has broken down, and they need your help (money).

— and now, be aware of a variety of salesmen who pretend at first to be lost or in need of some kind of help, and then they try to sell you goods. Do not allow yourself to be persuaded, under the pretext of seeing the goods, however attractive they may be, to enter the "salesman's" car.

— Watch out for drivers who do not indicate their intentions when on the road, especially when joining the traffic from a parking position.

— At some locations be aware of a plaque of motoscooters and alike, buzzing from every angle of vision, and snaking along the road with apparent lack of concern for their own safety.

— Motoring laws are strictly enforced by the Police Road Patrol. The minimum fine for traffic offences, like ; speeding is around £130 or, for exceeding the drink-driving level, from £250 — £500, an equivalent of which in French currency is expected to be paid in cash on the spot. The members of the Patrol are very helpful otherwise, as well.

— According to the French Police records, about 50% of all accidents involving British cars takes place within 80 km of the Channel. In conclusion; do not rush rather opt for the next crossing.

Identity checks

The French Police can stop people in the streets, including foreigners, in order to check their identity, and in case of dissatisfaction with the outcome of the identification, a person can be taken to the police station for as long as it would be necessry to establish an identity.
(Another good reason to look after your documents)

Minitel service

This is an information service, provided by telephone-based Minitel roadside computers which is available at some Rest Areas and often combined with "Bison Futé" enquiry desks and central booking offices. This service will help you to pinpoint traffic jams, indicate how much road tolls cost and even help you find hotels and restaurants.

Speed limits — maximum, unless otherwise posted

Toll motorways	130 km/h	110 km/h
Dual carriageways and motorways without tolls	110 km/h	100 km/h
Other roads	90 km/h	80 km/h
In towns	60 km/h	60 km/h

In towns, the speed limit restriction begins with the "town name sign" and the restriction ends with the "town name sign" crossed diagonally.

Please note:

1. You must not exceed 90 km/h during the first year after passing your driving test.

2. There is a new minimum speed limit of 80 km/h (50 mph) for the outside lane on motorways, during daylight, on level ground and with good visibility.

British Consulates

Address in Paris;109 rue de Faubourg St-Honore,75008 — Paris telephone;(1) 4266 — 9142.

There are also Consulates in the following towns; Bordeaux, Boulogne, Calais, Cherbourg, Dunkirk, Le Havre, Lille, Lyon, Marseille, Nantes and Perpignan.

— And finally, the French road network is clasified by;
  A — Motorway (Autorote),
  N — National roads,
  D — Regional roads (Departamentale),
  V — Local roads (Chemins vicinaux).

French National Holidays

(Jour Férié)

January 1	*Jour de L'An*	New Year's Day
May 1	*Fête du Travail*	Labour Day
May 8	VE Day	
July 14	*Fête Nationale*	Bastille Day
August 15	*Assumption*	Assumption
November 1	*Toussaint*	All Saints
November 11	*Anniversaire de L'Armistice*	Armistice Day
December 25	*Noel*	Christmas

Moveable dates

Lundi de Pâques	Easter Monday
Ascension	Ascension
Lundi de Pentecôte	Whit Monday

The week-ends incorporating July 14 and August 15, are the ideal dates to break your journey and stay in Paris. On the motorway and everywhere else will be very heavy traffic. Except Paris, hotels along the motorway are very likely to be fully booked, well in advance.

Days of the Week

Monday	*lundi*
Tuesday	*mardi*
Wednesday	*mercredi*
Thursday	*jeudi*
Friday	*vendredi*
Saturday	*samedi*
Sunday	*dimanche*

Months of the Year

January	*janvier*
February	*fevrier*
March	*mars*
April	*avril*
May	*mai*
June	*juin*
July	*juillet*
August	*août*
September	*septembre*
October	*octobre*
November	*novembre*
December	*decembre*

Numbers

1 — un (une)	21 — vingt et un
2 — deux	22 — vingt deux
3 — trois	23 — vingt trois etc.,
4 — quatre	30 — trente
5 — cinq	31 — trente et un
6 — six	32 — trente deux
7 — sept	33 — trente troix
8 — huit	40 — quarante
9 — neuf	50 — cinquante
10 — dix	60 — sixante
11 — onze	70 — soixante-dix
12 — douze	80 — quatre-vingt
13 — treize	90 — quatre-vingt-dix
14 — quatorze	100 — cent
15 — quinze	101 — cent-un
16 — seize	102 — cent deux
17 — dix-sept	200 — deux cents
18 — dix-huit	500 — cinq cents
19 — dix-neuf	1000 — mille
20 — vingt	2000 — deux mille

How to book your room in a hotel

Je voudrais reserver... *I would like to book...*
Une chambre avec ... *one room with...*

— un lit — *one bed, or*
— deux lits — *two beds, or*
— grand lit — *double bed*
— douche — *shower*
— salle de bain — *bathroom*
— pour ce soir — *for this evening*
— pour trois jours — *for three days*

Le petit dejeuner — *breakfast*
Le prix par jour — *rate per night*
La pension complète — *full board*
La demi-pension — *half board (bed and breakfast and evening meal)*
Une emplacement pour une voiture — *space for one car*

Some more expressions, but now from English to French:

Good morning — *bonjour*
Good afternoon — *bonjour*
Good evening — *bonsoir*
Good bye — *au revoir*

Please — *s'il vous plait*
How are you — *comment allez-vous*
Very well, thank you — *tres bien, merci.*
It is a nice day — *il fait beau*
It is hot — *il fait chaud*
It is cold — *il fait froid*
I do not speak French — *je ne parle pas français*
I do not know — *je ne sais pas*
Here is the key — *voici le clef*
To do the shopping — *faire des courses*
Good luck — *bon courage, bonne chance*
Underground — *metro*
Careful, look out — *attention*
To your health, cheers — *à votre santé*
Accommodation — *logement*
Money — *l'argent*
Excuse me — *excusez-moi*
Yesterday — *hier*
Today — *aujourd'hui*
Midday — *midi*
Tomorrow — *demain*
Change — *monnaie (more meaning of coins)*
Footbridge — *la passerelle*
Push — *poussez*
Pull — *tirez*

Some parts of the car and associated vocabulary:

Battery — *Batterie*
(Flat battery — *Batterie à vide*)
Bonnet — *Capot*
Car — *Voiture*
Carburettor — *Carburateur*
Distributor — *Distributeur d'allumage*
(Points — *Jeu de contacts*)
Door — *Porte*
Fan belt — *Courroie*
Fuse box — *Boite à fusibles*
Gasket (seal) — *Joint*
Gearbox - *Boite de vitesse*
Grease — *Lubricant*
Headlamp — *Phare*
Horn — *Avertisseur*
Hose — *Durite*
Ignition system — *Systèm d'allumage*
Number plate — *Plague de police*

Oil — *Huile*
Oil level — *Niveau d'huile*
Oil change — *Vidange*
Oil leak — *Fuite d'huile*
Petrol tank — *Reservoir d'essence*
Puncture — *Crevaison*
Radiator — *Radiateur*
Seat belt — *Ceinture de sécurité*
Side lamp — *Feu de position*
Spark plug — *Bougie*
Tyre — *Pneu*
Water — *Eau*
Wheel — *Roue*
Windscreen — *Pare-brise*

My car is broken down — *ma voiture est en panne*
Something is wrong with .... — *Quelque chose ne va pas ..*

the engine — *dans le moteur*
the brakes — *aux freins*

Car logbook — *carte grise*
Driving licence — *permis de conduire*
4-star petrol — *essence super (Supper)*
2-star petrol — *essence normale (Essence)*

Conversion tables and factors

Length

1 inch (in)	=	25.4 millimetres (mm)
	=	2.54 centimetres (cm)
1 foot (ft)	=	30.48 (cm)
	=	0.3048 metre (m)
1 yard (yd)	=	91.44 (cm)
	=	0.9144 (m)
1 mile	=	1.609 kilometres (km)
1 centimetre (cm)	=	0.394 inch (in)
1 metre (m)	=	1.094 yards (yd)
1 kilometre (km)	=	0.621 mile

Volume

1 UK ounce = 28.41 cm
= 28.41 millilitres (ml)
1 pint (pt) = 0.568 litre (l)
1 UK gallon (UK gal) = 4.546 litres
1 litre (l) = 0.22 UK gallon
= 1.76 pint

Weight

1 pound (lb) = 0.454 kilogram (kg)
1 hundredweight (cwt) = 50.8 kilograms (kg)
1 UK ton = 1016.05 kg
= 1.016 metric tonnes

1000 kg = 1 metric tonne (t)
1 kg = 2.2 pounds (lb)
1 metric tonne (t) = 2204.62 (lb)
= 0.984 UK ton

Pressure

1 pound per square inch
(lb/in) = .069 kg/cm
1 kg/cm = 14.2 (ib/in)

Tyre pressure

(ib/in)	(kg/cm)	(ib/in)	(kg/cm)
1	0.07	32	2.25
5	0.35	33	2.32
10	0.70	34	2.39
15	1.05	35	2.46
16	1.12	36	2.53
17	1.20	37	2.60
18	1.27	38	2.67
19	1.34	39	2.74
20	1.41	40	2.81
21	1.48	41	2.88
22	1.55	42	2.95
23	1.62	43	3.02
24	1.69	44	3.09
25	1.76	45	3.16
26	1.83	46	3.23
27	1.90	47	3.30
28	1.97	48	3.37
29	2.04	49	3.45
30	2.11	50	3.52
31	2.18	51	3.59

Temperature

Conversion of degrees Centigrate into Fahrenheit

C	0	5	10	15	20	25	30	35	40
F	32	41	50	59	68	77	86	95	104

Fuel consumption

Conversion of (miles/gallon) into (litres/100 kilometres)

miles/gallon	litres/100 km
10	28.25
15	18.84
20	14.13
25	11.30
30	9.42
35	8.07
40	7.06
45	6.28
50	5.65

1 (mile per gallon) = 282.54 (litre/100 km)

A VOUS PARIS

INTRODUCTION TO PARIS

(by a courtesy of the French Government Tourist Office in London)

The tall houses of Paris, the tree — lined boulevards, the stone bridges and precisely laid-out parks are as lovely on a snowy winter's day as in the summer sunshine, as enchanting in the pale light of dawn as in the twinkle street lights at dusk. It is an unfailingly beguiling city, and of the world's copital, perhaps the most agreeable to visit.

Not only enchanting to look at, it offers endless pleasures to pass the hours; beautiful paintings... haunting views... smart bars...ancient cafes drenched in atmosphere... opera... Turkish baths...museums...gardens...restaurants that perfect every conceivable type of cooking. Countless book and guides eulogise the marvels of Paris, and they enhance any trip.

The City is divided into 20 districts or *arrondissements*, numbered,very conveniently, from one to twenty.The numbering starts in the heart of Paris, then spirals, putting the twentiesth district - the *vingtième* - in the far east. Restaurants, bars, hotels and museums are all listed in guides according to their district, and it makes more sense of a map if you know roughly where each district lies.

The first incudes the Louvre, the Palais- Royal, the Tuileries gardens, the place Vendôme, the Ritz and the Comédie Francaise the elegant Rue de Rivoli, and plenty of hotels; then crosses the river Seine to encompass Sainte — Chapelle and half of the Ile de la Cité.

The *deuxième* runs north of the first and includes the Opéra area, where many of the city's most prestigious hotels and theatres are located and, in the east, a number of less expensive hotels.

The *troisième* is old Paris; the Marais, once the smartest area of Paris and now smartly restored after centuries of neglect. There are few hotels here but plenty in the fourth district, which takes in part of the Marais, the new Centre Pompidou,the other half of the Ile de la Cité, and the whole of the Ile St-Louis.

These four *arrondissements* are all on the right bank — or north of the river Seine. Getting to the fifth or cinquième means a hop across the river into the Latin Quarter. Here is the Sorbonne University, the busy Boulevard St-Michel with all the cafes, the Jeu de Paume gallery and, in the sixth, smart nightclubs.

Eiffel tower is situated squarely in the *septième*, along with Les Invalides, Napoleon's great tomb, a number of government buildings, and residential streets.

The eight district is fashionable, expensive and rather wild, homes of luxurious hotels, the Champ — Elysées, the Lido, and the Crazy Horse cabaret club, as well as the huge place de la Concorde, the presidential palace, and the very fashionable Rue du Faubourg St-Honoré.

The ninth containes plenty of contrast: department store, Theatres, the Opera, and blousy Pigalle. In the tenth only the Gare du Nord and the Gare de L'Est occupy visitors much, and in the residential eleventh, twelfth and thirteenth districts there is little of interest to outsiders.

The fourteenth has the huge Tour Montparnasse and a large Sheraton hotel; the fifteenth, mysterious little streets, full of interesting shops, and some modern luxury hotels; the sixteenth, smart Avenue Foch the Bois de Boulogne, and like the seventeenth, comfortable, old — fashioned hotels.

The eighteenth is dominated by Montmartre, and the lofty Sacre — Coeur, while the nineteenth and *vingtième* are mainly residential areas. And when you run out of numbers, you have the green and wooded country of the Ile — de — France which cradles Paris. Its Royal lands harbour châteaux and manor houses, cathedrals and churches, chapels and abbeys — and over a hundred museums.

New Paris

PLUS ÇA CHANGE PLUS C'EST LA M E ME CHOSE is a useful piece of French wisdom that applies to almost everything, except perhaps the French capital. Anyone doing the rounds there recently will have been aware of striking new silhouettes taking shape on the skyline and an element of surprise in some public spaces.

The intestinal tract of the Pompidou Art Centre, once dubbed "the oil refinery" has, by sheer dint of having been there several years, wormed its way into the affections of Parisians and tourists alike — just as the city's beloved trademark, the Eiffel Tower, rose above the insults hurled at its erection in the 19th century — "a great black factory chimney" they called it before the paint had time to dry.

PLUS ÇA CHANGE...
Pompidou is now an unmissable sight, both outside and in, for its exciting exhibitions, collections of 20th century art, and its looks which have proved that a building has a role as entertainer. Visitors are so amused by the escalators as they're processed through exterior glass tubes that, like befuddled actors, they miss their exits and entrances.

Nearby, the now virtually completed Forum shopping complex is a far cry from the blot on the landscape it was feared might accumulate here when the old Les Halles market area was ripped up. Since the various levels burrow downwards, the lovely old church of St-Eustache is clearly visible and the bonestructure of the Forum's conservatorial corridors echoes the lines of the Gothic church's flying buttresses. The Forum is also an enjoyable place to be: a shopper's club — sandwich of designer boutiques and BON MARCHE, CROISSANTERIES and other fast food dispensaries, emporia selling just-about-anything-you-can-think-of. And for those who still hanker after onion soup in the small hours, there are plenty of restaurants in the surrounding web of streets that still serve the brown, cheese-topped broth in varying strengths.

Latest addition to this area is the pool and fountains betwixt the Pompidou Centre and the shadowy church of St-Merri — an incongruous but delightful water gallery for the work of two sculptors: Tinguely, whose whimsical Health — Robinsonesque clockworks twirl in the centre, and Nicky de St-Phalle, whose brightly coloured fibre-glass sculptures never fail to raise a smile, an eyebrow or the temperature of passers-by. Luscious lips and a nubile torso fairly whack you between the eyes. They certainly lift the atmosphere of this once — faded little square where now new pavement cafes are spreading across the cobbles.

So brave and new it's not yet finished, is the vast science industry and culture complex at La Villette on the north-east outskirts of Paris. Here, some of the most visually stunning architecture of the Eighties wraps up this city-within-a-city designed for learning and leisure. Focal point is the Geode, a spectacular 117ft — wide spherical cinema, created by Fainsilber. Outside, its mirror-finish conjures fantastic moving pictures from the reflections of its surroundings.

The huge Centre of Science and Industry, opposite, summons every audio — visual and computerised aid to present the acceptable — and understandable — face of technology. Then there's the Grande Halle, a former cattle market revamped by architects Reichen and Robert as a venue for shows and exhibitions.

La Villette already has theatres and creative workshops, concert halls and conference centres, a bumper park and gardens where children can explore, discover and play. More is being added year by year — a City of Music next. You have to bear this in mind when you visit, for uncultivated parts still resound to a cacophony of construction. But this needn't worry you as the whole thing is so huge and there's so much to see you can easily stay clear of the bulldozers. How to get there? Metro Porte La Villette or take your car- there's a mammoth underground car park.

Transport in Paris

The following information will give you an idea of the price of travelling around Paris:

Buses

1 ticket	4.60 FF
Book of 10 tickets (carnet)	27.50

Underground system

2nd class:	1 ticket	4.60	FF
	Book of 10 tickets	27.50	
1st class:	1 ticket	6.80	FF
	Book of 10 tickets	42.00	

Before 9 a.m. and after 5 p.m. passengers holding a second class ticket are allowed to travel in first class carriages.

Carte orange (season ticket), 2nd class — 2 zones:

1 week	43.00	FF
1 month	152.00	

Tourist ticket

2 days	53.00	FF
4 days	80.00	
7 days	133.00	

The tourist ticket entitles you to unlimited travel on all R.A.T.P. network (on S.N.C.F. network different tariffs will apply), metro lines and R.E.R (A and B at the South of "Gare du Nord") in first class carriages, bus services except special bus routes. On Metro lines and R.E.R insert the magnetic card attached to the ticket in the slot of the electronic gate (except on R.E.R line B at the South of "Les Baconnets"). On regular bus routes the ticket must be shown to the driver.

Children under 4 travel free on buses and underground and between the age 4 and 10 have a 50% reduction.

Entertainment and sightseeing in Paris (approximate prices):

Theatre seats

Opera	40.00 FF	to	440.00 FF
Comedie Francaise	35.00	to	110.00
Odeon	22.00	to	94.00
Other theatres	30.00	to	220.00

Cinema seats

First release	28.00 FF	to	33.00 FF
(students, Senior Citizens, and Mondays)	20.00	to	22.50

Entrance prices for cabarets;

Folies Bergere	75.00 FF	to	324.00 FF
The Lido (Champagne and Show)			340.00
Dinner and Show			495.00
The Moulin Rouge, Champagne and Show			340.00
Dinner and Show			495.00
To Crazy Horse Show + 2 drinks			505.00
The Paradis Latin Champagne and Show			330.00
Dinner and Show			485.00
The Bateaux Mouches Dinner and cruise			420.00
Dinner and Show			460.00

Museums and historic monuments;

Entrance fees for National museum vary between 9 and 16 FF. The Louvre: 16 FF, free on Sundays. All National Museums offer 50 % reductions on Sundays and Public Holidays.

Conciergerie — Sainte — Chapelle	16.00 FF
Arc de Triomphe, by stairs	9.00
Eiffel Tower : 2nd floor, by stairs	7.00
by lift	22.00
3rd floor, by lift	37.00
Tour Montparnasse (59 floor)	26.00
children	17.00
Notre — Dame: the church	free
the towers	9.00

Reduced rates of admission for children, students and senior citizens are available.

There are numerous tourist companies which offer sightseeing tours, lasting for a duration of a few hours to a full day, featuring, tightly scheduled excursions; to see Paris by day and, to see Paris by night.

The hotels of Paris shown in the Guide will be able to advise you in detail, on how to tackle the city of Paris, efficiently, in all aspects of its attractions. Some of the hotels (e.g. Arcade — Cambronne) houses a Tourist Information Service Desk which may arrange everything for you.

*PRINTEMPS

THE MOST PARISIAN DEPARTMENT STORE
LE PLUS PARISIEN DES GRANDS MAGASINS

FOLIES BERGERE

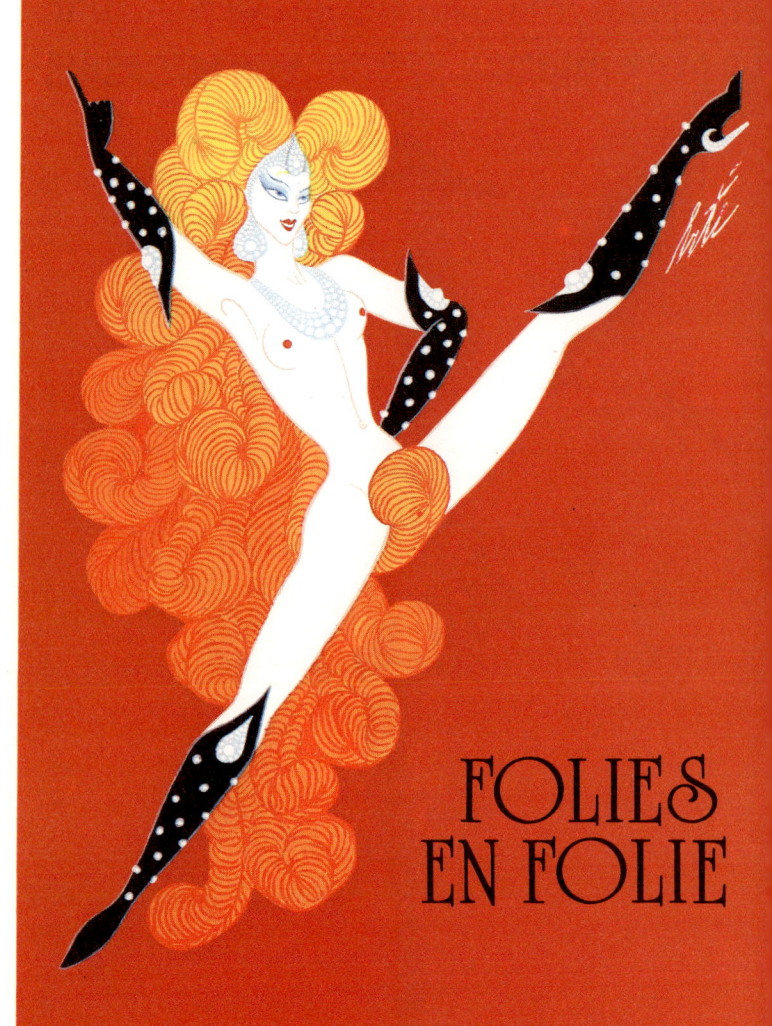

FOLIES EN FOLIE

**LA NOUVELLE REVUE DE HÉLÈNE MARTINI
MISE EN SCÈNE ET COSTUMES
DE MICHEL GYARMATHY**

32, rue Richer, 75009 PARIS - 42 46 77 11

FOLIES BERGÈRE

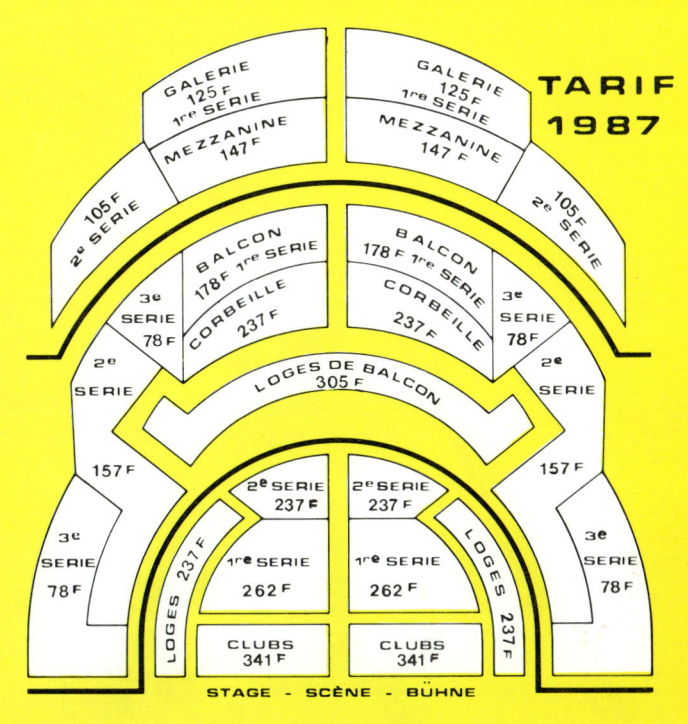

TARIF 1987

Seating chart:
- GALERIE 1re SÉRIE — 125 F
- MEZZANINE — 147 F
- 2e SÉRIE — 105 F
- BALCON 1re SÉRIE — 178 F
- CORBEILLE — 237 F
- 3e SÉRIE — 78 F
- 2e SÉRIE — 157 F
- LOGES DE BALCON — 305 F
- LOGES — 237 F
- 2e SÉRIE — 237 F
- 1re SÉRIE — 262 F
- 3e SÉRIE — 78 F
- CLUBS — 341 F

STAGE - SCÈNE - BÜHNE

32, rue Richer - 75009 PARIS Métro Cadet ou Rue Montmartre

spectacle tous les soirs à 21 h
RELACHE LUNDI

Informations et Réservations

Tous les jours de 11 h à 18 h 30
au Théâtre ou par téléphone **42 46 77 11**
Par correspondance : 8, rue Saulnier, 75009 PARIS
Télex 641 533 FOLIBER

---

show every evening at 9 p.m.
CLOSED ON MONDAY

Informations and Reservations

Every day from 11 a.m. till 6.30 p.m.
at the Theatre or by phone **42 46 77 11**
By mail : 8, rue Saulnier, 75009 PARIS
Telex 641 533 FOLIBER

MARTINET, Paris - 47.70.34.99

The locations of the hotels in Paris

★ ★ ★ ★ de Luxe   Telephone   Page

A Pullman St.Jacques   4589-8980   54

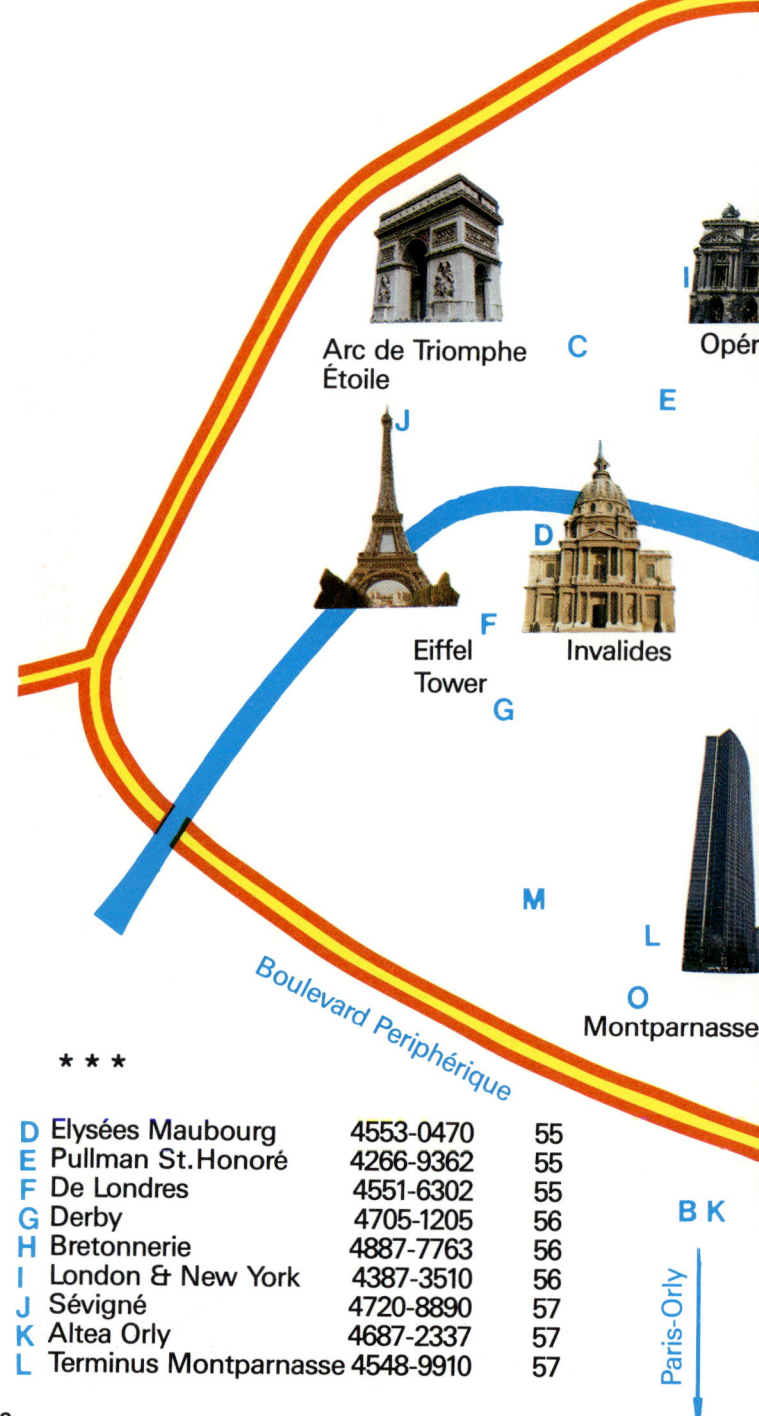

Arc de Triomphe
Étoile   C   Opéra
                          E
          J
                      D
                  Invalides
      Eiffel F
      Tower
              G

                      M   L
                                O
                             Montparnasse

Boulevard Periphérique

★ ★ ★

D	Elysées Maubourg	4553-0470	55
E	Pullman St.Honoré	4266-9362	55
F	De Londres	4551-6302	55
G	Derby	4705-1205	56
H	Bretonnerie	4887-7763	56
I	London & New York	4387-3510	56
J	Sévigné	4720-8890	57
K	Altea Orly	4687-2337	57
L	Terminus Montparnasse	4548-9910	57

B K

Paris-Orly

* * * *

| B | Pullman Paris-Orly | 4687-3636 | 54 |
| C | Pullman Windsor | 4563-0404 | 54 |

LA GÉODE

N

Louvre

H

Notre-Dame

A

* *

M	Arcade-Cambronne	4567-3520	58
N	Arcade-La Villette	4268-2370	58
O	Arcade-Montparnasse	4567-3520	58

PULLMAN SAINT-JACQUES **** de Luxe
17 Boulevard Saint-Jacques,
75014 — Paris
Tel.(1) 4589-8980, Telex: 270740

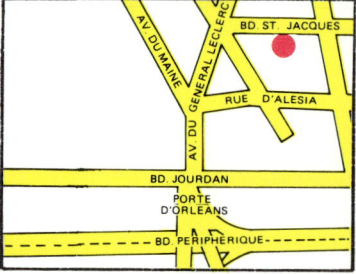

800 rooms ● bathrooms ● air-conditioning ● radio ● colour TV ● mini-bar ● direct line telephone ● 5 restaurants — japanese, chinese and famous "Cafe Francais" ● 2 bars ● 17 conference rooms ● travel agency car rental ● cinema ● shopping arcade ● beauty salon ● garage ● bus to airport

PULLMAN PARIS-ORLY ****
20 Avenue C. Lindbergh
94656 — Rungis Cedex
Tel.(1) 4687-3636, Telex: 260 738

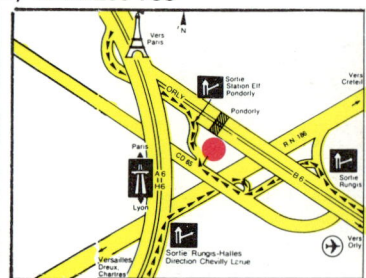

206 rooms ● details, page 14 ● room service ● TV with video circuit ● restaurant ● parking facilities ● hotel shuttle bus free ● garden ● bar ● boutique ● sauna bath ● open-air swimming pool ● close to Rungis wholesale market ● 20 min drive from Paris and near the Orly airport.

PULLMAN WINDSOR ****
14, Rue Beaujon,
75008 — Paris
Tel.(1) 4563-0404, Telex: 650 — 902

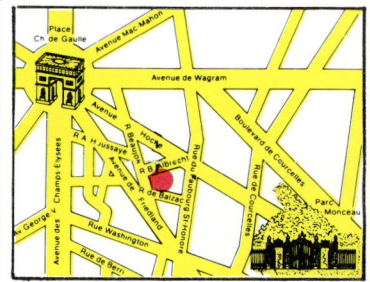

135 rooms ● details page 14 ● TV with video circuit ● restaurant ● bar ● meeting rooms.

HOTEL ELYSÉES-MAUBOURG ***

35 Boulevard de Latour Maubourg,
75007 Paris
Tel.(1) 4556-1078, Telex:206 227 F

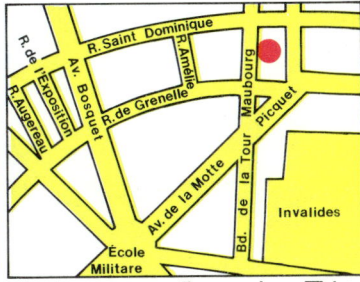

30 rooms with fully equipped private bathroom ● radio ● colour TV ● mini-bar ● personal safe box in each room ● direct telephone ● sauna ● small garden ● bar ● rooms with video in English and cable TV- at your disposal; cable TV (channel 4) and video film (channel 8). A new film each night at 9 p.m. and 11 p.m.

PULLMAN ST.HONORE ***

15 Rue Boissy — d'Anglas,
75008 — Paris
Tel.(1) 4266-9362, Telex: 240366

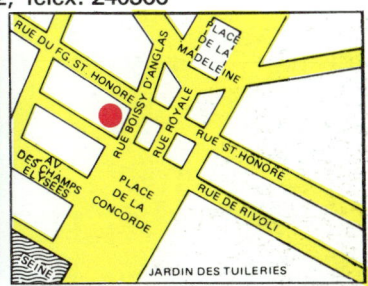

112 rooms ● duplexes and suite ● bathroom ● radio ● colour TV with video circuit with in house movie channel ● mini-bar ● direct telephone ● bar ● parking nearby.

HOTEL DE LONDRES ***

1 Rue Augereau,
75007 — Paris,
Tel.(1) 4551-6302, Telex: 206 398F

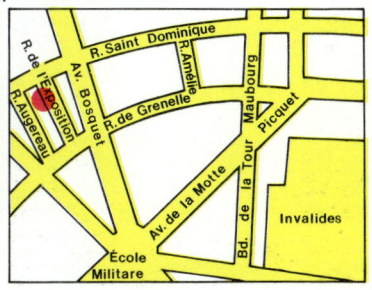

30 rooms with private bathroom ● competely refurbished and renovated ● colour TV ● lift ● radio ● mini-bar ● telephone direct.

55

DERBY-HOTEL ***
5 Avenue Duquesne,
75007 — Paris
Tel.(1) 4705-1205, Telex: Derby 206236

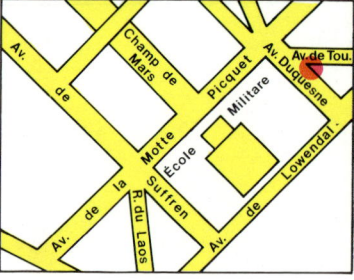

44 rooms with private bathrooms, WC ● colour TV ● direct telephone ● sound-proofed ● personal safety deposit box in each room ● private bar ● small garden.

HOTEL DE LA BRETONNERIE ***
22 Rue Ste Croix de la Bretonnerie,
75004 — Paris
Tel.(1) 4887-7763

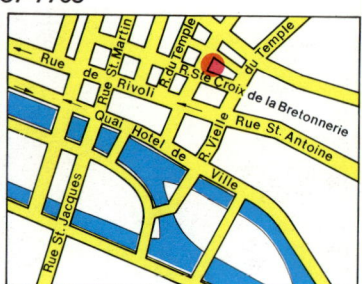

31 rooms with fully equipped bathrooms ● this unique hotel, recommended in a 17th century mansion house will make you feel a real inhabitant of Old Paris ● direct-line telephone ● period furniture.

HOTEL LONDRES & NEW YORK ***
15 Place de Havre,
75008 — Paris
Tel.(1) 4387-3510, Telex: Hotelny 650 117

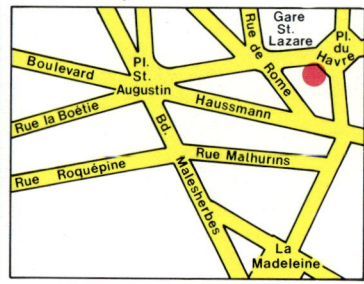

70 rooms with bathrooms or shower, WC ● direct telephone ● mini-bar ● colour TV ● telex service.

HOTEL DE SÉVIGNÉ ★★★
6 Rue de Belloy,
75116 — Paris
Tel.(1) 4720-8890, Telex:610219 F

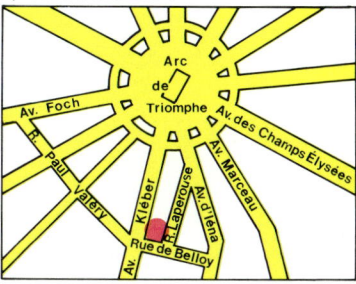

30 rooms with bathrooms ● colour TV ● radio ● direct telephone ● mini-bar ● bar ● laundry and dry cleaning ● safe ● car rental ● parking facilities.

ALTEA HOTEL ★★★
429-94547 Orly Aerogare Cedex,
Tel.(1) 4687-2337, Telex:204 345

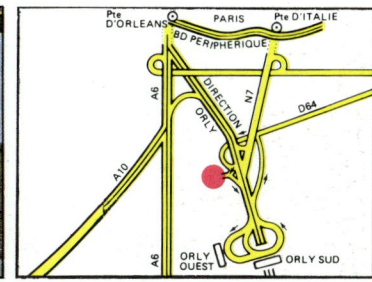

200 rooms with fully equipped bathrooms ● sound proofed ● TV with video ciccuit ● air-conditioned ● radio ● restaurant ● bar ● parking ● free shuttle service to the airport ● 800 m from Orly air terminals ● close to the International Rungis market.

HOTEL TERMINUS MONTPARNASSE ★★★
59 Boulevard du Montparnase,
75006-Paris
Tel.(1) 4548-9910, Telex:Motel 202636 F

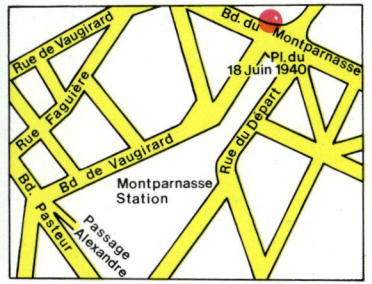

63 rooms with bath or shower, WC ● colour TV ● direct line telephone ● automatic morning call ● reception room ● bar ● public car park nearby.

HOTEL ARCADE PARIS **

2 Rue de Cambronne,
75740 — Paris, Cedex 15
Tel.(1) 4567-3520, Telex: Arcapar 203842

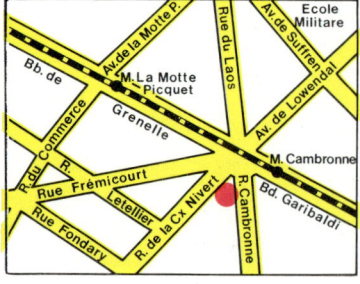

530 rooms

TYPICAL EXAMPLE OF THE ARCADE HOTELS

All rooms with shower and WC ● telephone ● alarm clock ● colour TV on request ● restaurant ● bar ● nursery ● tourist and entertainment information ● boutique – duty free ● parking facilities.

HOTEL ARCADE PARIS-LA VILLETTE **

Opens in June 1987
31-35 Quai de L'Oise
75019 — Paris
Tel.(1) 4268-2370, Telex: 642241

285 rooms

HOTEL ARCADE PARIS-MONTPARNASSE **

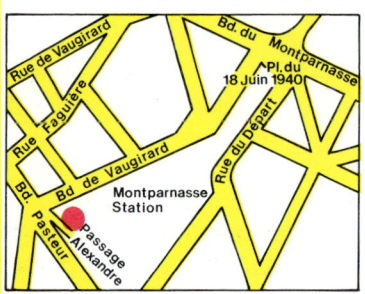

Opens possibly in June 1987
15 Passage Alexandre
75015 — Paris

31 rooms

Until the opening date contacts should be made with the **Hotel Arcade Paris-Cambronne**
Tel.(1) 4567 — 3520, Telex: 203842

✱PRINTEMPS

Welcome. On the ground floor of the Nouveau Magasin, over ten multilingual interpreters are ready to help you at the Welcome Service. They know Printemps by heart and can:

— guide you to the departments you are looking for,
— assist with all formalities associated with payment and shipping of your purchases,
— help you to change currency,
— explain how you can benefit from the export discount.

They will also be happy to give you any additional information useful for your stay in Paris free of charge.

Printemps, gifts by the thousands. At "Primavera" you will be inspired to decorate your home. At the "Boutique Douce" rare liqueurs or delicacies. For the table, top names in silverware, crystal and china.

Printemps has all the fashion in Paris. All the great names and designers are here with their latest creations: clothing, lingerie, beauty care products and perfumes.

Printemps is also a man's world. "Brummel" is entirely devoted to mail fashion, with a large selection of famous names from the "new wave" designers, to traditional elegance.

YOUR GUIDE TO LE GUIDE

Calais

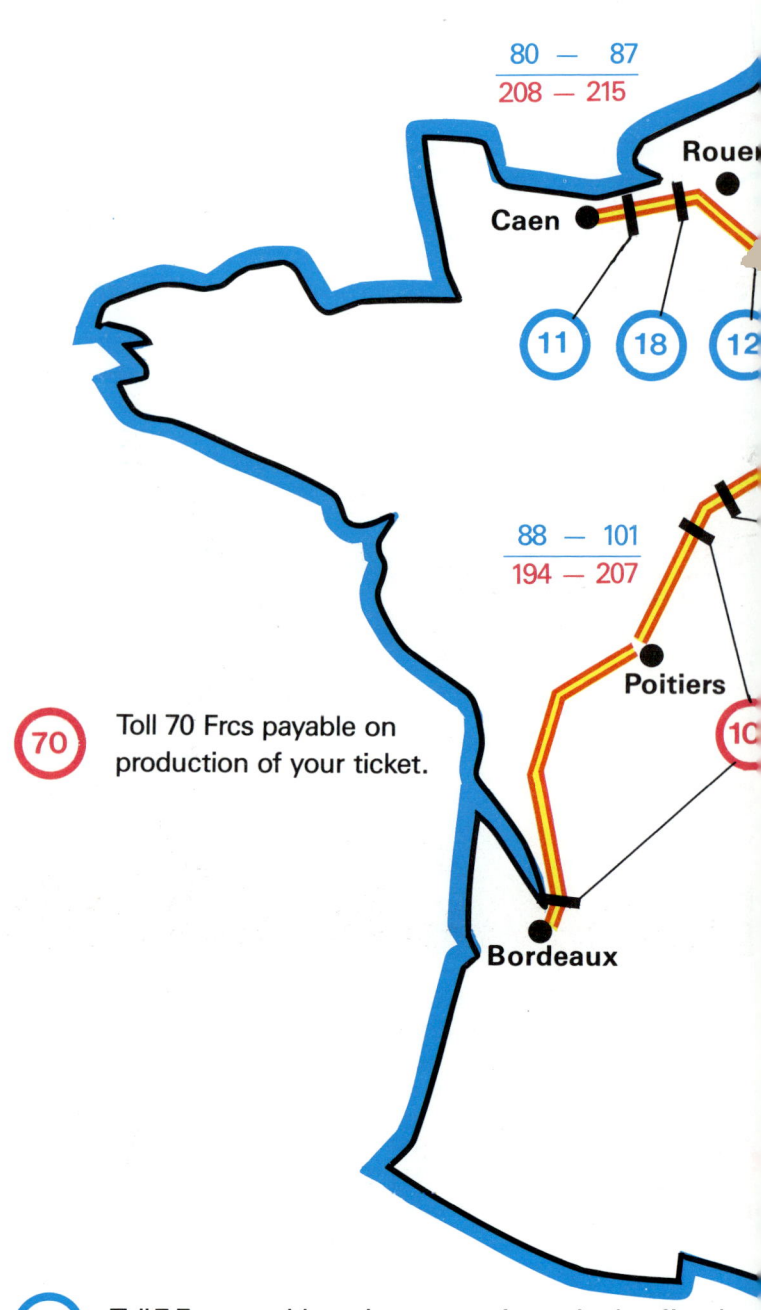

$$\frac{80 - 87}{208 - 215}$$

Rouen

Caen

(11) (18) (12)

$$\frac{88 - 101}{194 - 207}$$

Poitiers

(10)

(70) Toll 70 Frcs payable on production of your ticket.

Bordeaux

(7) Toll 7 Frcs payable at the automatic service barrière de péage, have your coins ready. Use seperate, marked lane if change is required.

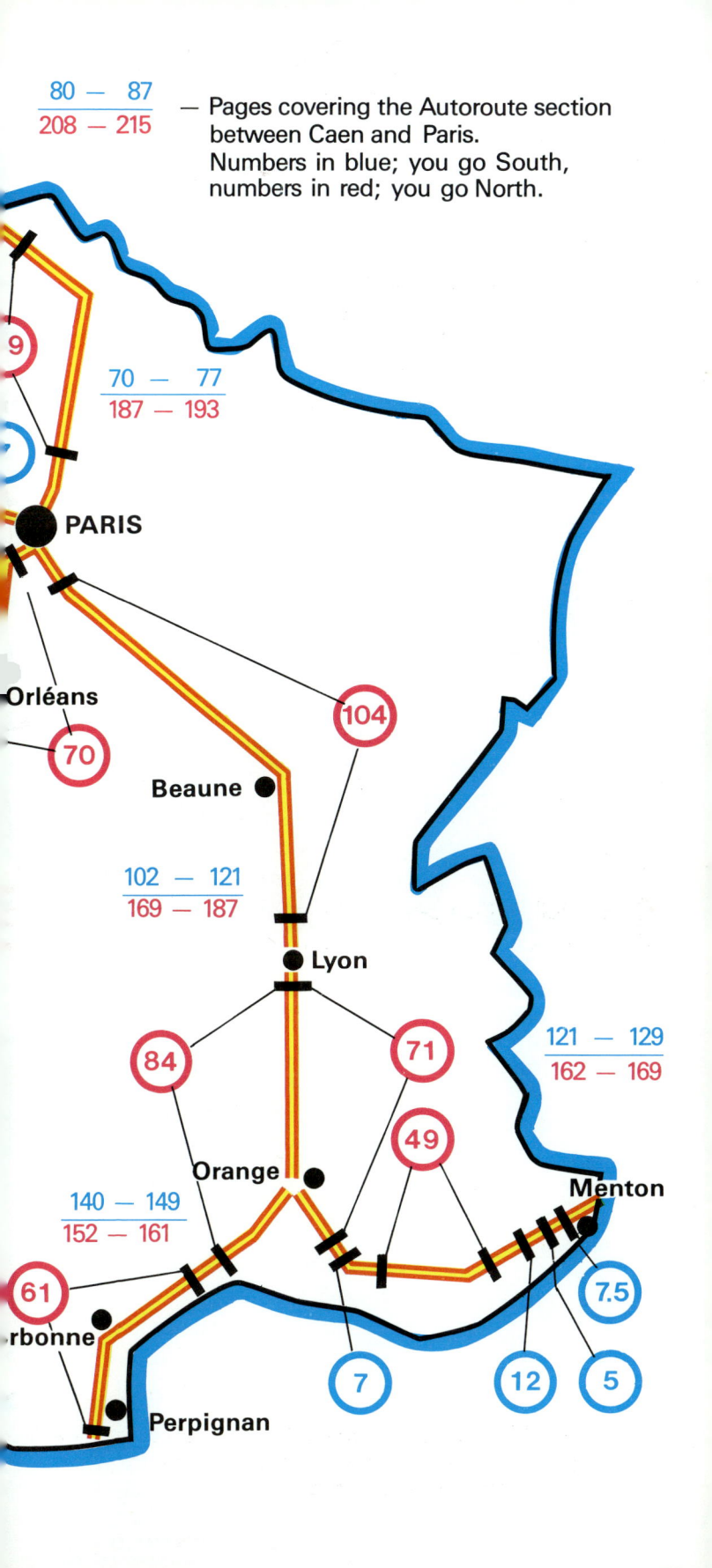

80 — 87
208 — 215
— Pages covering the Autoroute section between Caen and Paris.
Numbers in blue; you go South, numbers in red; you go North.

70 — 77
187 — 193

PARIS

Orléans
(70)

(104)

Beaune

102 — 121
169 — 187

Lyon

(84) (71)

121 — 129
162 — 169

(49)

Orange
140 — 149
152 — 161

Menton

(61)
rbonne

(7.5)

(7) (12) (5)

Perpignan

61

L'ARCHE RESTAURANTS

RESTAURANT FORMULAS - LEGEND

A - BAR - SANDWICHERIE
B - SELF-SERVICE
C - GRILL - SERVICE AT TABLE

Nearest town

ON MOTORWAY A.1

L'ARCHE	de	RESSONS-Est	A-B	COMPIEGNE
L'ARCHE	de	RESSONS-Ouest	B	COMPIEGNE
L'ARCHE	d'	ASSEVILLERS-Est	B	PERONNE
L'ARCHE	d'	ASSEVILLERS-Ouest	A-B-C	PERONNE

ON MOTORWAY A.31

L'ARCHE	de	SANDAUCOURT	B	VITTEL

ON MOTORWAY A.4

L'ARCHE	de	VERDUN	A-B-C	VERDUN

ON MOTORWAY A.6

L'ARCHE	de	VENOY-Ouest	A-B	AUXERRE
L'ARCHE	de	VENOY-Est	B-C	AUXERRE
L'ARCHE	de	MAISON DIEU	B	AVALLON
L'ARCHE	de	SAINT-AMBREUIL	B	CHALON S/S
L'ARCHE	de	SAINT-ALBAIN	A-B-C	MACON

ON MOTORWAY A.9

L'ARCHE	de	FABREGUES	A-B-C	MONTPELLIER

SMILE AND RECEPTION INCLUDED

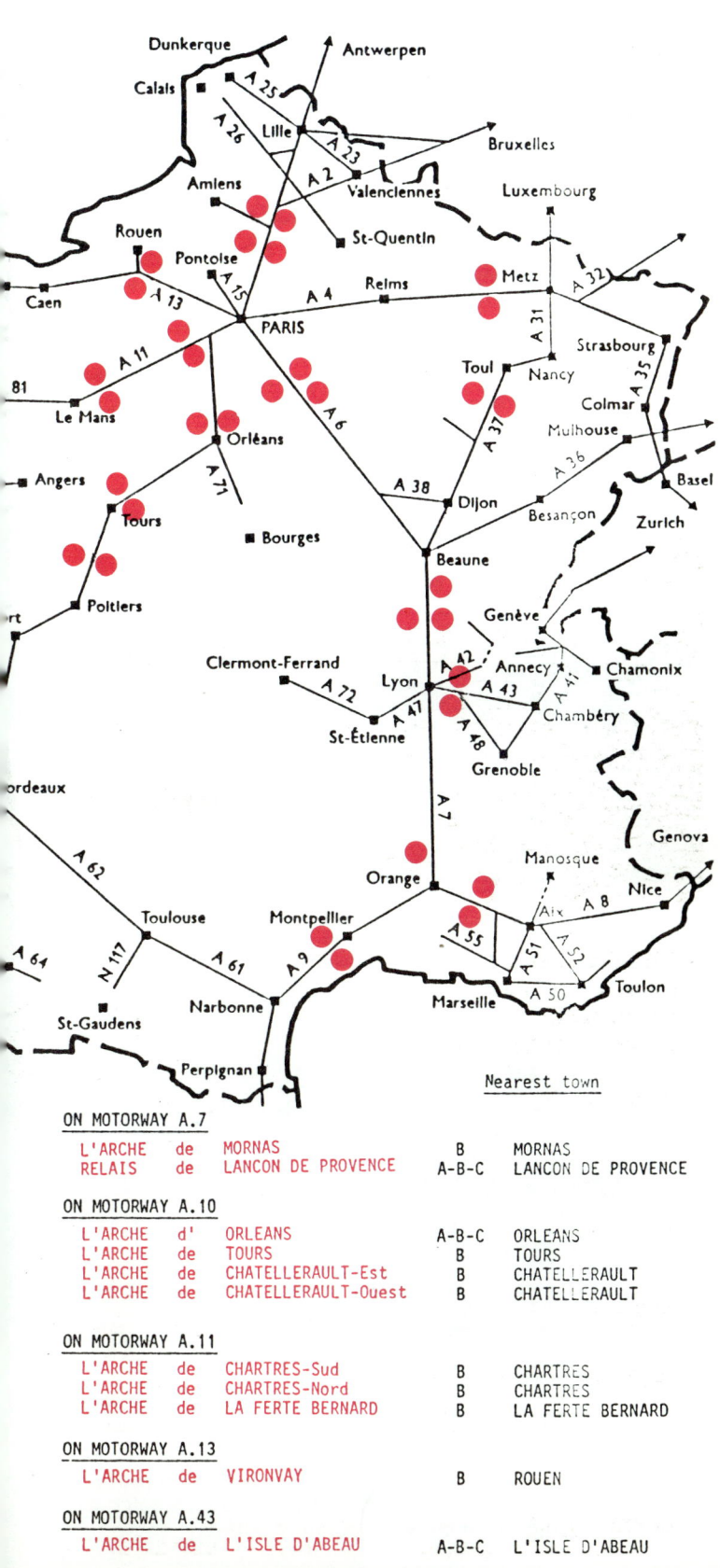

		Nearest town		
ON MOTORWAY A.7				
L'ARCHE	de	MORNAS	B	MORNAS
RELAIS	de	LANCON DE PROVENCE	A-B-C	LANCON DE PROVENCE
ON MOTORWAY A.10				
L'ARCHE	d'	ORLEANS	A-B-C	ORLEANS
L'ARCHE	de	TOURS	B	TOURS
L'ARCHE	de	CHATELLERAULT-Est	B	CHATELLERAULT
L'ARCHE	de	CHATELLERAULT-Ouest	B	CHATELLERAULT
ON MOTORWAY A.11				
L'ARCHE	de	CHARTRES-Sud	B	CHARTRES
L'ARCHE	de	CHARTRES-Nord	B	CHARTRES
L'ARCHE	de	LA FERTE BERNARD	B	LA FERTE BERNARD
ON MOTORWAY A.13				
L'ARCHE	de	VIRONVAY	B	ROUEN
ON MOTORWAY A.43				
L'ARCHE	de	L'ISLE D'ABEAU	A-B-C	L'ISLE D'ABEAU

HOTEL PULLMAN LE PIGONNET ★★★★
5 Avenue du Pigonnet
13090 — Aix-en-Provence
Tel.4259-0290, Telex: 410629

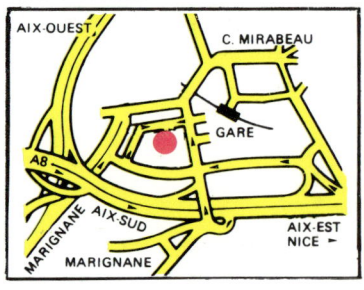

50 rooms with fully equipped bathrooms ● restaurant ● bar ● telephone ● swimming pool ● parking ● conference rooms.

PULLMAN HOTEL ★★★★
129 Rue Servient-Part-Dieu Nord,
69003 — Lyon
Tel.7862-9412, Telex:380088

245 rooms ● details, page 14 ● TV with video circuit ● restaurant ● bar ● parking facilities ● hotel shuttle bus ● Europe's tallest hotel, overlooking the high-speed-train station.

HOTEL NOVOTEL ★★★★
Autoroute A6, Porte de Lyon
69570 — Dardilly
Tel.7835-1341, Telex: 330962 F

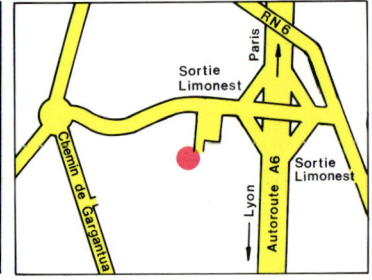

107 rooms with fully equipped bathrooms ● colour TV ● video circuit ● radio ● automatic alarm clock ● direct line telephone ● restaurant ● air-conditioning and soundproofed ● room service ● parking free ● bar ● restaurant ● buffet.

HOTEL MERCURE ★★★
Autoroute A7
13680 — Lancon-de-Provence
Tel.9053-9070, Telex:440183 F

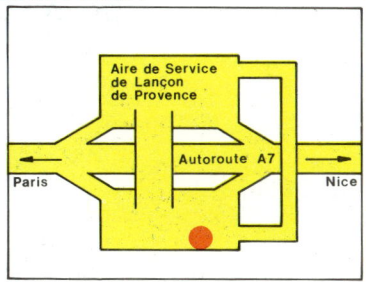

100 rooms (including 1 for disabled people and 2 suites) with fully equipped bathrooms ● colour TV (partly) ● direct line telephone ● mini-bar ● air-conditioning ● sound proofing ● catering from 7 p.m. to midnight ● swimming pool ● buffet brekfast ● bar-open until midnight ● free car park.

ALTEA HOTEL ★★★
26 Rue de Coubertin,
71000 — Macon
Tel.8536-2806, Telex:800830

63 room ● details, page 14 ● restaurant ● bar ● parking facilities ● garden ● boutique ● 100 m away from in-door and open-air swimming pool ● on the bank of Saone River ● surrounded by green country side.

ALTEA HOTEL ★★★
22 Boulevard de la Marne,
21100-Dijon
Tel.8072-3113, Telex:350293

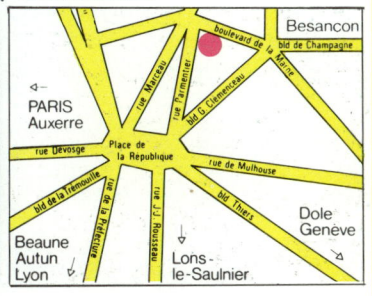

124 rooms ● details,page 14 ● TV with video circuit ● room service ● restaurant ● bar ● parking facilities ● open-air swimming pool ● a few steps from the City Centre.

ALTEA HOTEL ★★★
A.S.P. Darvault, Autoroute A6,
77140 — Nemours
Tel. 6428-1032, Telex: 690 243

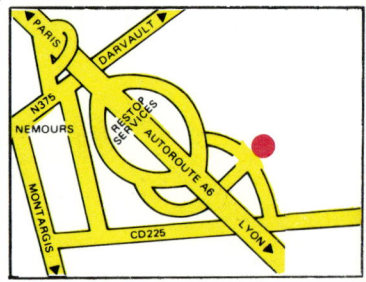

102 rooms with fully equipped bathroom ● radio ● TV ● telephone ● mini-bar ● motorway restaurants on near-by service area ● children play ground.

ALTEA BEAUNE HOTEL ★★★
21203 — Beaune
Tel. 8021-4509, Telex: 350 627

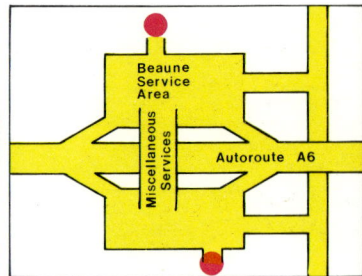

150 rooms with fully equipped bathrooms ● radio ● TV ● 2 self service cafeterias ● mini-bar ● restaurant ● bar ● located in a wooded park ● parking in front of your apartment.

HOTEL MERCURE ★★★
80200 — Assevillers Peronne
Tel. 2284-1276, Telex: 140 943 F

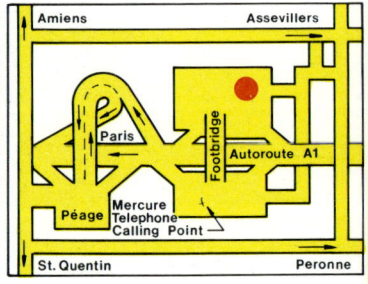

100 rooms with fully equipped bathroom (1 room and 2 suites for disabled people) ● colour TV (partly) ● direct telephone ● mini-bar ● swimming pool ● bar ● buffet ● restaurant-self service.

HOTEL IBIS **

Aire du Soleil Levant,
Autoroute A6, 89290 Champs S/Yonne
Tel. 8640-3131, Telex: 351817

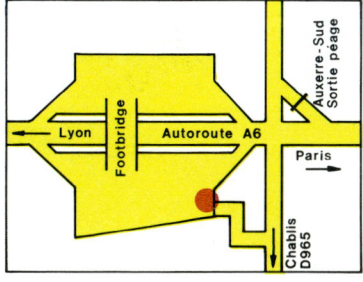

72 rooms with fully equipped bathroom ● TV with video circuit ● direct telephone ● motorway restaurants on nearby Service Area.

HOTEL "LE RELAIS" **

66 Boulevard C. Senlecq
62610 — Ardres
Tel. 2135-4200

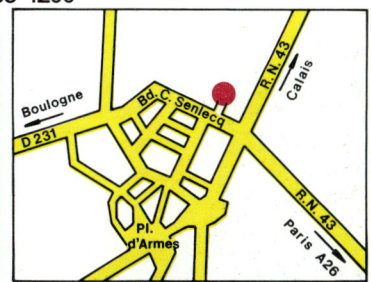

11 rooms with bath or shower and WC ● telephone ● English pub-like bar ● spacious restaurant and very attractive ● family suite for 5 persons ● pretty garden ● private parking ● conveniently located on the route between Calais and A26 — Autoroute to Paris.

HOTEL VICTORIA **

8 Rue du Cdt Bonningue (corner Rue de Madrid)
62100 — Calais
Tel. 2134-3832

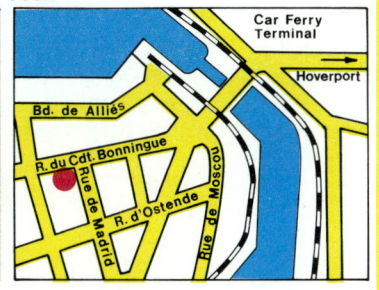

15 rooms with baths or showers and WC ● direct line telephone ● automatic morning call ● breakfast in rooms ● parking in the street ● conveniently located.

This sign-logo reads:

KINDNESS, COURTESY, QUALITY.

So wherever you come across this sign; a restaurant, a hotel, a garage, a car or any other place, it would be most likely that the implied connotation is precisely correct. It is in the interest of all of the users of this guide that the LE GUIDE sign is displayed appropriately. Please help.

The actual Routes of the Guide

(going south)

CALAIS

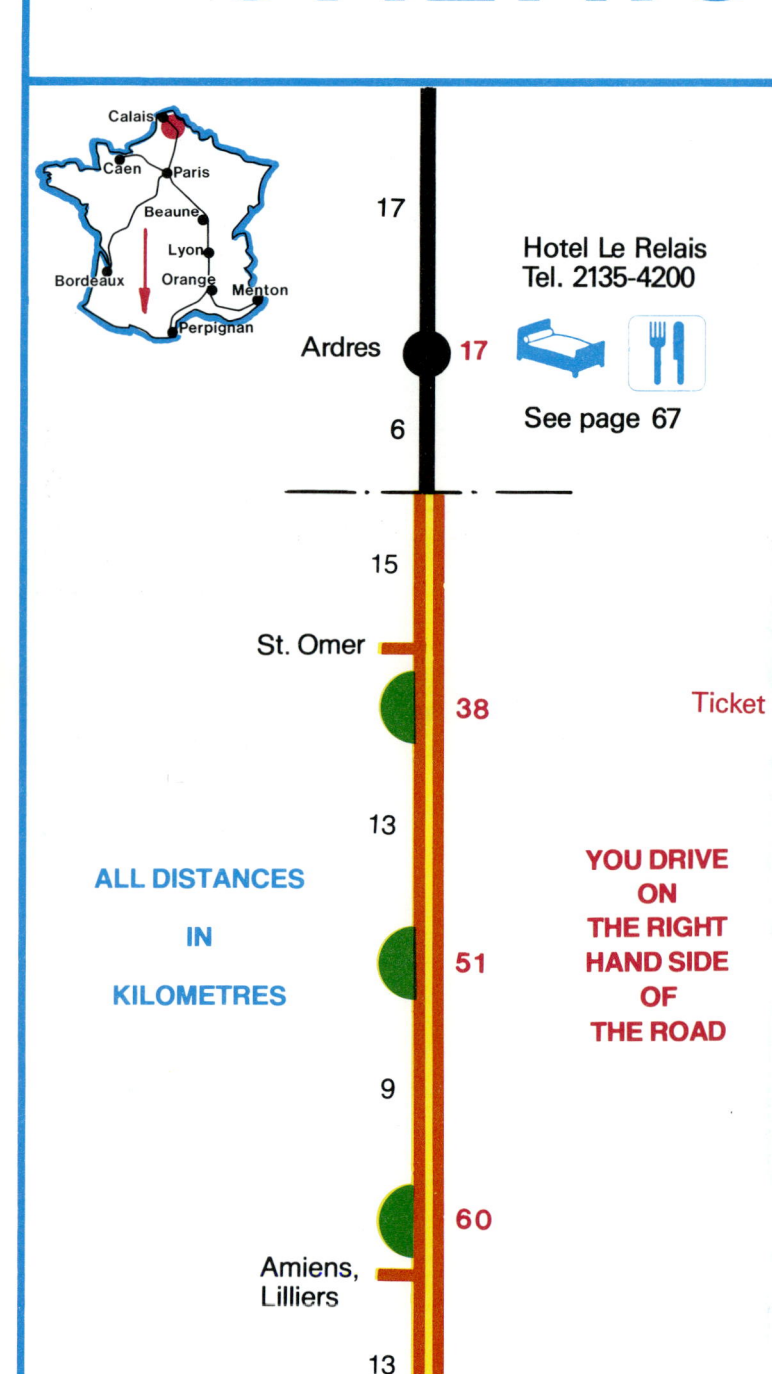

17

Ardres 17

Hotel Le Relais
Tel. 2135-4200

See page 67

6

15

St. Omer

38   Ticket

13

ALL DISTANCES

IN

KILOMETRES

51

**YOU DRIVE
ON
THE RIGHT
HAND SIDE
OF
THE ROAD**

9

60

Amiens,
Lilliers

13

73

Bethune

73

22

PORT

Aire de **Barrière de péage**

WC 📞 ♿ ℹ️

Open space type of area with tables and benches, grassy, small and pleasant.

Aire du **Grand Riez**

WC ♿ 🎢

As above, climbing frame, lit.
SOS — at side of the Area.

Aire du **Rely**

Very open, spacious, lot of grassy spots, newly developed.
SOS — at the side.

Aire du **Reveillon**

WC 🎢

Enclosed, forested, tables and benches, some among trees, lit at night, climbing frame, very nice.
SOS — at the side.

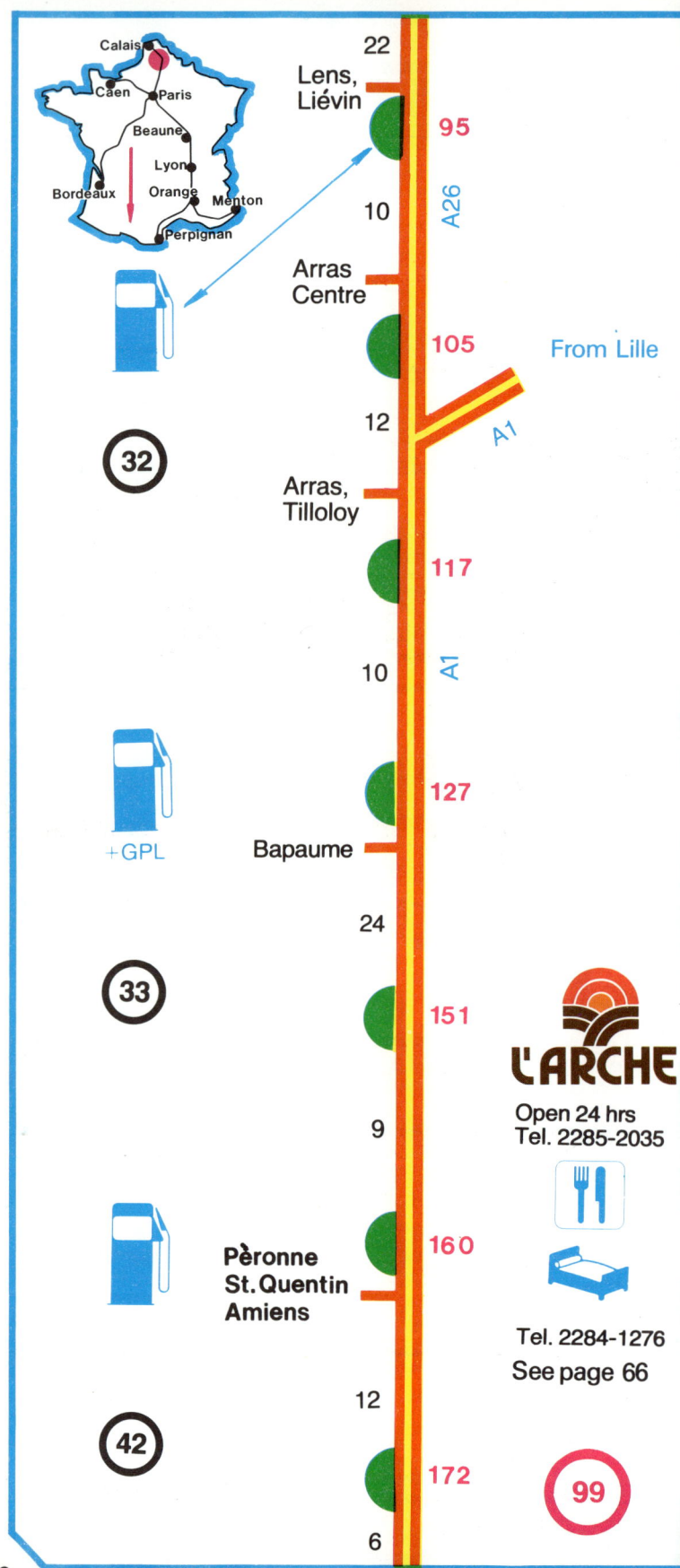

	22	
Lens, Liévin		95
	10	A26
Arras Centre		105
	12	From Lille / A1
(32)		
Arras, Tilloloy		117
	10	A1
+GPL		127
Bapaume		
	24	
(33)		151
	9	
Pèronne St. Quentin Amiens		160
(42)	12	172
	6	

L'ARCHE

Open 24 hrs
Tel. 2285-2035

🍴 🛏

Tel. 2284-1276
See page 66

(99)

Aire de Souches

Just parking facilities. Small.
SOS — at side.

Aire des Trois Crettes

Open type with few tables and benches. Lit at night, spacious.
SOS — towards the exit.

Aire de Wancourt-Ouest

Open space type of area, few tables and benches, pleasant.

Aire de St. Léger

As above. Hot drinks available from dispensing machines.
SOS — located just before the entry to the Area.

Aire de Maurepas

Small with tables and benches, lit at night, grassy and nice
SOS — at the side.

Aire d Assevillers

Ample parking facilities. Cafeteria, grill, boutique there is a footbridge to the other side of the m-way Rest Area.
SOS — at the side.

Aire de Hattencourt

Open space type of area. Tables and benches. Nice.
SOS — at the side.

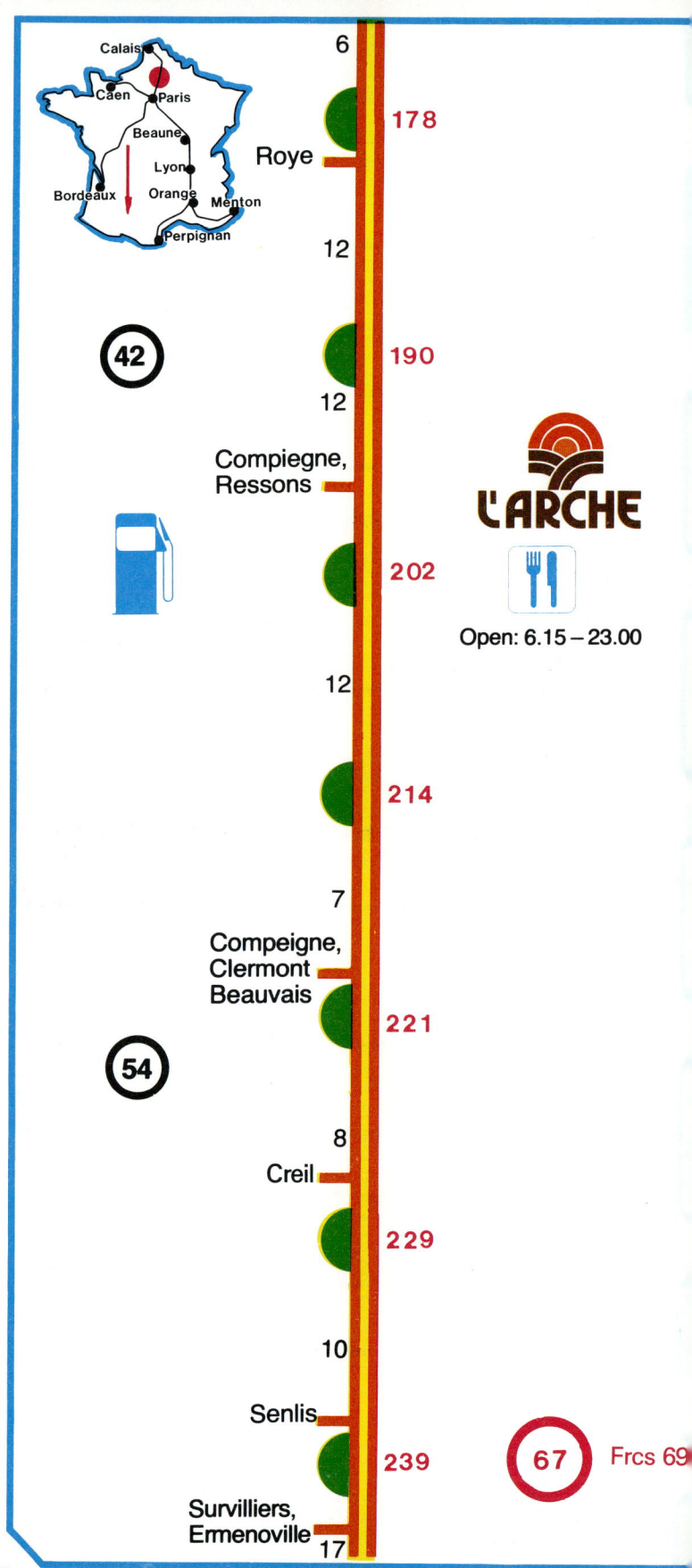

	6	
Roye		178
	12	
(42)		190
	12	
Compiegne, Ressons		
		202
	12	
		214
	7	
Compeigne, Clermont Beauvais		221
	8	
Creil		
		229
	10	
Senlis		
		239
Survilliers, Ermenoville	17	

L'ARCHE

🍴

Open: 6.15 – 23.00

(67) Frcs 69

74

Aire de Goyencourt-Ouest

WC ♿ 🚻

There are tables and benches. Some of the sets are under cover. Nice.
SOS.

Aire de Tilloy-Ouest

WC ♿ 🚻

Plenty of tables and benches, most are among trees. Lit at night, climbing frames. Very nice.
SOS — at the side towards the exit.

Aire de Ressons-Ouset

🚻 ☎ ♿ 🎁 ☕ ⛽ 💱 🚻

Usual facilities of petrol station complex. The exit to Compiegne combined with the entrence to the Rest Area.

Aire de Bois d'Arsy

WC ☎ 🚻

Spacious, tables and benches among trees and in the open space. Swings for children, climbing frames, lit. Nice.
SOS.

Aire de Longueil

WC

Very small but nice, few tables and benches, some trees. Situated on a hill.
SOS — just past the Area

Aire de Roberval-Ouest

WC

Tables and benches, some trees, very small area but pleasant.
SOS — at the entry.

Aire de Barrière de péage

WC ☎ ♿

Open space type of area. Exit for Senlis actually takes place at the "barrière de péage".

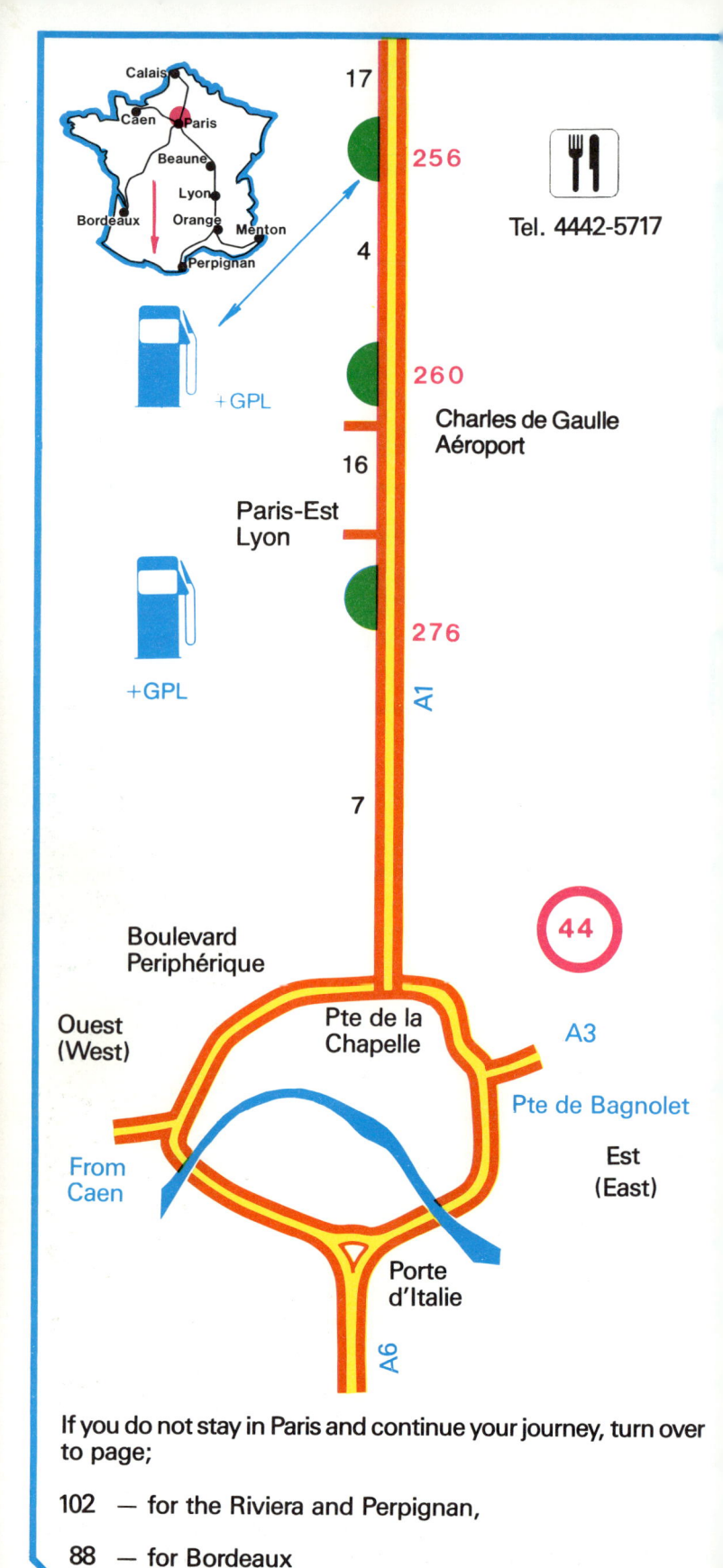

17

256

Tel. 4442-5717

4

+GPL

260

Charles de Gaulle
Aéroport

16

Paris-Est
Lyon

276

A1

+GPL

7

44

Boulevard
Periphérique

Pte de la
Chapelle

A3

Ouest
(West)

Pte de Bagnolet

From
Caen

Est
(East)

Porte
d'Italie

A6

If you do not stay in Paris and continue your journey, turn over to page;

102 — for the Riviera and Perpignan,

88 — for Bordeaux

76

Aire de **Vemars**

Wide selection of services. Self-service cefeteria and restaurant.
SOS.

Aire de **Chennevières**

WC

There are tables and benches among trees, very tidy small. Pleasant.
SOS — not far from the exit.

Aire de la **Courneuve**

Limited services as indicated.
SOS — near the entrance to the Area.

But now, having passed the Rest Area — Aire de Chennevieres and depending on, whether you stay in Paris or drive past you continue your journey as follows;-

You stay in Paris.

Since there are alternatives to follow, you need to decide upon your choice, depending on your intended destination in Paris.

You may;

1. leave the motorway at the exit "Paris-Est, Lyon" and join the Boulevard Peripherique at the Pte de Bagnolet ("Pte" — short form for "Porte", which means "gate" in this particular instance)

2. drive straight on, and before reaching Pte de la Chapelle you follow;

— the sign "Pte de Clignancourt" if you want to go Ouest (West) or,

— if you want to go Est (East) you follow the sign 'Pte d'Aubervilliers" which is next to Pte de la Villette, the nearest, convenient location of one of the Arcade hotels just outside of the City of Science and Industry with it's famous now "GÉODE" — a unique spherical giant structure, housing one of the biggest hemispheric screens in the world, a "must" to visit when in Paris, or,

— straight on, following the sign "Paris".

You need to be equipped with a good map, covering Paris with its great majority of streets offering "one way" only traffic.

I take the opportunity here, to advise you to acquire the Michelin **PLAN DE PARIS** (blue cover, 1cm = 100 metres) and you will not get lost in Paris

You drive past Paris

Take the exit for "Paris-Est, Lyon" and at the next choice of alternatives take the route for "Paris-Sud", leading you to the Pte de Bagnolet, and continue along the Boleuvard Peripherique round Paris, until you reach the pte d'Italie at which it is necessary to leave the Boulevard for your journey to the Sun. Do not concentrate your attention on the Pte d'Italie and KEEP in lane for LYON.

If you miss the above mentioned exit for "Paris-Est, Lyon" you are still O.K. joining the Boulevard at the location of Pte de la Chapelle. Just before this Gate, you have 3 possibilities but must not take the Pte de la Chapelle, otherwise you will enter the City of Paris.

If it happens, that you went straight on , turn round as soon as you realize your error, and follow the sign "Boulevard Periphérique" and then one of the two alternatives; "EST"- East or "OUEST"- West. Est seems to be the obvious choice but either will take you to the A1- Autoroute du Soleil if you KEEP in lane for LYON.

On the Boulevard Periphérique keep in lane,at least second from the right hand side. The extreme right hand side lane driving can easy lead to some frustration as the incoming traffic joins the Boulevard in a manner, as if, there was nobody else driving. But the "Priorite a droite" rule explains evrything. See "Some Tips and Further Information" chapter for further comments.

If you are heading for Bordeaux, you should follow the same route as for LYON until you have left the Boulevard and come across a choice for "Lyon" and "Chartres, Orleans".

If you happen to drive for Bordeaux using the western part of the Boulevard you may be tempted to take an earlier exit for Orleans. Unless you know the route well, do not try it if time is of importance. It is apparent that on the way you have to go through local traffic.

In the immediate vicinity of Pte d'Italie you will face awkward, small radius bends entering into suddenly darkened tunnels. Take care.

CAEN

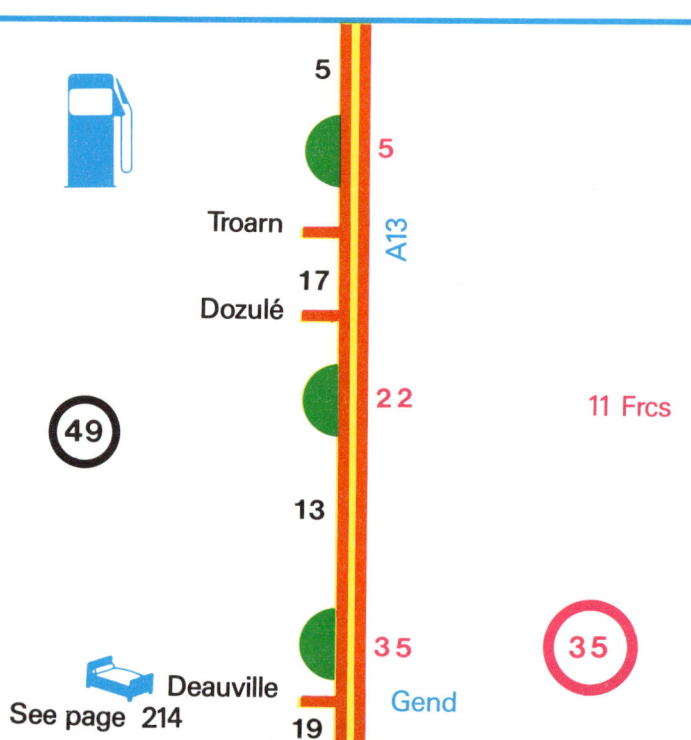

5
5
Troarn
A13
17
Dozulé

(49)
22
11 Frcs

13

35 (35)
Deauville Gend
See page 214
19

80

PULLMAN GRAND HOTEL * * * *de Luxe

Promenade Marcel — Proust,
14390 — Cabourg

Tel. 3191-0179,

Telex: 171364

70 rooms and suites ● bathroom ● colour TV ● radio ● telephone ● restaurant ● piano ● bar ● reception — conference rooms ● numerous sport facilities ● City swimming pool close to hotel ● parking facilities ● direct access to the beach.

REMEMBER

YOU DRIVE ON THE RIGHT HAND SIDE OF THE ROAD

Aire Sud de **Kiberville**

| WC | ☎ | ♿ |

Spacious, grassy area.
SOS — at the side.

Aire de **Barrière de péage**

| ☎ |

Just parking spaces. Very small.

Aire de **Beaumont**

| WC | 🪑 |

Small, grassy. Some trees, tables and benches, very pretty. Recommended.
SOS — just past the Rest Area.

81

19

54

4

Le Havre, Beuzeville

58

18 Frcs

20

(43)

78

Bourg-Achard

19

97

8

Maison-Brulée

(34)

105

Rouen

From Rouen, Les Essarts

17

Elbeuf

122

Le Vaudreuil   Louviers, Evreux

See page 208

9

131

(42)

2

(96)

(49)

Aire Sud de **Beuzeville**

Spacious, some tables and benches, grassy, pleasant.
SOS — located toward exit.

Aire de **Barrière de péage**

Very small with few parking spaces. More sort of a parking bay.

Aire du **Moulin**

Small with tables and benches, very nice.
SOS — just past the Rest Area.

Aire de **Bosqouet**

Just parking facilities. Snack-bar.
SOS — just past the Area.

Aire Sud de **Robert-le-Diable**

SOS — by the side, towards the end of the Rest Area. Located actually on the Area, not easy to spot from the Motorway.

Aire Sud de **Bord**

There are tables and benches among trees.
SOS — at the side of Area.

Aire de **Vironvay**

L'ARCHE

Spacious in parking facilities. Interconnected with the other side of Rest Area. Cafeteria.
SOS — at the side of Area.

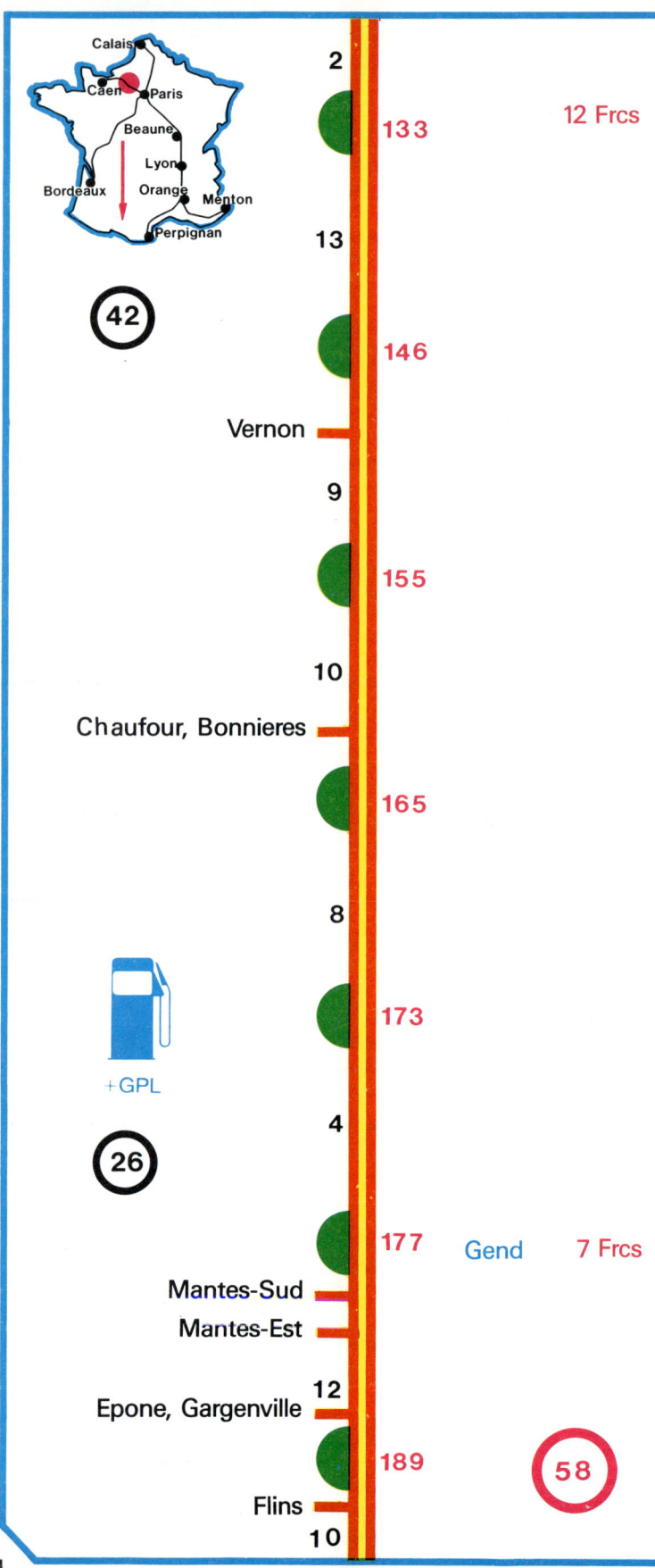

2	133	12 Frcs
13	146	
Vernon		
9	155	
10		
Chaufour, Bonnieres	165	
8	173	
+GPL		
(26)		
4	177	Gend 7 Frcs
Mantes-Sud		
Mantes-Est		
12		
Epone, Gargenville	189	(58)
Flins		
10		

(42)

Aire de **Barrière de péage**

SOS — not far, having passed the Area.

Aire Sud de **Bauchene**

Partly forested. Tables and benches.
SOS — at the entry to the Area.

Aire Sud de **Douains**

Very basic, just parking spaces.
SOS — at side, towards the entry.

Aire Sud de la **Villeneuve en Chevrie**

Small, arranged at two levels. There are few tables and benches among trees at the upper level.
SOS — at the side.

Aire de **Rosny-sur-Seine**

Few tables and benches, generaly parking spaces.
SOS — at the side of Area.

Aire de **Barrière de péage**

Just parking facilities. Gendarmerie.

NO NAME -Rest Area

SOS — not far from the exit, past the Rest Area.

85

Meulan, Les Mereaux

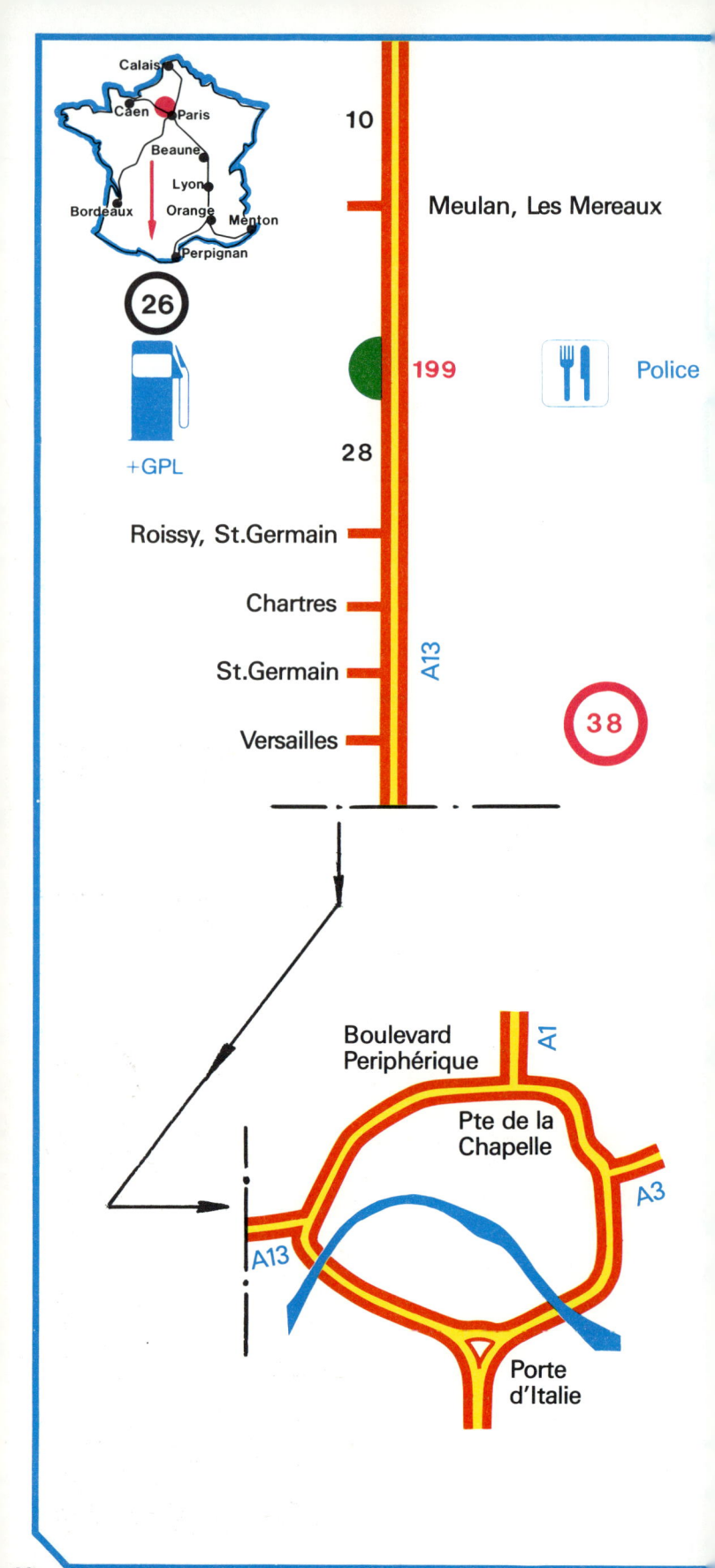

10

199

Police

28

Roissy, St.Germain

Chartres

St.Germain

Versailles

A13

38

+GPL

26

Boulevard Periphérique

A1

Pte de la Chapelle

A3

A13

Porte d'Italie

Aire Sud de **Morainvilliers**

Ample Rest Area, footbridge to the other side of Motorway Rest Area

If you do not stay in Paris and continue your journey to the South, turn over to page ;-

102 — for the Riviera and Perpignan,

88 — for Bordeaux

Take "Paris-Sud" before joining Boulevard Periphérique and follow the sign "Lyon" whether you go for Bordeaux or the Riviera.
Read further comments on page 78 and 79.

If you go for Bordeaux, you may opt for an earlier exit for Chartres which leads to the Autoroute A10 but the details are not available for this edition.

Continued from Calais

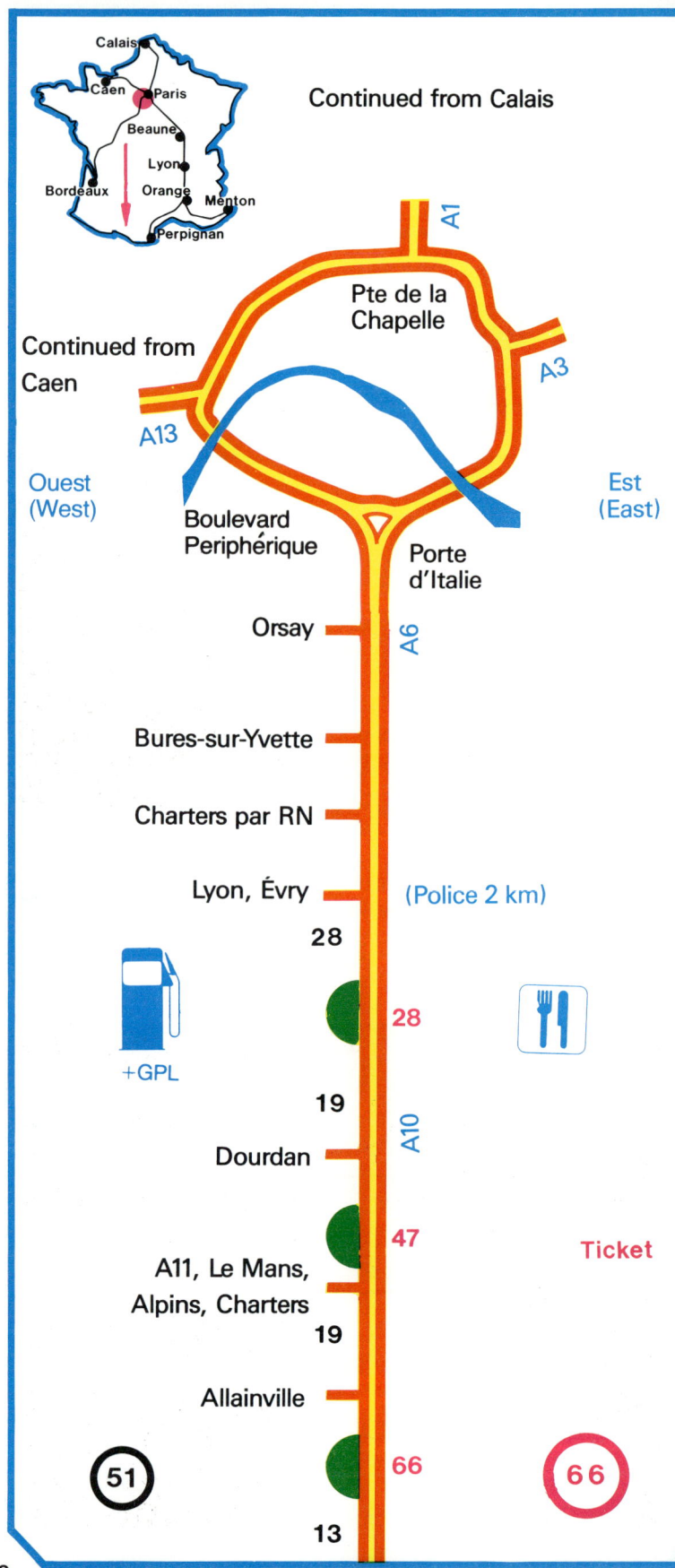

Continued from Caen

Ouest (West)

Est (East)

A1

Pte de la Chapelle

A3

A13

Boulevard Peripherique

Porte d'Italie

Orsay

A6

Bures-sur-Yvette

Charters par RN

Lyon, Évry

(Police 2 km)

28
28
19
A10
Dourdan
47
A11, Le Mans, Alpins, Charters
19
Allainville
66
13

+GPL

Ticket

(51)   (66)

L'ARCHE RESTAURANTS

Aire de Limours-Janvry

Just parking spaces. Cafeteria, currency exchange at the cash desk.

Aire de Barrière de péage

Few tables and benches. Pleasant.

Aire de Boutroux

Spacious with some tables and benches, grassy, small trees, interesting.

89

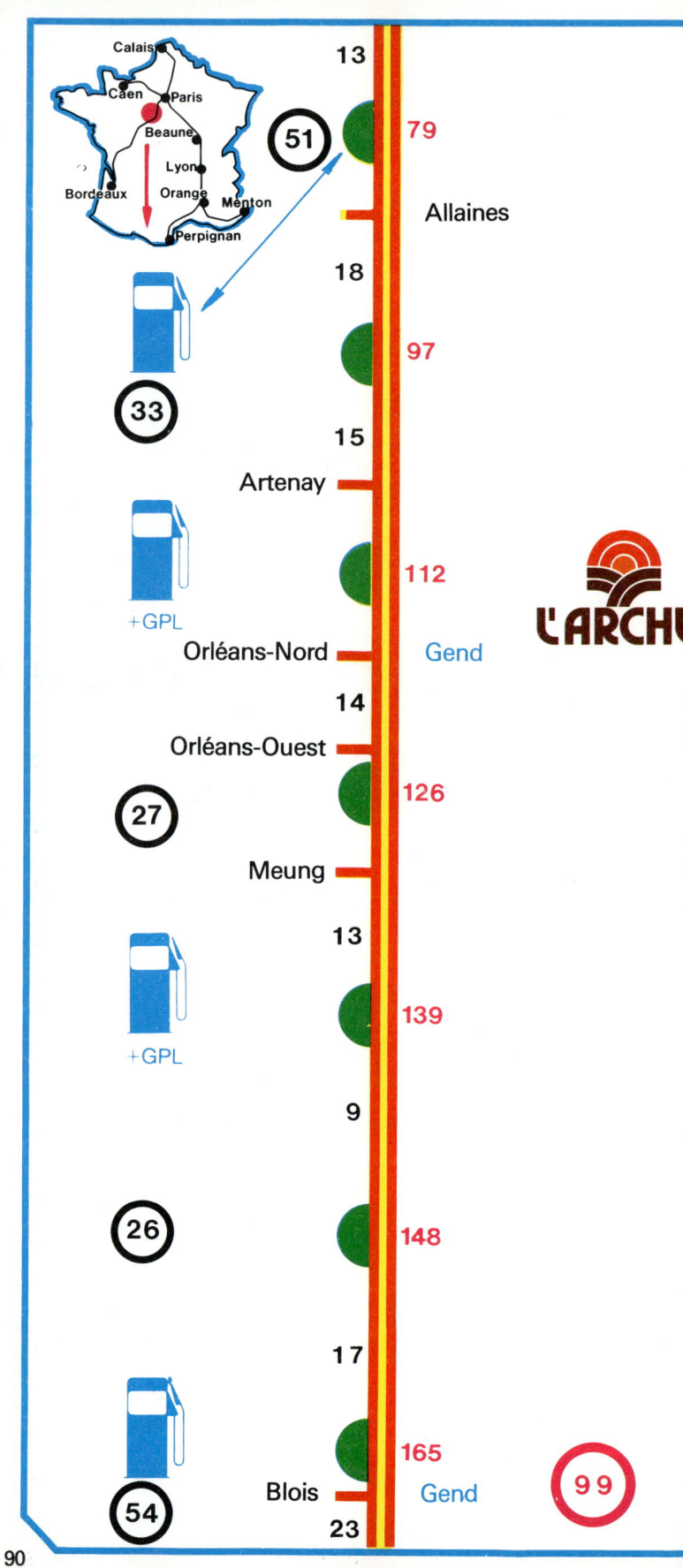

(51)	13	79
		Allaines
(33) ⛽	18	97
	15	Artenay
⛽ +GPL		112 Gend
		Orléans-Nord
	14	Orléans-Ouest
(27)		126
		Meung
⛽ +GPL	13	139
(26)	9	148
⛽	17	165
(54)		Blois Gend
	23	

L'ARCHE

(99)

Aire de **Francheville**

Bar, buffet, boutique.

Aire de **Héron-Cendré**

WC

Spacious, jungle-like with tables and benches.

Aire d' **Orléans-Saron**

Bar, grill, boutique. Footbridge to the other side of the motorway Service Area.
SOS — at the side.

Aire de **Bellevue**

WC

SOS at the side of the Area.

Aire de **Meung-Sur-Loire**

Few tables and benches. Pleasant.
SOS — at the same distance from the entry.

Aire de **Fougeres**

WC

Open type of area, a lot of tables and benches in a row. Pleasant.
SOS — at the side.

Aire de **Blois-Villerbon**

Cafeteria, bar.
SOS — not far from exit.

23

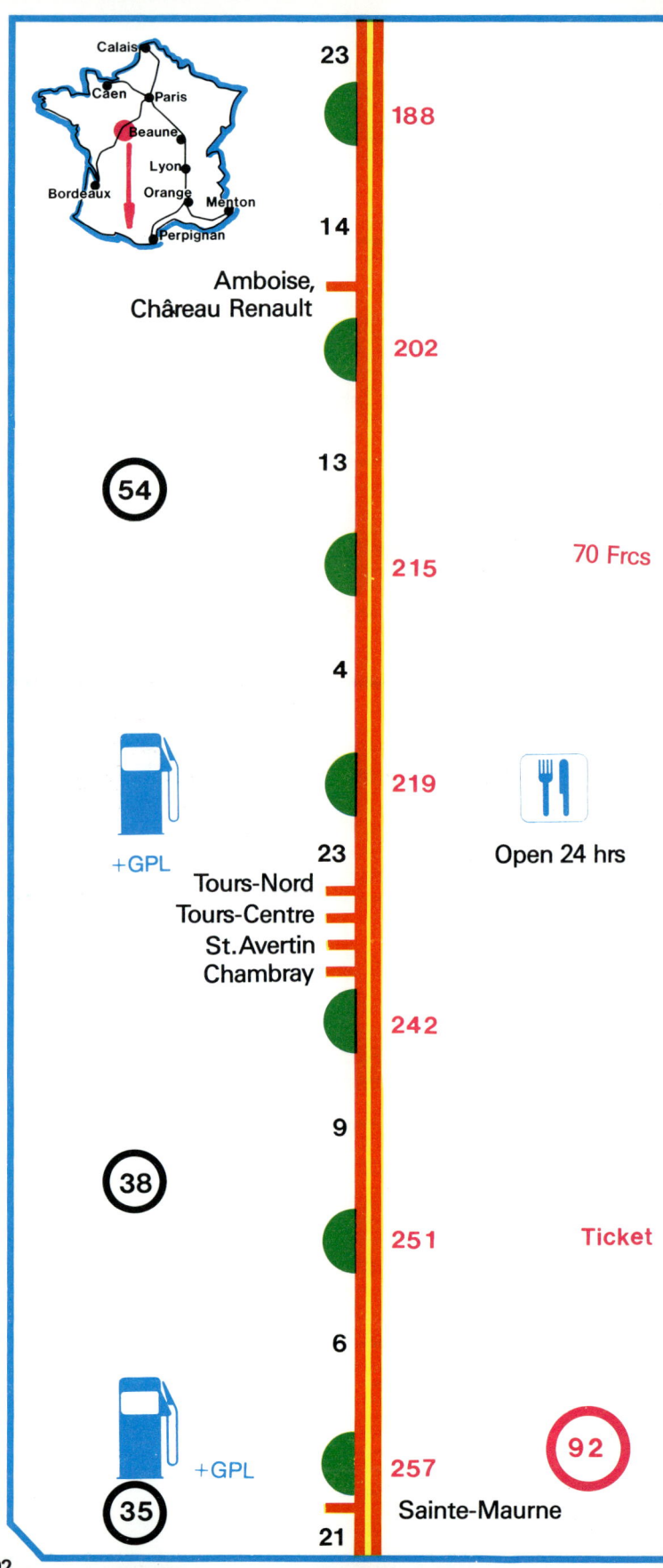

188

14

Amboise,
Château Renault

202

13

(54)

215

70 Frcs

4

+GPL

219

Open 24 hrs

23

Tours-Nord
Tours-Centre
St. Avertin
Chambray

242

9

(38)

251

Ticket

6

+GPL

257

(92)

(35)

Sainte-Maurne

21

Aire de la Chatière

WC

Tables and benches in the open and among trees. Small and pleasant.
SOS — 300 m past the Area.

Aire de la Courte Epée

WC

Forested, a lot of tables and benches.

Aire de Barrière de péage

WC

Open type area. Few tables and benches.
SOS — 300 m from the entry.

Aire de Tours-Longue Vue

L'ARCHE

Interconnected by a footbridge. There are; Bar, buffet, boutique, sandwich bar.
SOS — at the exit end.

Aire du Village-Brule

WC

Forested with a lot of tables and benches. Spacious.
SOS — at the side.

Aire de Barrière de péage

WC

There are some tables and benches.

Aire de St.Maure de Touraine

SOS — at the side of Area.

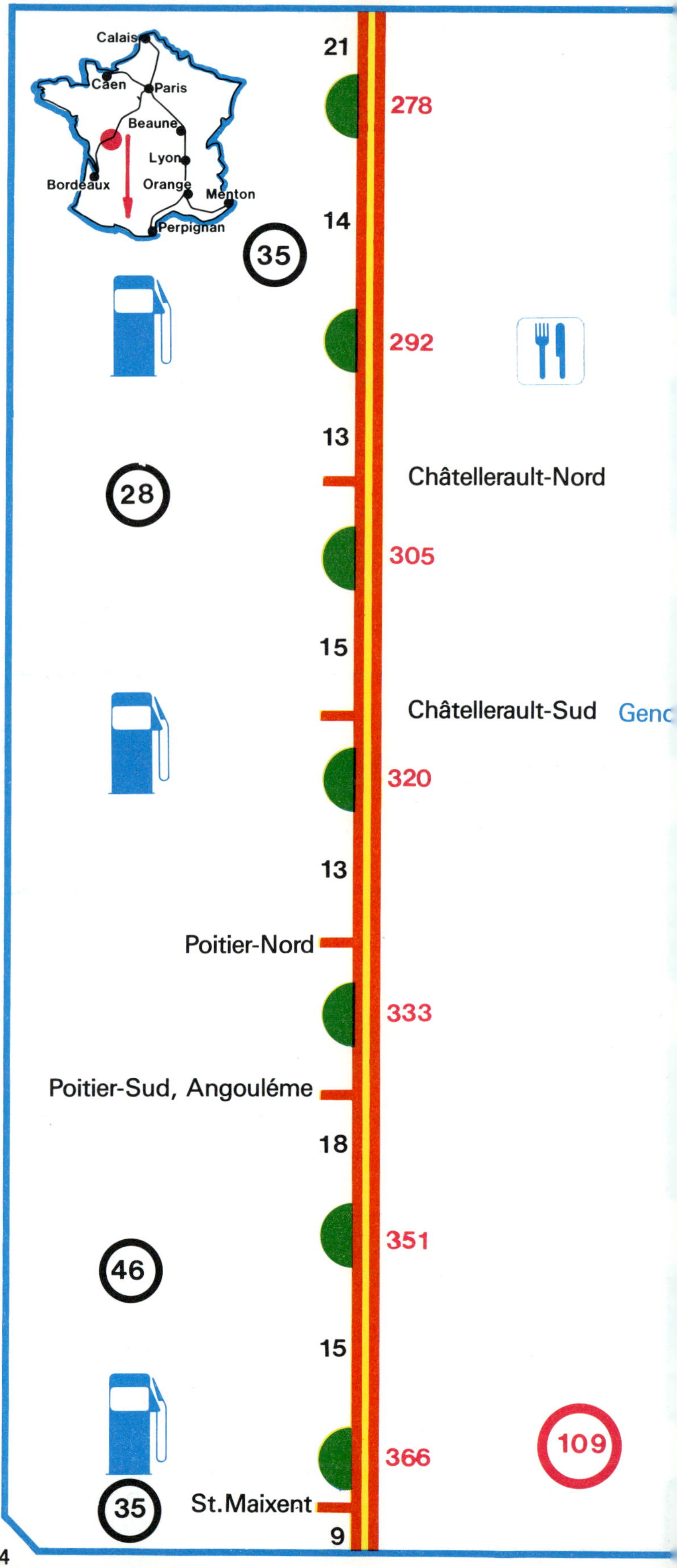
Calais
Caen
Paris
Beaune
Lyon
Bordeaux
Orange
Menton
Perpignan
21
278
14
35
292
13
Châtellerault-Nord
28
305
15
Châtellerault-Sud
Genc
320
13
Poitier-Nord
333
Poitier-Sud, Angouléme
18
351
46
15
366
109
35
St.Maixent
9

Aire de Maille

WC

Forested with a lot of tables and benches. Very pleasant.
SOS — at the entry to Area.

Aire de Chatellerault Antran

L'ARCHE

Just parking facilities.

Aire des Meuniers

WC

SOS — at the side of the Area.

Aire de Poitiers Jaunay-Clan

SOS — at the side of the Area.

Aire des Gent-Saptiers

WC

Open type, tables and benches. Pleasant.
SOS — at the side.

Aire de Coulombiers-Nord

WC

Open type, some trees, lit at night, tables and benches. Nice.
SOS — at the entry.

Aire de Rouillé-Pamproux

Take care at the entry — small radius bend. Take first one on the right hand side. Tables and benches, it is very nice indeed.
SOS — at the side.

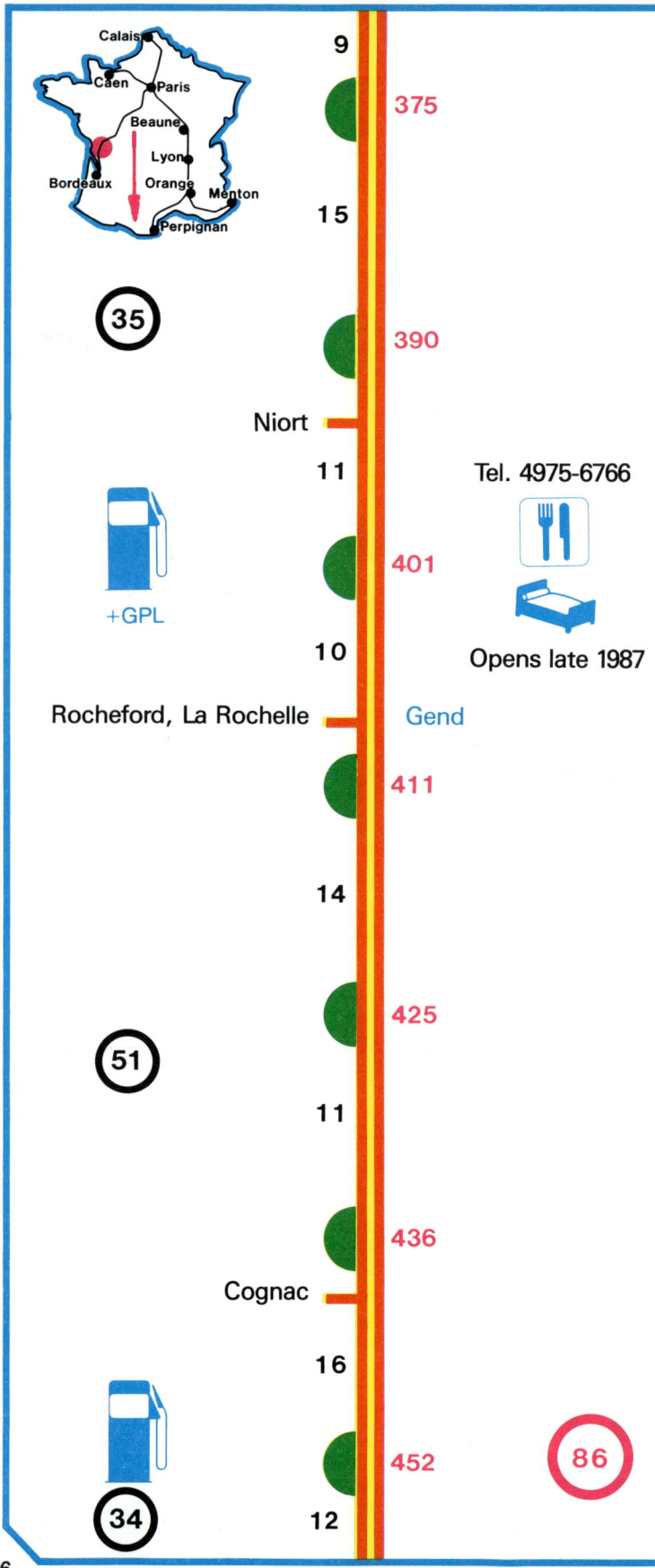

9

375

15

(35)

390

Niort

11

Tel. 4975-6766

401

Opens late 1987

10

Rocheford, La Rochelle   Gend

411

14

425

(51)

11

436

Cognac

16

452   (86)

(34)

12

96

Aire de Ste Eanne-Nord

| WC | ☎ | 🛇 |

Open type of area, swings, tables and benches. Very nice.
SOS — at the side towards exit.

Aire de Ste Néomaye-Nord

| WC | ☎ | 🛇 |

Open type space. Lit at night, swings, tables and benches.
Rather small. Recommended.
SOS — at the side.

Aire des Les Ruralies

| 🚻 | ☎ | ♿ | 🎁 | ☕ | 🍼 | 💱 | 🛇 | ℹ️ | ✉️ |

Tables and benches. Interconnected with the other side. Very complex Area. Museum, strongly recommended.
SOS.

Aire de Gript-Nord

| WC | ♿ | 🛇 |

Open type space, tables and benches. Very nice.
SOS — at the side towards the entry.

Aire de Doeuil s/le Mignon

| WC | ♿ | 🛇 |

Quite spacious with tables and benches. Very pleasant.
SOS — at the exit end.

Aire de Lozay

| WC | ♿ | 🛇 |

Tables and benches, swings, rocking things. Lit at night, open space area, spacious.
SOS — at the exit end.

Aire de Fenioux

| 🚻 | ☎ | ♿ | 🎁 | 🛇 |

Spacious, open space area, tables and benches. Lit at night, swings, climbing nets. Nice.
SOS — at the side.

12

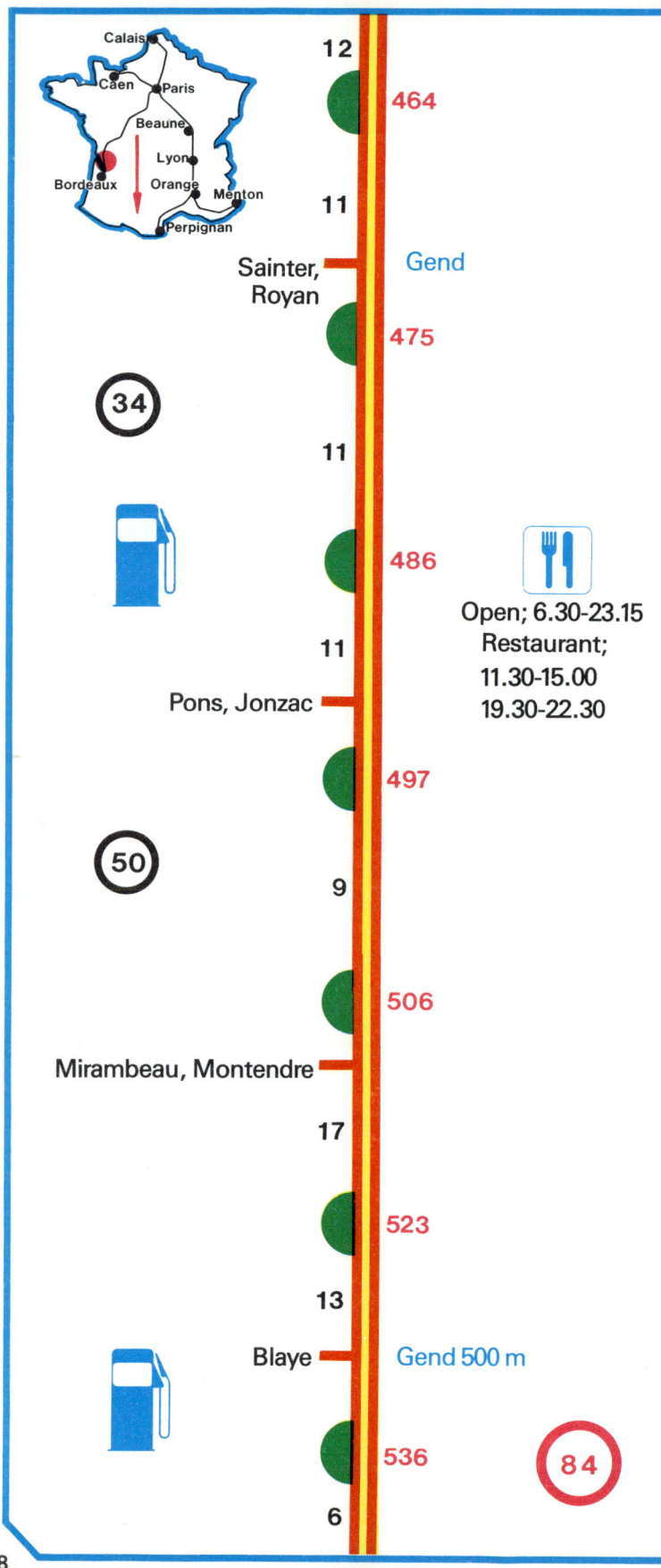

464

11

Sainter, Royan   Gend

475

(34)

11

486

Open; 6.30-23.15
Restaurant;
11.30-15.00
19.30-22.30

11

Pons, Jonzac

497

(50)

9

506

Mirambeau, Montendre

17

523

13

Blaye   Gend 500 m

536

6

(84)

98

Aire de Port d'Envaux
[WC] [☎]

In two parts; open space and forested. Tables and benches. Rather nice.
SOS — at the side by the entry.

Aire de Chermignac
[WC] [☎] [🛍]

Open space type of area with tables and benches.
SOS — at the side of Area.

Aire de St-Léger
[🚻] [☎] [♿] [⛽] [☕] [💉] [📺] [🛍]

Very spacious, picnicking-area, tables and benches. Swings climbing frames. Very elegant, recommended.
SOS — at the exit end.

Aire de St-Palais
[WC] [☎] [🛍]

Tables and benches among trees and in the open. Small tidy and very nice.
SOS — not far from the entry.

Aire de St.Ciers
[WC] [☎] [🛍]

Tables and benches among trees and in the open space. Lit at night, spacious, very pleasant. Recommended.
SOS — at the side, near the entry.

Aire de St.Cabrais
[WC] [☎] [🛍]

Tables and benches among trees and in the open space. Lit at night.
SOS — at the side of Area.

Aire de Saugon
[🚻] [☎] [♿] [⛽]

As above. Recommended.
SOS — at the side.

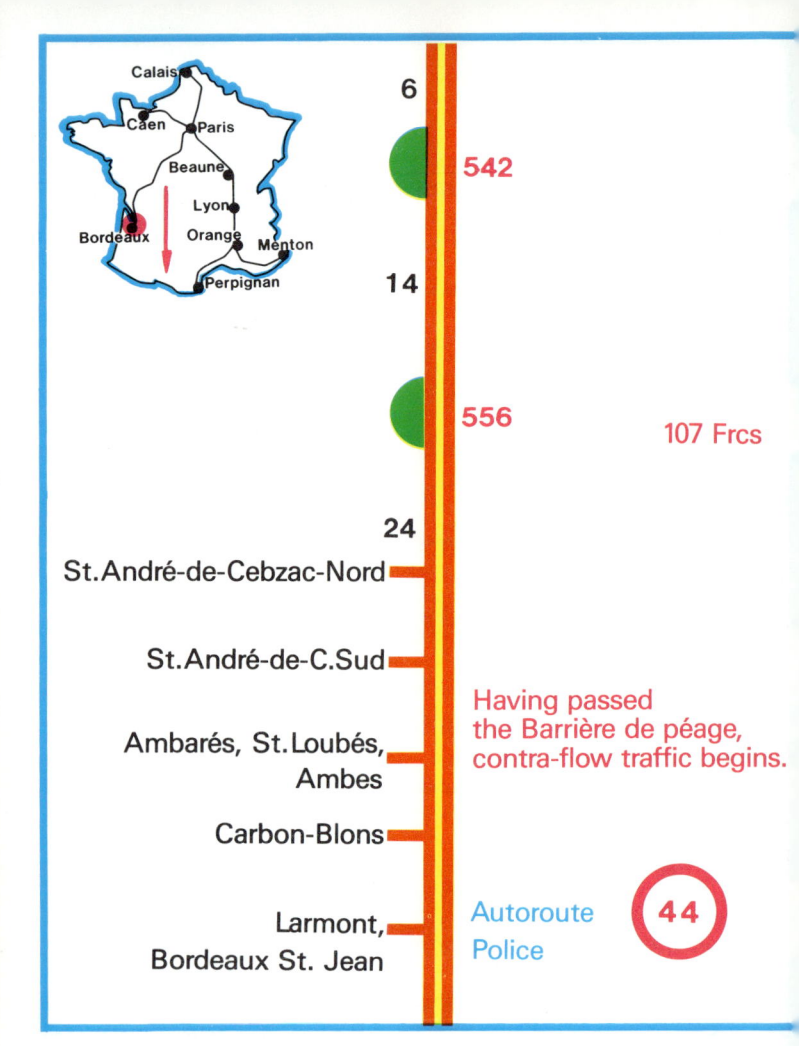

6		
		542
14		
		556
		107 Frcs
24		
St. André-de-Cebzac-Nord		
St. André-de-C. Sud		
Ambarés, St. Loubés, Ambes		Having passed the Barrière de péage, contra-flow traffic begins.
Carbon-Blons		
Larmont, Bordeaux St. Jean		Autoroute Police (44)

BORDEAUX

PULLMAN HOTEL ★★★★
Quartier Meriadeck, 5 Rue R — Lateulade,
33000 — Bordeaux
Tel. 5690-9237, Telex: 540565

196 rooms ● details page 14 ● TV with video circuit ● restaurant ● bar ● parking ● a large hotel in the centre of Bordeaux 12 km from Bordeaux — Merignac airport.

Aire de **St. Christoly**

WC

Tables and benches among trees and in the open space. Spacious. Recommended.
SOS — at the entry.

Aire de **Barrière de péage**

WC 📞 ♿

Just parking spaces.

ALTEA HOTEL ★★★★
7 Rue Labeda
31000 — Toulouse
Tel. 6121-2175, Telex: 530550

95 rooms • details page 14 • radio • TV • direct telephone • mini-bar • restaurant • bar • parking.

Continued from Calais

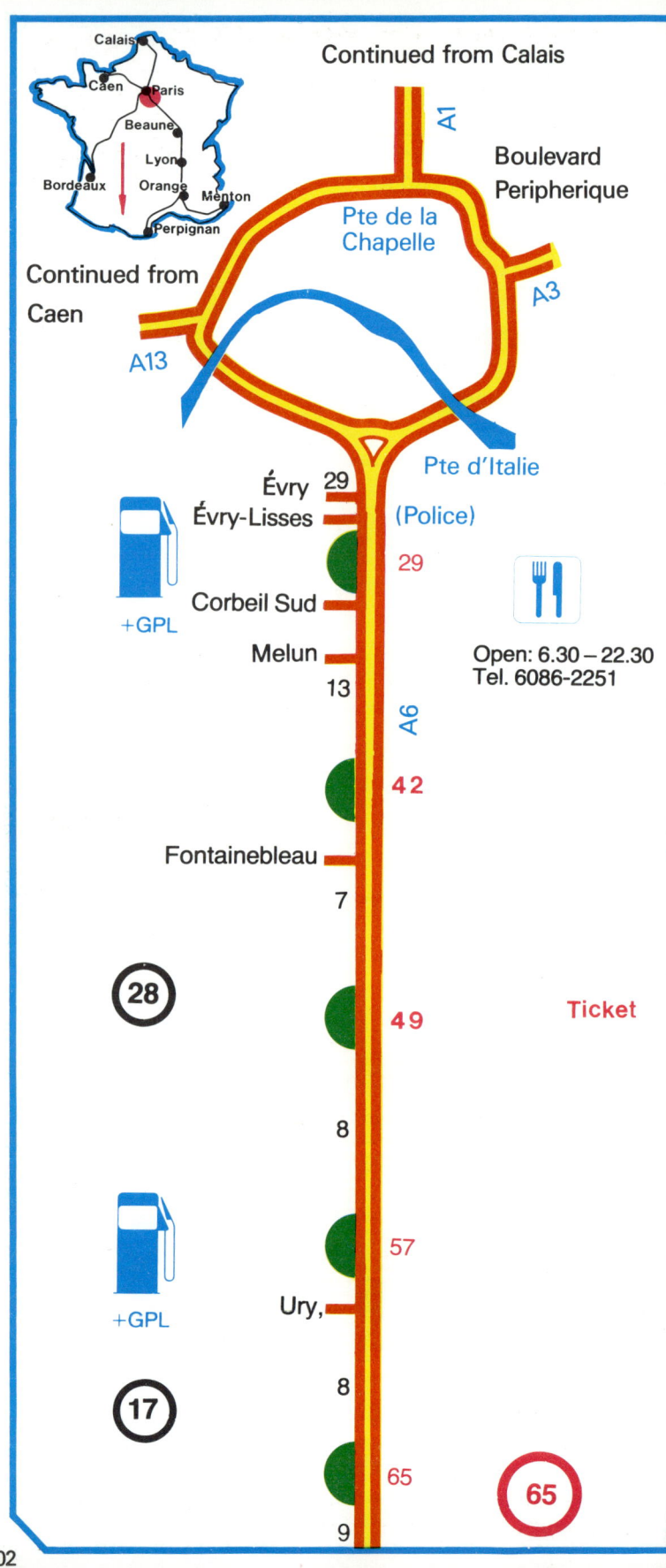

A1

Boulevard Peripherique

Pte de la Chapelle

A3

Continued from Caen

A13

Pte d'Italie

Évry 29
Évry-Lisses
(Police)
29
Corbeil Sud
Melun
13
A6
42
Fontainebleau
7

(28)

49

8

57
Ury,

+GPL

(17)

65
9

Open: 6.30 – 22.30
Tel. 6086-2251

Ticket

(65)

102

Aire de Lisses

Just parking facilicies. Cafeteria, boutique. Combined entry to te Rest Area with the exit from the m-way.
SOS — at side.

Aire de Nainville

Forested, tables and benches among trees. Small but nice.
SOS — 200 m from the entry.

Aire de Barrière de péage

Just parking facilities. Spacious.

Aire d' Achèries

There are tables and benches.
SOS.

Aire de Villiers

Very nice woodland type of area. There are tables and benches. Spacious. First best.
SOS — actually on the Rest Area at the very end, difficult to be spotted from the motorway.

Nemours
9

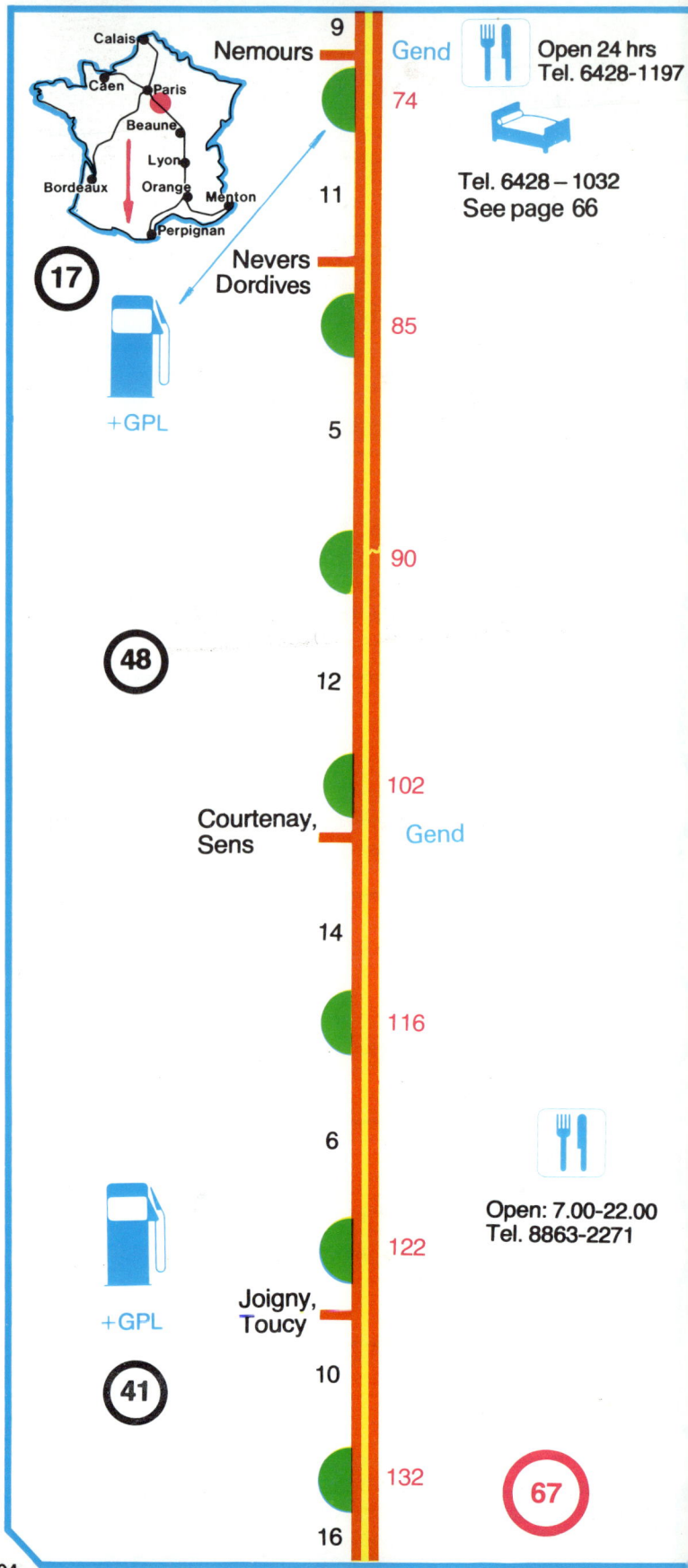

Gend
74

Open 24 hrs
Tel. 6428-1197

Tel. 6428 – 1032
See page 66

11

Nevers
Dordives

85

(17)

+GPL

5

90

(48)

12

102

Courtenay,
Sens

Gend

14

116

6

Open: 7.00-22.00
Tel. 8863-2271

122

+GPL

Joigny,
Toucy

(41)

10

132

(67)

16

104

Aire de Nemours

Ample services provided, typical for petrol station complex. Few tables and benches, interconnected with the other side of the m-way Rest Area.
SOS — at the side. Info-Route.

Aire de Sonville

Small, but very nice. Forested and partly open area. Plenty of tables and benches.
SOS — at the side.

Aire du Liard

Forested, tables and benches, very nice. Partly open space.
SOS — at side.

Aire du Parc Thierry

It is a jungle type of area with plenty of tables and benches among the trees obviously.
SOS — towards the exit.

Aire des Chataigniers

Large, jungle like type, as above. Very nice.
SOS — at side.

Aire de la Réserve

Open space arranged just for parking. There is a bar, buffet, cafeteria.
SOS — at side.

Aire de la Racheuse

Forested area. Small with tables and benches.
SOS.

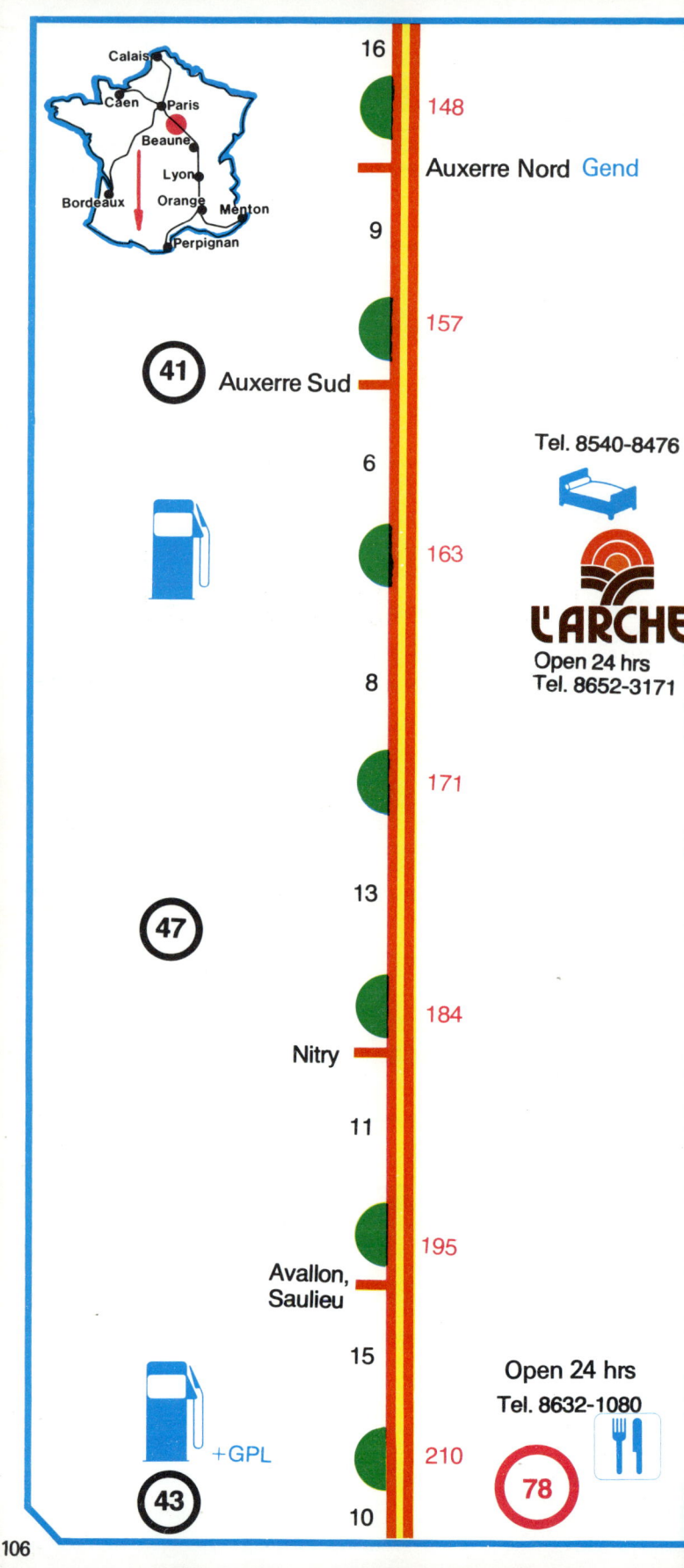

	16	148	Auxerre Nord Gend
(41) Auxerre Sud	9	157	
⛽	6	163	Tel. 8540-8476 🛏 L'ARCHE Open 24 hrs Tel. 8652-3171
	8	171	
(47)	13	184	Nitry
	11	195	Avallon, Saulieu
⛽ +GPL (43)	15 10	210	Open 24 hrs Tel. 8632-1080 (78) 🍴

106

Aire de la Biche

|WC| |♿|

Forested area but no tables or benches provided. Nice.
SOS — at side.

Aire des Bois Impériaux

|WC| |🏛|

Small with tables and benches.
SOS — at the side by the exit.

Aire de Venoy Grosse Pierre

|🚻| |☎| |♿| |🗑| |☕| |🧴| |💱| |✉|

Very spacious, few tables and benches, footbridge to the other side of motorway. Bar, self-service, stamps at the boutique. Collection 9.10 a.m. letter box by the cafeteria.
SOS — towards the entry.

Aire de la Grosse Tour

|WC| |🏛|

Very small with tables and benches. In two parts; forested and open space. Nice.

Aire de Couée

|WC| |♿| |🏛|

Small, forested with tables and benches. Nice.
SOS — at the entry.

Aire de Montmorency

|WC| |♿| |🏛|

Forested, a lot of tables and benches.
SOS — 400 m past the Area.

Aire de Chaponne

|🚻| |☎| |♿| |🗑| |☕| |💱|

Just parking spaces. Grill, self-service.
SOS — at the side.

10
220

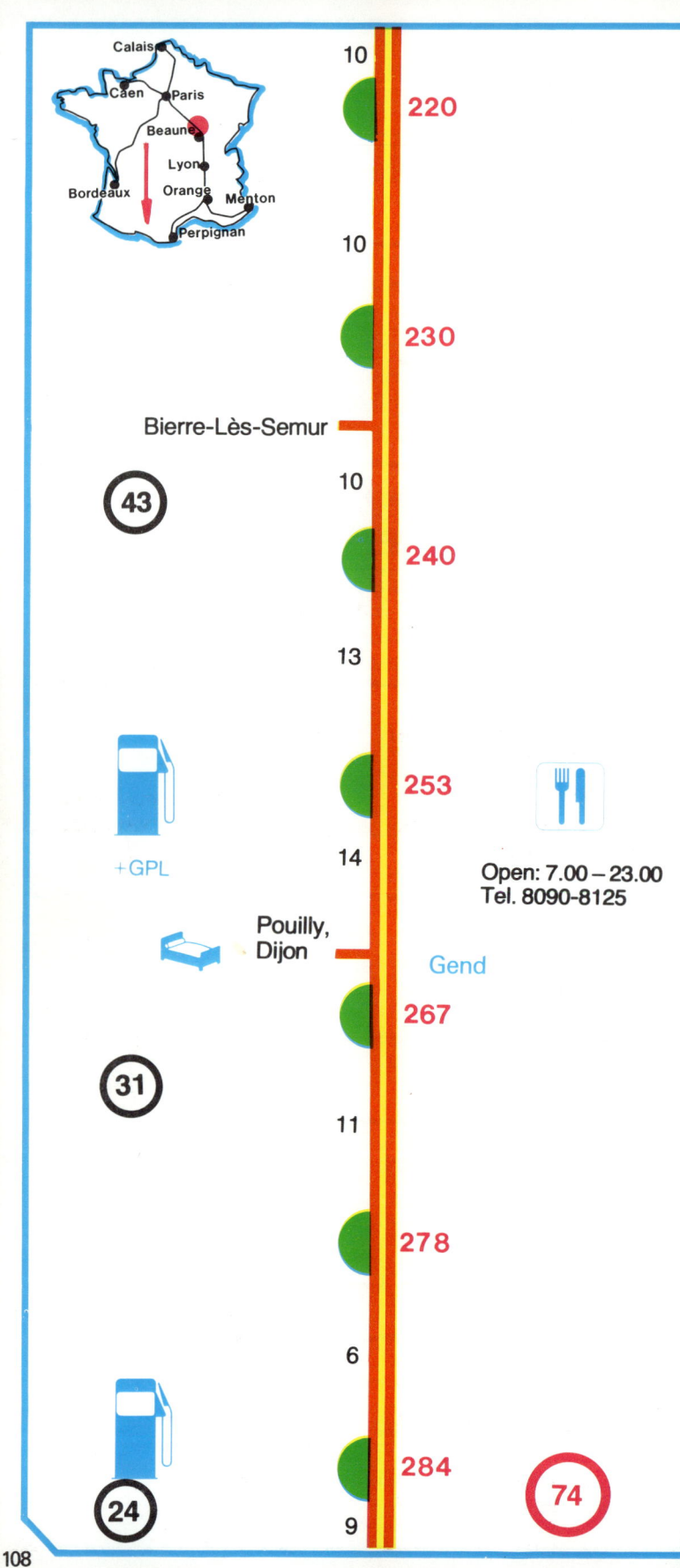

10
230

Bierre-Lès-Semur

(43)

10
240

13

253

+GPL

14

Pouilly, Dijon

Gend

Open: 7.00 – 23.00
Tel. 8090-8125

267

(31)

11

278

6

(24) 284 (74)

9

Aire d' Epoisses

WC ♿ 🎪

Open type area, tables and benches. Very nice, recommended.
SOS — at side.

Aire de Ruffey

WC

Open type and grassy area. No tables nor benches.
SOS — at side towards the entry.

Aire de Fermenot

WC 🎪

Spacious with tables and benches among trees. Nice.
SOS — at the entry.

Aire du Chien Blanc

🚻 📞 ♿ 🗑 ☕ 💱 🎪

Open spaces, very spacious, newly arranged, very modern, tidy and very nice. There are tables and benches. Recommended.
SOS — at side.

Aire de Chaignot

WC 🎪

There are tables and benches among trees. Jungle like.
SOS — at side.

Aire de la Garenne

WC ♿ 🎪

Pleasant, situated on the side of a hill with a panoramic view. Tables and benches.
SOS — at side.

Aire de la Forêt

🚻 📞 ♿ 🗑 🎪

Very spacious, which is not apparant at first. Located beyond the petrol station.
SOS — at side.

109

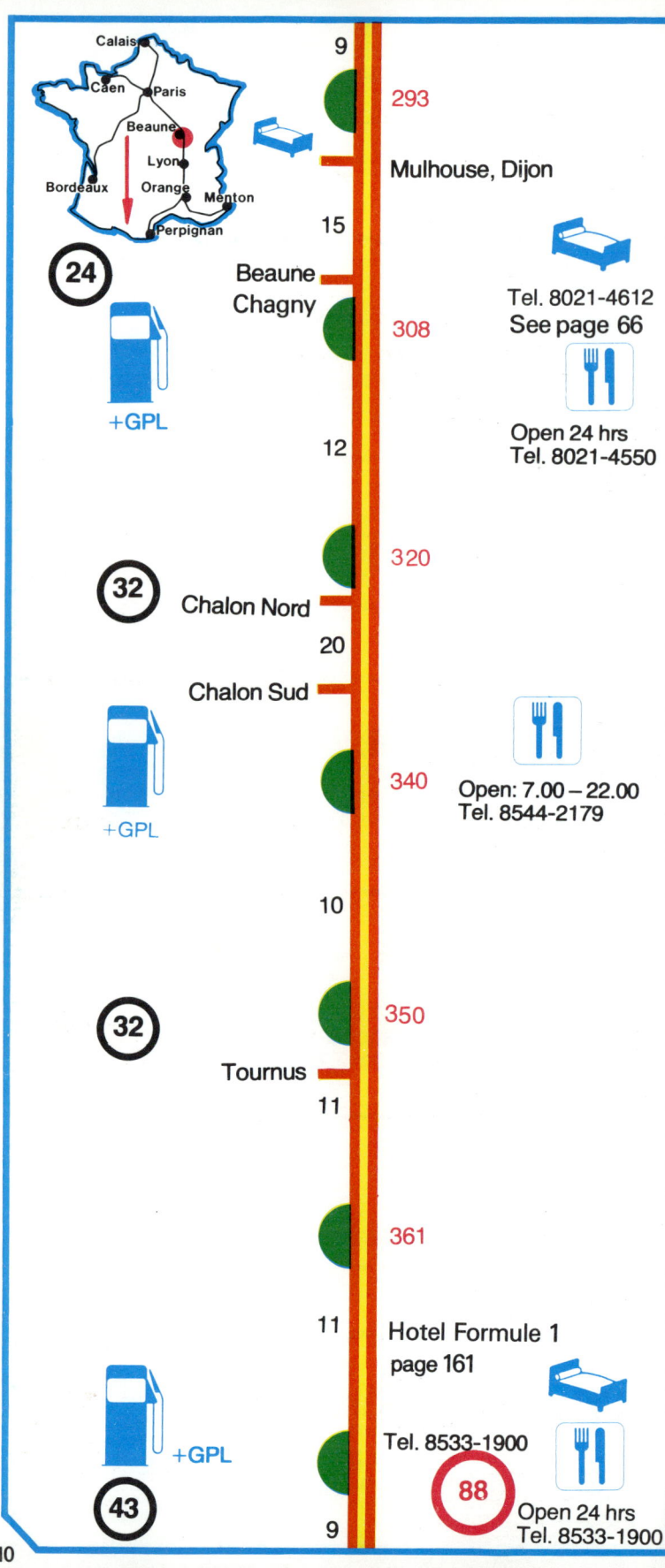

	9	293	🛏️ Mulhouse, Dijon
㉔ +GPL	15	308	Beaune Chagny — 🛏️ Tel. 8021-4612 See page 66 — 🍴 Open 24 hrs Tel. 8021-4550
	12	320	
㉜	20		Chalon Nord
+GPL		340	Chalon Sud — 🍴 Open: 7.00 – 22.00 Tel. 8544-2179
	10	350	
㉜	11	361	Tournus
+GPL ㊸	11 9	88	Hotel Formule 1 page 161 — Tel. 8533-1900 — 🛏️ 🍴 Open 24 hrs Tel. 8533-1900

Aire du Rossignols

WC

Small and pleasant, woodland type, there are tables and benches and some grassy spots.
SOS — by the entry.

Aire de Beaune Tailly

There is THE ARCHEODROME. Tel. 8021-4825 open throughout the year from 10.00 a.m. to 8.00 p.m. (May-Sept) and 10.00 a.m.- 6.00 p.m.(Oct.- Apr.)
SOS — at side.

Aire de le Curney

WC

There is an impressive Memorial to the victims of the "Beaune" accident 31 July, 1982. See page 112. Spacious and forested, tables and benches.
SOS — at side.

Aire de la Ferté

Just car spaces provided. There is a bar and a buffet.
SOS — at side.

Aire de Jugy

Open space type type of area, small and pretty. There are tables and benches.
SOS — at side.

Aire de Farges

WC

As above.
SOS — at side.

Aire de Mâcon St. Albain (71)

L'ARCHE

Spacious. Some tables and benches. Typical services for a petrol station complex. Cafeteria. Grill, bar.
SOS — by the entry. MAISON DES PAYS
RELAIS de BOURGOGNE - BRESSE - 85·33·19·40

THE BEAUNE MEMORIAL TO

Stop here for a moment, and try to comprehend the contents of these pages. Think for a while and pay your respects to those killed and injured in road accidents.

MÉMORIAL POUR L'AVENIR

Érigé par l'Association du Mémorial National
des Victimes de la Route

Au-delà du souvenir du terrible accident de "BEAUNE" du 31 Juillet 1982, les nombreuses associations de victimes et de prévention qui ont contribué à l'érection de ce monument, veulent exalter l'espoir et provoquer une prise de conscience de l'opinion publique sur le fléau que représentent les accidents de la circulation.

Oeuvre de Françoise JOLIVET
Aménagement et Maîtrise d'Oeuvre de Jacques VALENTIN,
architecte

VICTIMS OF ROAD ACCIDENTS

To do so validates the purpose of this memorial and will help us all to enjoy accident free holidays.

MEMORIAL FOR THE FUTURE

Erected by the National Memorial Association for Road Victims.

"To go further than the memory of the dreadful accident near Beaune on the 31st July, 1982, the many associations for victims and road safety who contributed to this memorial wish to inspire hope and stimulate the conscience of public opinion against the scourge which traffic accidents have become."

And if you translate the word "scourge" into the likely meaning of the word, "barbarian conquerers", this would exactly mean what traffic accidents have become.

	9	**Mâcon Nord**
		381
	12	**Mâcon Sud**
(43) 🛏		393
	10	
⛽		403
	Belleville	🍴 Open: 7.00 – 23.00 Tel. 7466-4949
	12	
		4 15
(27)	7	
	Villefranche	
		422 Gend 104 Frcs
	Neuville	
	10	A6
⛽ +GPL	Anse	432
	10	
(12)	Limonest, Dardilly, Porte de Lyon	442
	2	(70)

114

Aire de Sennecé

WC

Small and smart.
SOS — at side.

Aire de Crèches

WC ♿ /⚏

Open space type of area, nests of tables and stools or benches, very modern. Attractive.
SOS — at the side.

Aire de Dracé

🚻 ☎ ♿ 🎁 ☕ 🎮

Open space, tables and benches, lot of grassy area, pleasant. Restaurant, cafeteria.
SOS — at the entry.

Aire de Patural

WC ♿

Very small with tables and benches. Very open. Pleasant.
SOS — by the entry.

Aire de Barrière de péage

WC ☎ ♿

Just parking spaces. In the stage of development. Gendarmerie

Aire des Chêres

🚻 ☎ ♿ 🎁 ☕ ⛽

Spacious, open type of area with tables and benches.
SOS — at side.

Aire de la Porte de Lyon, Limonest, Dardilly

The same, exit slip road.
There is an impressive nest of many hotels and a camping site and a petrol station with a very well stocked shop. Petrol is priced very competitively. It is not a Rest Area.

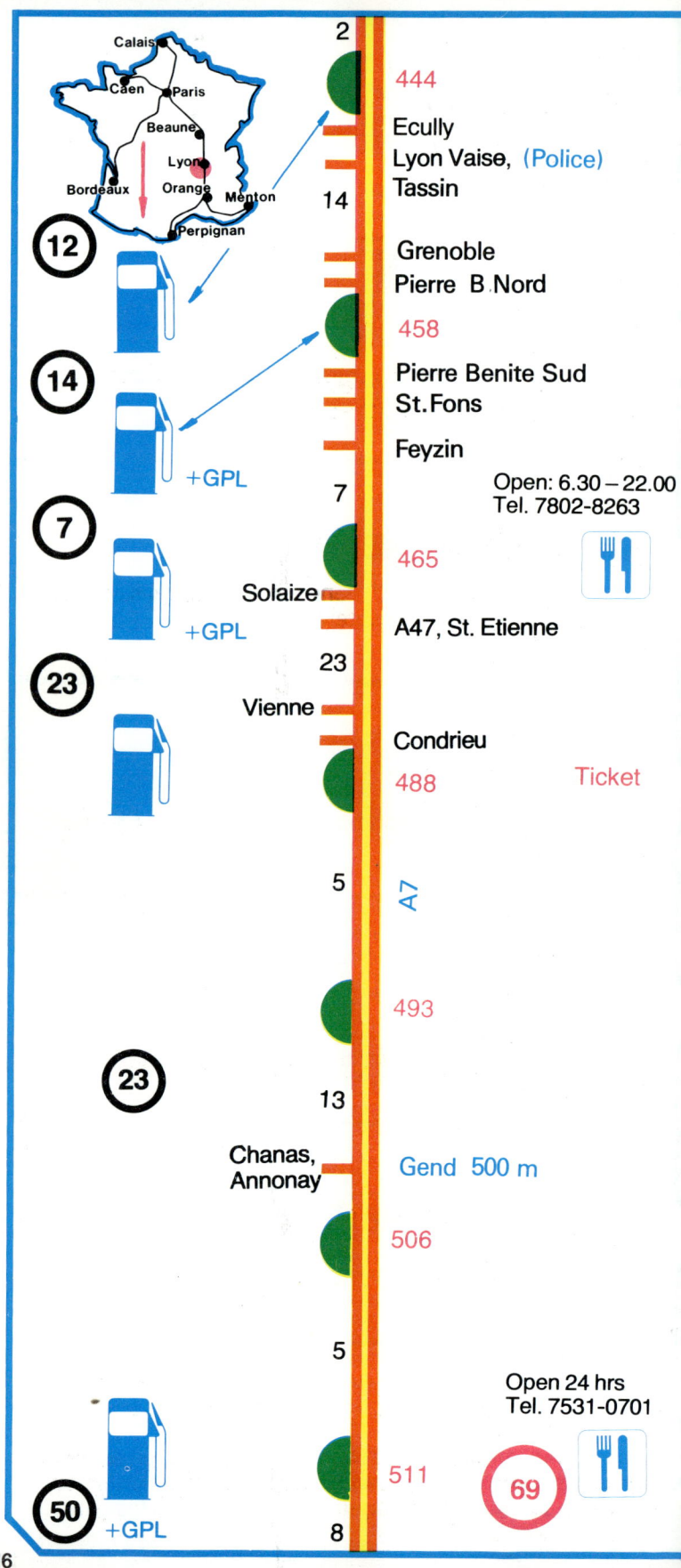

	2	444
		Ecully
		Lyon Vaise, (Police)
		Tassin
⑫	**14**	Grenoble
		Pierre B. Nord
		458
⑭ +GPL		Pierre Benite Sud
		St. Fons
		Feyzin
		Open: 6.30 – 22.00
		Tel. 7802-8263
⑦ +GPL	**7**	465
		Solaize
		A47, St. Etienne
㉓	**23**	Vienne
		Condrieu
		488 Ticket
	5	A7
		493
㉓	**13**	Chanas, Annonay Gend 500 m
		506
	5	
㊿ +GPL		511 69
	8	Open 24 hrs
		Tel. 7531-0701

116

Aire de Dardilly

Just parking facilities.
SOS — at side.

Aire de Pierre Bénite Nord

As above. Exit for Pierre Benite and entry to the Rest Area is combined.
SOS — just before entry.

Aire de Solaize

As above. Spacious.

Aire de Barrière de péage

As above.

Aire d' Auberives

Pique-nique jeux d'enfants area. Best so far. (Suitable for parties with young children). Lit at night.
SOS — at side.

Aire de Chanas

No facilities. Very small, few tables.
SOS — at side.

Aire de St. Rambert d'Albon

Pique-nique area, tables and benches. Very pretty with attractive type of trees. Footbridge to the other side of the motorway. Recommended.
SOS — at side. Info-route.

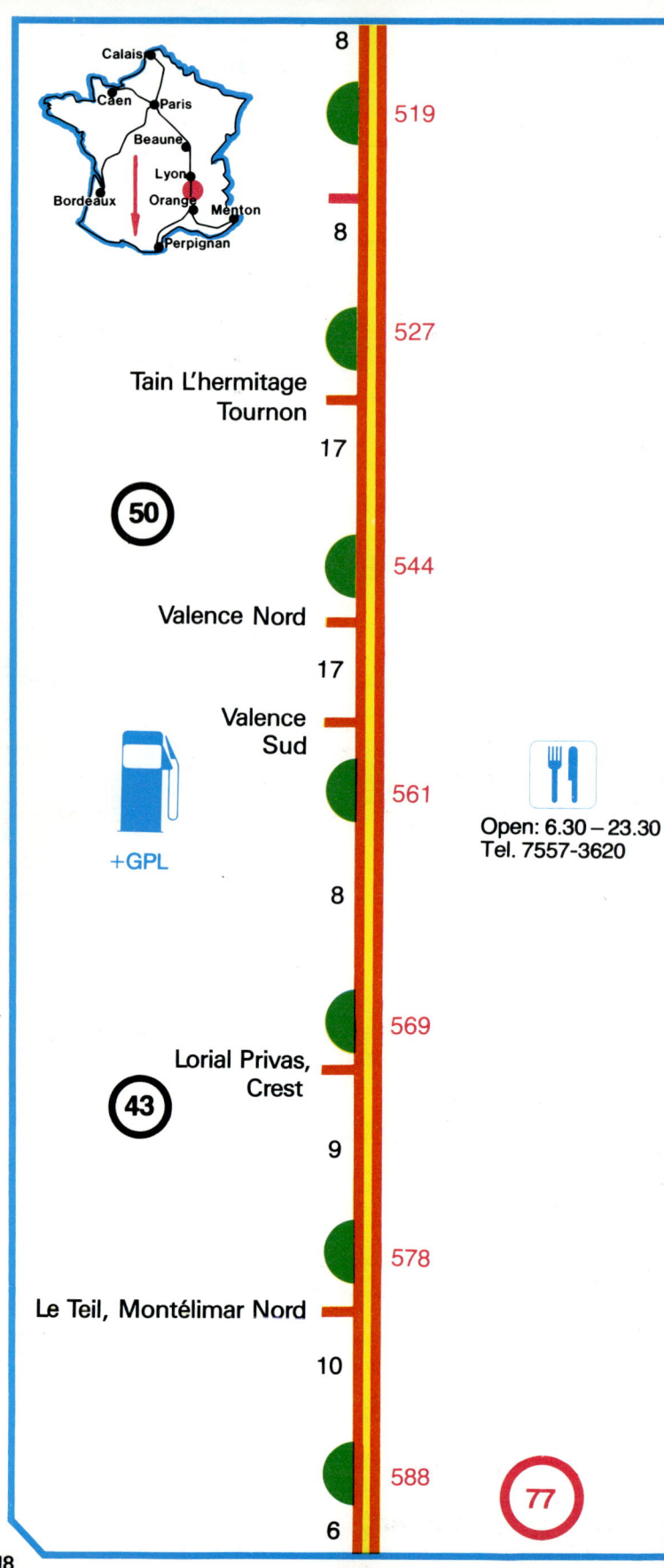

8

519

8

527

Tain L'hermitage
Tournon

17

(50)

544

Valence Nord

17

Valence
Sud

561

+GPL

Open: 6.30 – 23.30
Tel. 7557-3620

8

569

Lorial Privas,
Crest

(43)

9

578

Le Teil, Montélimar Nord

10

588

(77)

6

118

Aire de **Blacheronde**

WC ☎ ♿

Very small, few benches, some trees. Pleasant.
SOS — at side.

Aire du **Bornaron**

🚻 ☎ 🏬

Pique-nique jeux d'enfants. Large, very nice. Recommended.
SOS — at side.

Aire de **Pont de l'Isère**

WC ☎

Very small, grassy with tables and benches. Recommended.

Aire de **Portes-Lès-Valence**

🚻 ☎ ♿ 🗑 ☕ ⛽ 🛒 🏬

Pique-nique jeux d'enfants. There are tables and benches, average.

Aire de **Bellevue**

WC ☎

Very small with nests of tables and stools, some trees, attractive.

Aire de **Bras de Zil**

WC ☎

Rather spacious with attractive trees, there are tables and benches. Very pretty. Recommended.
SOS — at side.

Aire de la **Coucourde**

WC ☎ 🏬

Pique-nique jeux d'enfants, very spacious, forested and grassy. Attractive.
SOS — just past the Area.

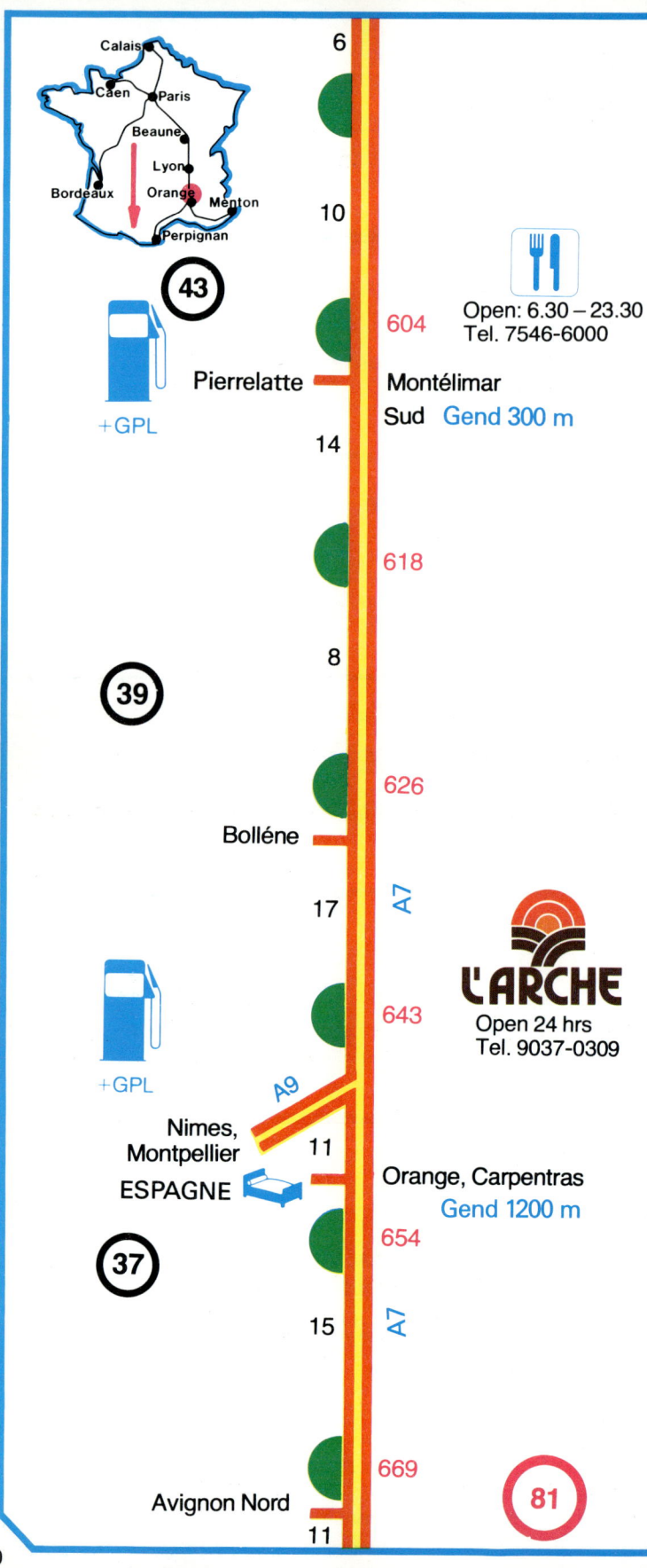

6

604

10

Pierrelatte — Montélimar Sud Gend 300 m

Open: 6.30 – 23.30
Tel. 7546-6000

14

618

(43)

8

(39)

626

Bolléne

17

A7

643

L'ARCHE
Open 24 hrs
Tel. 9037-0309

A9

Nimes, Montpellier
ESPAGNE

11 Orange, Carpentras
    Gend 1200 m

654

(37)

15 A7

669

Avignon Nord

11

(81)

Aire de Savasse

WC ☎

Open type of area, tables and benches. Very elegant area.

Aire de Pierrelatte

🚻 ☎ ♿ ⛽ ☕ 🖊️ 🛒 🛍️ ℹ️ ✉️

Pique-nique jeux d'enfants. It is quite a forest. There is a bar ,grill, cafeteria, self-service. Interconnected. Attractive.
SOS — at side.

Aire de Montélimar

WC ☎

Small, open type of area with some trees. There are tables and benches. Attractive.

Aire du Bois des Lots

WC ☎

Very small but pleasant. There are tables and benches. Lit at night.
SOS — at the entry.

Aire de Mornas-Village

🚻 ☎ ♿ ⛽ ☕ 🖊️ 💱 🛍️ ℹ️

Average, self-service, grill. Few and tables and benches.
SOS — at side.

Aire d' Orange Le Grès

WC ☎ 🛍️

Pique-nique jeux d'enfants.
SOS — at side, actually on the area.

Aire du Fournalet

WC ☎

Pique-nique jeux d'enfants, rather small area.

Open: 6.30 – 22.00
Tel. 9022-5968

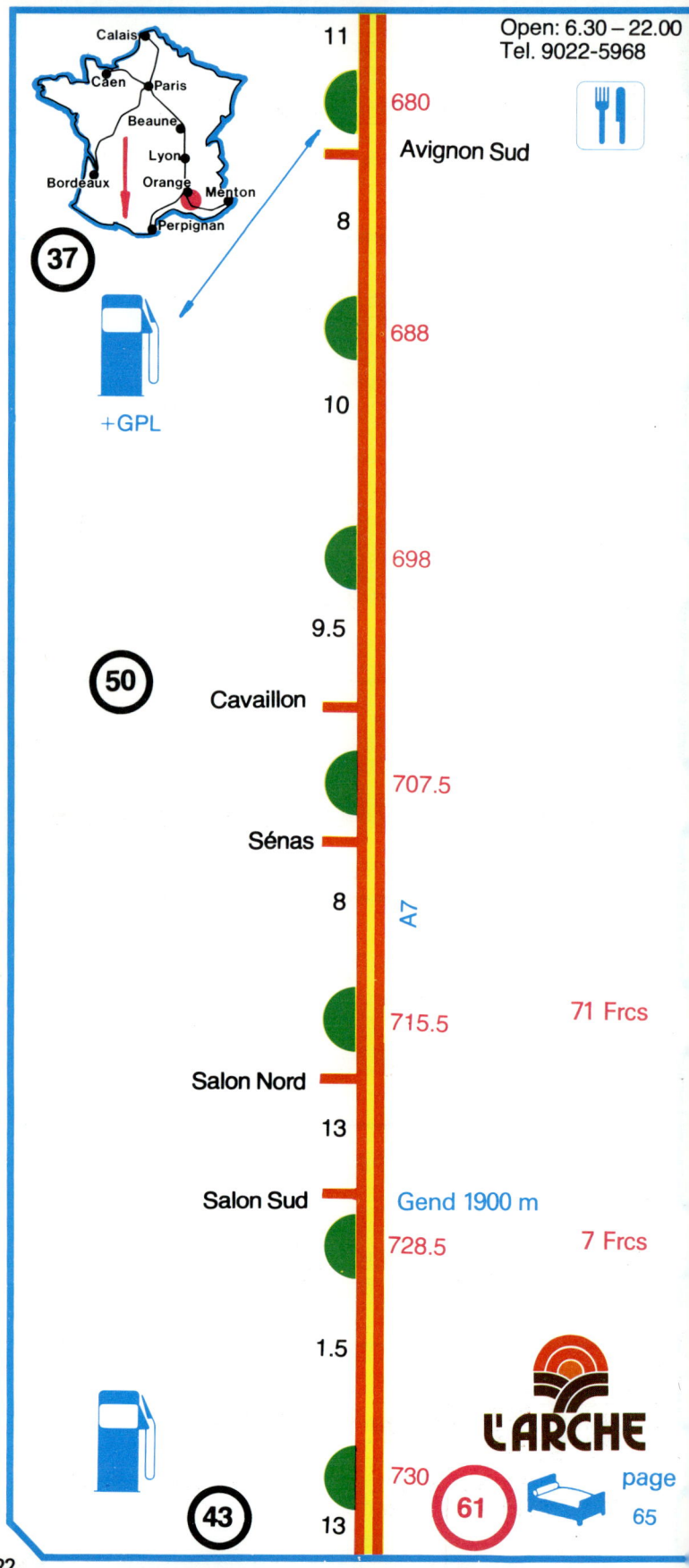

11

680
Avignon Sud

8

688

10

698

9.5

(50)

Cavaillon

707.5

Sénas

8

A7

715.5   71 Frcs

Salon Nord

13

Salon Sud   Gend 1900 m

728.5   7 Frcs

1.5

L'ARCHE

730   page 65

(43)   61

13

+GPL

(37)

122

Aire de **Morières**

Pique-nique jeux d'enfants. Recommended. Info-Route.

Aire de **Cabannes**

Very small, open space type of area, few benches. Lit.
SOS — a few hundred metres past the Area.

Aire de **Cavaillon**

As above, tables and benches. Nice.
SOS — at side.

Aire de **Sénas**

Small, open space, tables and benches and rather elegant.
SOS — at side.

Aire de **Barrière de péage**

Just parking spaces facilities.

Aire de **Barrière de péage**

As above. In a stage of development.

Aire de **Lançon de Provence**

There are tables and benches. Interconnected. Attractive
SOS — at side. Info-Route.

	A7 13	Marseille, Berre
		743
	A51	Aix Ouest Marseille
	21	Aix Sud
Aix Est		
(43) Le Canet		
		764 Ticket
Marseille, Toulon 🛏	A8	
	9	
⛽		773 Open: 6.00 – 22.00 Tel. 4229-2338
	15	
(29) St. Maximin		788 Gend 500 m
	14	
⛽ Brignoles		802 Open: 6.30 – 23.00 Tel. 9469-1726
	18	
(40) Le Luc		820 Gend 700 m Tel. 9473-0221
	22	🛏
⛽ +GPL		842 (112) Open 24 hrs Tel. 9473-0221
(35)	21	

Aire de Ventabren-Sud
[WC] [☎]

Pique-nique jeux d'enfants.

Aire de Barrière de péage
[WC] [☎]

Just parking facilities.

Aire de l' Ark
[🚻] [☎] [♿] [🎁] [☕] [⛽]

Very spacious but just parking facilities.

Aire de Barcelonne
[WC] [☎] [🏛]

Tables and benches under cover. Very pretty.
SOS — at side.

Aire de Brignoles-Cambarette
[🚻] [☎] [♿] [🎁] [☕] [⛽] [ℹ]

Interconnected by a tunnel. Just parking facilities.
SOS — at side,

Aire de Roudal
[WC] [☎] [♿] [🏛]

Sited on the side of a hill, rather spacious and pleasant. Recommended.
SOS at side by the entry.

Aire de Vidauban-Sud
[🚻] [☎] [♿] [🎁] [☕]

Just parking facilities. Cafeteria.
SOS — at the side by the entry.

18

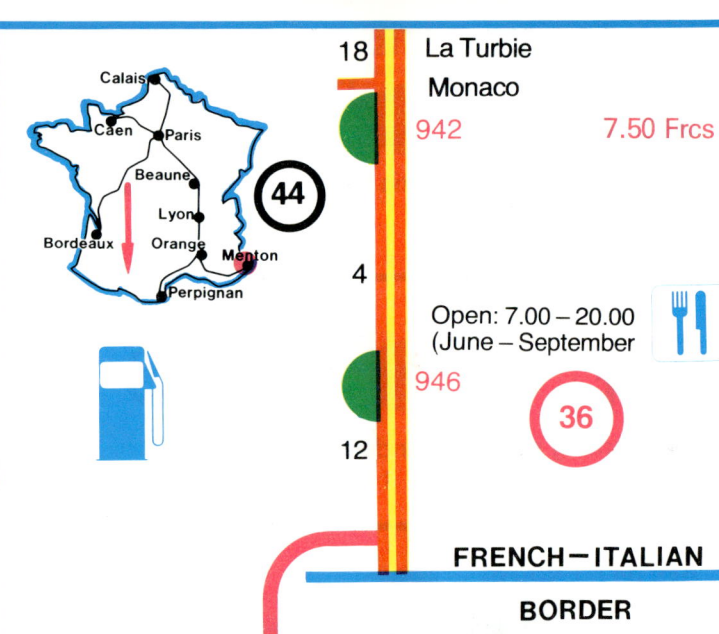

La Turbie
Monaco

942

7.50 Frcs

(44)

4

Open: 7.00 – 20.00
(June – September

946

36

12

FRENCH — ITALIAN

BORDER

MENTON
PERLE de la FRANCE
(E. RECLUS)
est heureuse de
vous accueillir

Aire de **Barrière de péage**

[WC] [☎]

As above.

Aire de **Beausoleil**

[♂♀] [☎] [♿] [🎁] [☕] [💵]

Sited on the side of a hill, by the Sea, very nice, modern with a panoramic view of Monaco.
SOS — just before entry.

THE HOTELS

OF

THE RIVIERA

The hotels appearing in this section are located between Menton at the Italian border and the West End of the coast and are shown in that order, town by town.

EUROP HOTEL ★★★
35 Avenue de Verdun,
06500 — Menton
Tel. 9335-5992

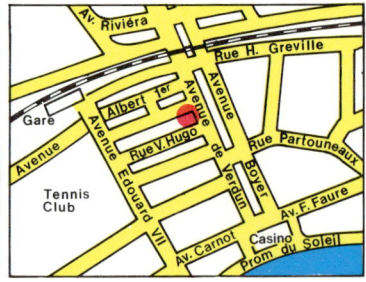

33 rooms with bath or shower, WC • telephone • radio • TV • mini-bar • lift • air-conditioned • sound-proofed • bar • garage in the hotel • casino and beaches nearby.

HOTEL LES RELAIS BLEUS ★★
57 Porte de France
06500 — Menton
Tel. 9357-6060

58 rooms with fully equipped bathrooms • colour TV • direct line telephone • automatic morning call • mini-bar • domestic animals accepted • restaurant • private parking in the basement.

HOTEL EDWARD'S ★★
7 et 9 Avenue Riviera,
06500 — Menton
Tel. 9335-7479

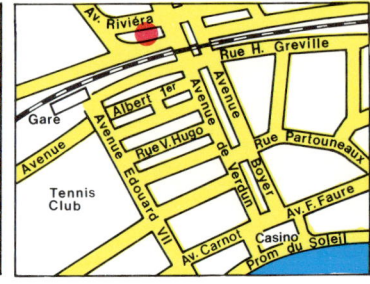

27 rooms with bath or shower, WC or C de T • telephone • solarium • private garden • lift • the beaches and casino nearby.

HOTEL VICTORIA ★★★
7 Promenade du Cap
06190 — Roquebrune Cap-Martin
Tel.9335-6590

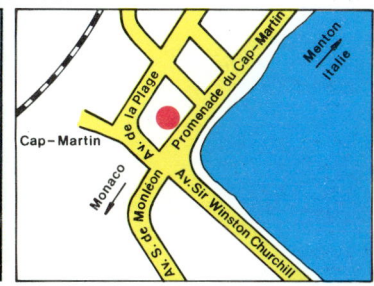

30 rooms with bath, shower and private toilets ● colour TV ● breakfast only ● many restaurants nearby ● ample parking facilities ● closed garage for 8 cars ● exceptional view over the Menton Bay and the approach to Italy.

HOTEL BEAUREGARD ★
10 Rue Albert 1er,
06500 — Menton
Tel.9335-7408

20 rooms with bathroom shower or C de T ● television room ● restaurant ● attractive garden ● shops, casino and beaches closeby.

LA VIEILLE AUBERGE
06500 — Ste Agnes
Tel.9335-9202

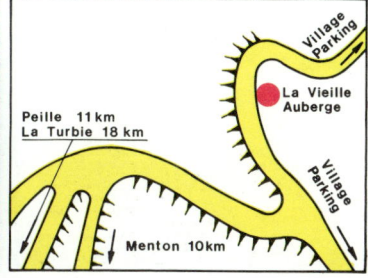

7 rooms with C de T ● elegant and tidy ● bar ● tea-room ● specialites provencales ● restaurant with its terrace area and exceptional panoramic view ● the dishes and service are of high quality ● rooms reasonably priced and food to do with it is excellent ● parking ● good value. ● Aperitifs and liquers de montagne shop.

INTER-HOTEL ALEXANDRA ★★★
93 Avenue Sir Winston Churchill,
06190 Roquebrune Cap-Martin
Tel.9335-6545, Telex:OREM 470673 F 1548

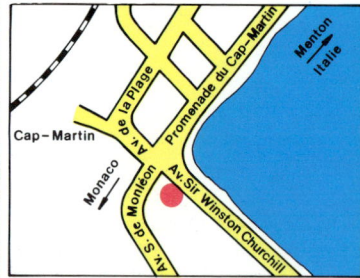

40 rooms with fully equipped bathroom ● air-conditioned ● colour TV ● mini-bar ● direct telephone ● lift ● solarium ● lounge bar ● parking reserved and garage spaces ● exceptional view over the Menton Bay and the approach to Italy.

HOTEL WESTMINSTER ★★
14 Avenue Lois Laurens
Roquebrune Cap-Martin
Tel.9335-0068

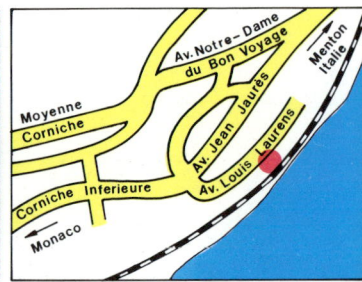

30 rooms with bathroom or shower, WC ● telephone ● TV room ● attractive garden on a hill with panoramic view on the bay ● bar ● 200 m from the beach.

HOTEL "LE NAPOLEON" ★★
7 Avenue de la Victoria
06320 — La Turbie
Tel.9341-0054

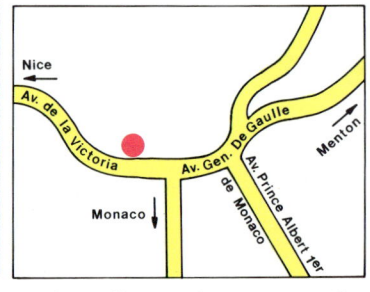

24 rooms with bathrooms and toilets ● large flowered terrace ● radio ● restaurant ● bar ● telephone ● TV on request ● casino 7 km at Monaco

HOTEL MIRAMAR ***
1 bis Avenue Kennedy,
Monte Carlo, Principalite de Monaco
Tel.9330-8648

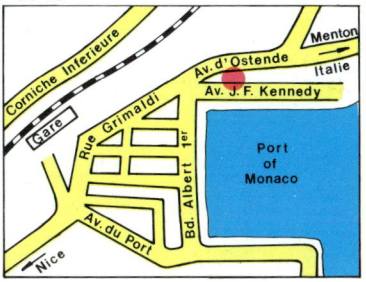

14 rooms with bathroom, WC ● air-conditioning ● balcony ● hotel stands on the shore, overlooking the sea and the port of Monaco ● large terrace on the roof ● car park opposite of the hotel ● casino 300 m away ● swimming pool nearby ● 5 min to the beach.

HOTEL WEST END ***
31 Promenade des Anglais
06000 — Nice
Tel.9388-7991,Telex:460879

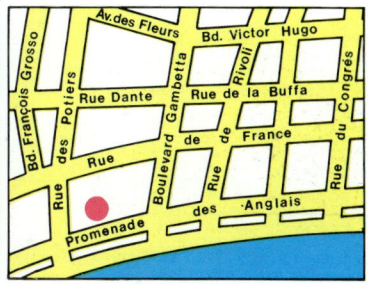

101 rooms with fully equipped bathrooms ● colour TV ● direct line telephone ● automatic morning call ● restaurant ● bar ● mini-bar ● reception room ● banqueting and conference rooms ● public car park behind the hotel.

HOTEL PARIS-NICE **
58 Rue de France,
06000 — Nice
Tel.9388-3861

28 rooms equipped with bathrooms and private toilets ● telephone ● TV room ● half-day and full day sight-seeing tours ● half board and full board on request ● car park nearby ● appears to be the nearest 2-star hotel to beaches at Nice and Promenade des Anglais.

PULLMAN HOTEL ★★★
28 Avenue Notre-Dame,
06000 — Nice
Tel.9380-3024, Telex:470662

200 rooms • details, page 14 • TV with video circuit • restaurant • bar • sauna bath • parking facilities • 5 min from the Promenade des Anglais • tropical garden and swimming pool.

HOTEL DE MULHOUSE ★★
9 Rue Chauvain,
06000 — Nice
Tel.9392-3669, Telex:970579 TURAZUR

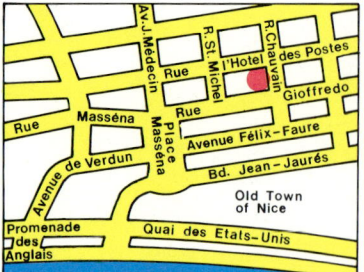

50 rooms with bathroom or shower, WC • telephone direct • automatic morning call • cafeteria on 6th floor • television room • 200 m from the Massena square

HOTEL "LA BELLE MEUNIERE" ★
21 Avenue Durante,
06000 — Nice
Tel.9388-6615

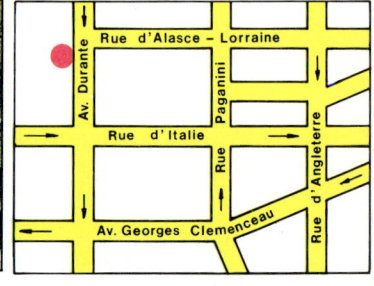

17 rooms with C de T or shower and WC • elegant and tidy • detached, villa-type • parking facilities • less than 10 min to the Promenade des Anglais

PULLMAN BEACH HOTEL ★★★★ de Luxe

13 Rue de Canada,
06400 — Cannes
Tel. 9338-2232, Telex: 470034

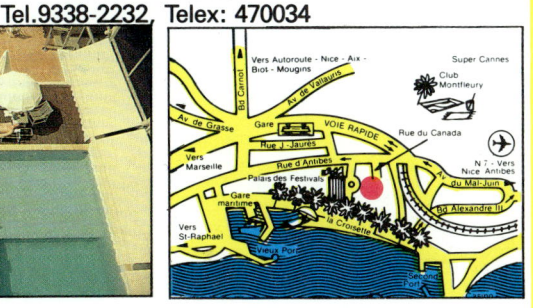

95 rooms ● details, page 14 ● TV with video circuit ● restaurant ● bar ● parking facilities ● open-air swimming pool ● the latest of the luxury hotels ● close to the new Festival and Congress Hall ● 50 m away from the Croisette.

ALTEA HOTEL ★★★★

Boulevard Amiral-Vence,
83200 — Toulon
Tel. 9424-4157, Telex: 400 347

93 rooms ● details, page 14 ● restaurant ● TV bar ● garden ● parking facilities ● open-air swimming pool ● bowling (French) ● overlooking the famous Toulon roadstead.

PULLMAN ILE ROUSSE ★★★★ de Luxe

Boulevard Louis-Lumière,
83150 — Bandol
Tel. 9429-4686, Telex: 400372

55 de luxe rooms ● bathroom ● radio ● colour TV and video programme ● telephone ● lift ● balcony ● 2 restaurants on the beach ● bar ● 3 conference rooms ● open air swimming pool with sea water ● solarium numerous sport facilities ● garage ● direct access on the beach.

PULLMAN HOTEL BEAUVAU ★★★★
4 Rue Beauvau,
13001 — Marseille
Tel. 9154-9100, Telex: 401778

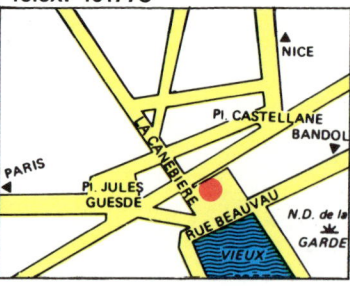

72 rooms with bath or shower ● air-conditioned ● colour TV ● radio ● mini-bar ● lift ● numerous restaurants nearby ● located in the front of the "Vieux Port" near the Canebiere.

ALTEA HOTEL ★★★★
Centre Bourse, Rue Neuve St. Martin
13001 — Marseille
Tel. 9191-9129 Telex: 401886

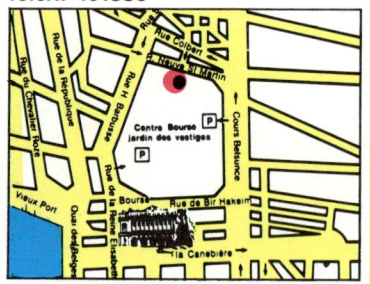

200 rooms ● details page 14 ● TV with video circuit ● restaurant ● bar ● meeting rooms ● located near the old port overlooking the Jardin des Vestipes.

HOTEL CAMARGUE ★★★
Route d'Istres,
13270 — Fos-sur-Mer
Tel. 4205-0057, Telex: 410812

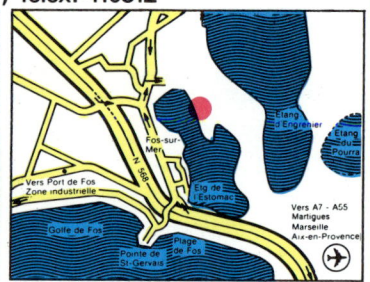

146 rooms ● details page 14 ● restaurant ● bar ● swimming pool ● conference rooms ● parking.

ALTEA HOTEL ★★★
Rue du Port
34280 — la Grande-Motte
Tel.6756-9081, Telex: 480241

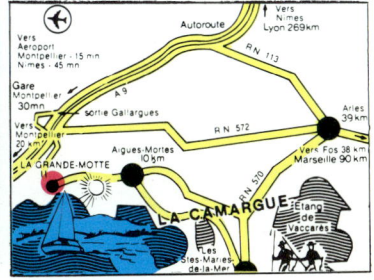

135 rooms ● details page 14 ● restaurant ● bar ● parking ● on the yacht harbour in the heart of the well known Languedoc — Roussillon resort area.

ALTEA HOTEL ★★★
Le Polygone, 218 Rue du Bastion — Ventadour,
34000 — Montpellier
Tel.6764-6566, Telex: 480362

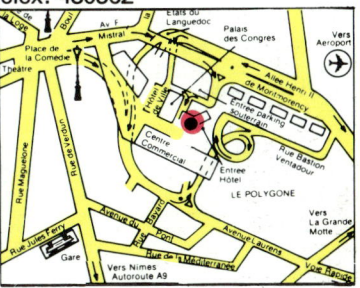

116 rooms ● details page 14 ● restaurant ● bar ● parking ● a modern hotel in the heart of Polygone business district 3 min from the Palace de la Comedie.

39

7

643

9

A7

662

8

A7

For Menton and Italy

Open 24 hrs
Tel. 9037-0309

+GPL

27

670

A9

8

28

678

Remoulins

2

35

+GPL

Calais
Caen
Paris
Beaune
Lyon
Bordeaux
Orange
Menton
Perpignan

140

Continued from page 121

Aire de **Mornas-Village**

This Rest Area's name is shown here for your reference only

Aire de **Roquemaure-Ouest**

Small with tables and benches.
SOS — at the side of Area.

Aire de **Tavel-Nord**

Tables and benches among trees and in the open space.
Pique — nique site, forested, spacious and nice.
SOS — just past the Area.

Aire de **Estezargues-Nord**

Pique — nique site incorporated, some pretty spots with attractive trees. Spacious, tables and benches.
SOS — at the side of Area.

12

690

(28)

8

698

Nimes-Est

16

Nimes-Ouest, Garons

714

8

(34)

722

Galargues

5

727   84 Frcs

5

Tel. 6771-1401

732

open; 7.00-22.00

+GPL

(33)

7

739   (61)

Vendargues

8

142

Aire de Ledenon-Nord
WC ☎ ♿

Completely open space type of area, few tables and benches pleasant.
SOS — at the side.

Aire de Nimes-Marguerittes
🚻 ☎ ♿ 🎁 ☕

There is a Pique- nique site with some tables and benches. Open space, pleasant.
SOS — about 500 m past the Rest Area.

Aire de Milhaund-Nord
WC ☎

Small with tables and benches.
SOS — at the side.

Aire de Vergèze-Nord
WC ☎ 🎪

Pique — nique site, swings, see — saws, sort of a wooden castle for children to play. There are tables and benches.
SOS — at the exit.

Aire de Barrière de péage
WC ☎ ♿

Just parking facilities.

Aire de Vidourle
🚻 ☎ ♿ 🎁 ☕ ⛽ 💱 ℹ️ ✉️

Ample parking facilities. Info-Route.

Aire de Nabriges
WC ☎ 🎪

There are tables and benches in the open space and among trees, swings and climbing frames.
SOS — at the side of Area.

143

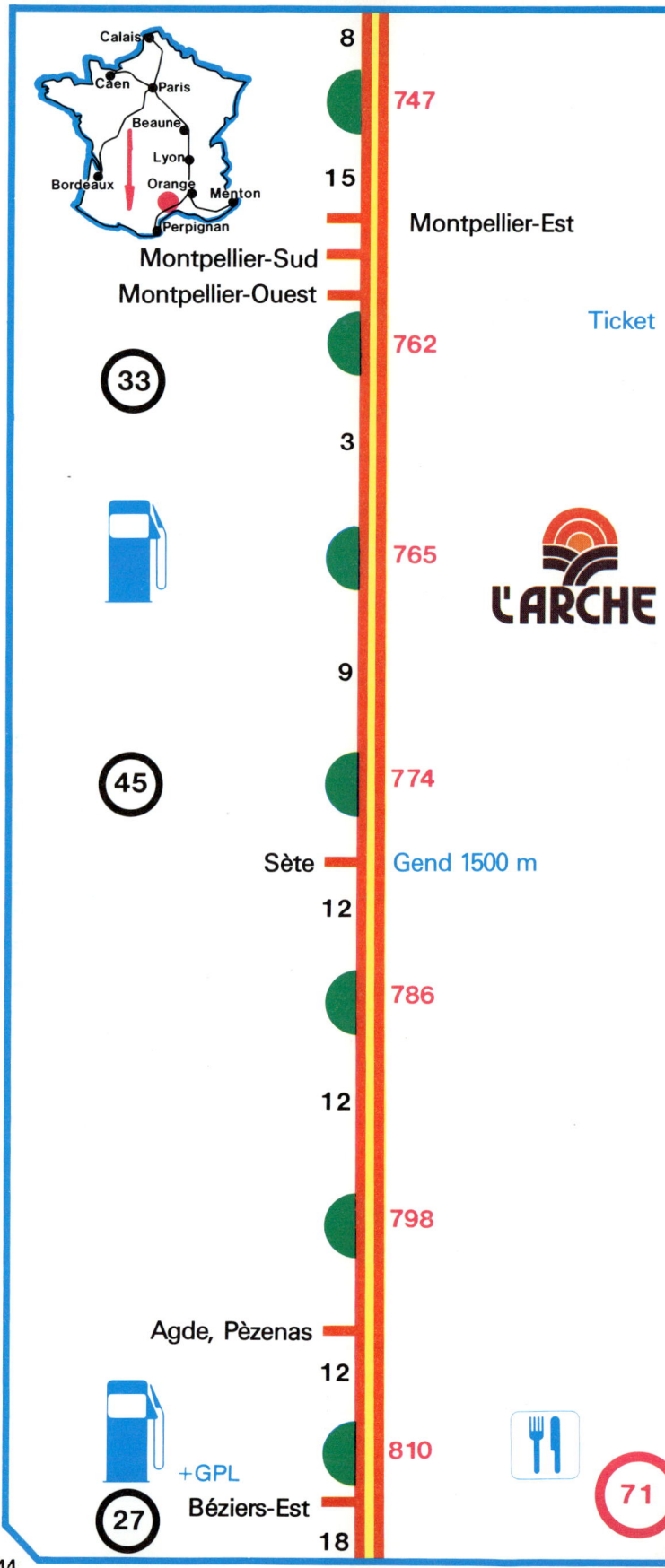

	8	
		747
	15	
	Montpellier-Sud	Montpellier-Est
	Montpellier-Ouest	
		Ticket
(33)		762
	3	
⛽		765
	9	
(45)		774
	Sète	Gend 1500 m
	12	
		786
	12	
		798
	Agde, Pèzenas	
	12	
⛽ +GPL		810
(27)	Béziers-Est	
	18	

L'ARCHE

🍴

(71)

144

Aire de **St. Aunes-Nord**

WC ☎

Tables and benches, small and pretty.
SOS — at the side.

Aire de **Barrière de péage**

WC ☎ ♿

Just parking bay for a few cars.

Aire de **Montpellier-Fabregues**

🚻 ☎ ♿ ⛽ ☕ 🍼 💰 🛍 ℹ️

Just parking facilities with some tables and benches. The other side of the M-way Rest Area accesible by car over a bridge.
SOS — at the exit.

Aire de **Gigean**

WC ☎

Open space type of area, yet with some trees. There are tables and benches.
SOS — at the side.

Aire de **Meze**

WC ☎

Forested with a pique — nique site incorporated. There are tables and benches.

Aire de **Florensac**

WC ☎

Just parking spaces.
SOS — at the side of Area.

Aire de **Béziers-Montblanc**

🚻 ☎ ♿ ⛽ ☕ ℹ️

Generally, car parking facilities. Info-Route.
SOS — at the side.

18 Béziers-Ouest

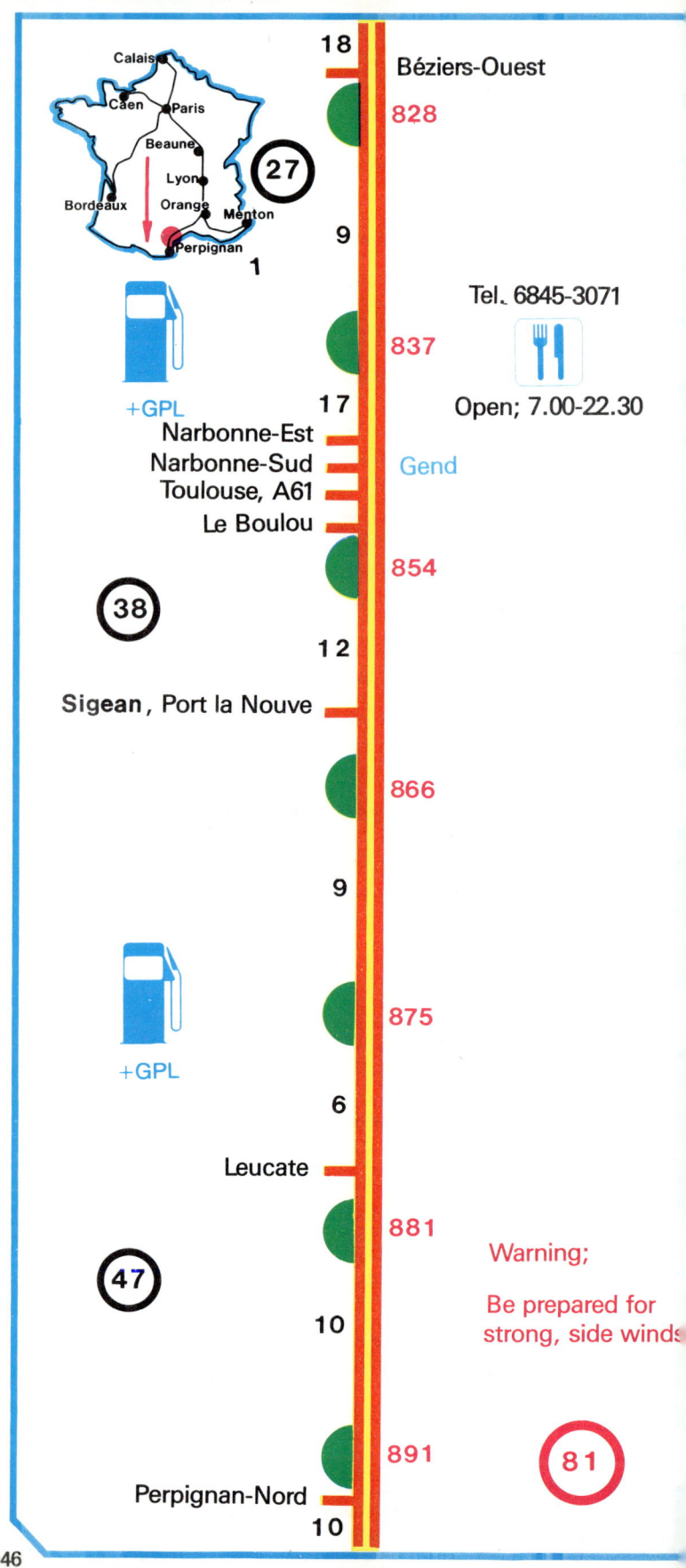

828

(27)

9

837

Tel. 6845-3071

Open; 7.00-22.30

17
Narbonne-Est
Narbonne-Sud   Gend
Toulouse, A61
Le Boulou

854

+GPL

(38)

12

Sigean, Port la Nouve

866

9

875

+GPL

6

Leucate

881

(47)

Warning;

Be prepared for
strong, side winds

10

891

(81)

Perpignan-Nord

10

146

Aire de Lespignan
WC ☎

Open space, with tables and benches. Small and pleasant.
SOS — at the side of Rest Area.

Aire de Narbonne-Vinassan
🚻 ☎ ♿ 🎁 ☕ 🍼 🚐 ℹ️ 🎠

Pique — nique jeux d'enfants, tables and benches. modest in size. Cafeteria, restaurant, self — service.
SOS — at the side. Info-Route.

Aire de Prat de Cest
WC ☎

Slightly forested, on a raised ground. Tables and benches. Incorporates a picnic site.
SOS — at the entry to the Area.

Aire des Gasparets
WC

Tables and benches among trees, combined with a picnic site.
SOS — at the side of Area.

Aire de Lapalme
🚻 ☎ ♿ 🎁

Some tables and benches.
SOS — at the side. Info-Route.

Aire de Fitou-Ouest
WC

Very much open type area, lit at night, just few benches.
SOS — at the side of the Rest Area.

Aire de Chateau de Salses
WC ☎ 🎠

Tables and benches, open type with bushy trees. Tunnel to the other side of Motorway Services. Very nice.

10

901

Gend

11

Perpignan-Sud

912

(47)

10

Tel. 6821-7430

922

+GPL

Open; Grill 11.00-22.00
Self-service 7.00-18.00

7

Le Boulou

929

(38)

8

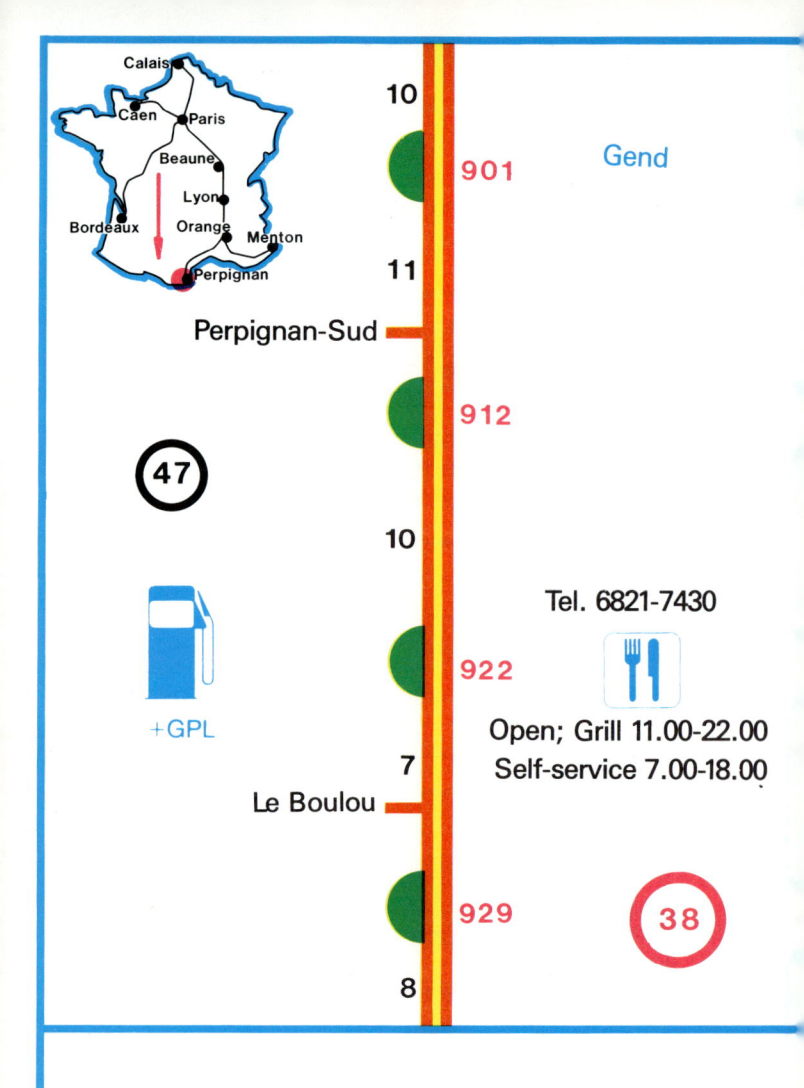

SPAIN

148

Aire de Rivesaltes

WC ☎

Grassy, attractive trees, pleasantly arranged site. Very pretty.
SOS — located at the entry.

Aire Ouest de Pavillons

WC ☎

Open type, lit at night. Tables and benches, pretty.
SOS — at the entry.

Aire du Village Catalon

🚻 ☎ ♿ 🗑 ☕ ⛽ 🛒 🎠 ✉

Very spacious, away from the Petrol Station Complex. Well sign — posted. Unusually big picnicking area with shops nearby. Info-Route.

Aire de Barrière de péage

WC ☎

Just parking bay.

The actual Routes of the Guide

(going north)

Aire de Pia
WC ☎

Few tables and benches, some trees. Lit at night. Nice
SOS — at the side of Area.

Aire Est des Pavillons
WC ☎

Forested, few benches, very pleasant.
SOS — at the side.

Aire du Village Catalon

🚻 ☎ ♿ 🎁 ☕ 🛒 ℹ️ ✉️

Very spacious area with picnicking facilities away from
petrol station complex. Sign-posted. Info-Route.

Aire de Barrière de péage
WC ☎

Just parking bay for cars.

HOTEL GRILL ★★
les Relais Bleus
13 Chemin de Gargantua,
69570 — Dardilly
Tel.7866-1366, Telex: 375071

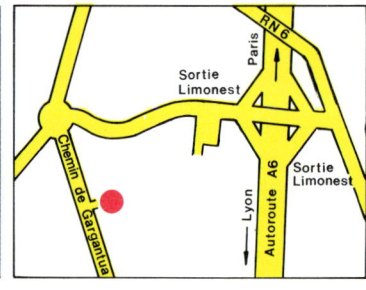

48 rooms with fully equipped bathrooms ● colour TV ● automatic
morning call ● direct-line telephone ● mini-bar ● domestic animals
accepted ● restaurant (open 12.00 — 14.00 and 19.00 — 22.00) ●
parking free.

(35)

Perpignan-Sud

10
35
11

24
9

🍴

15
7

Ticket
8
8

(48)

+GPL

A9

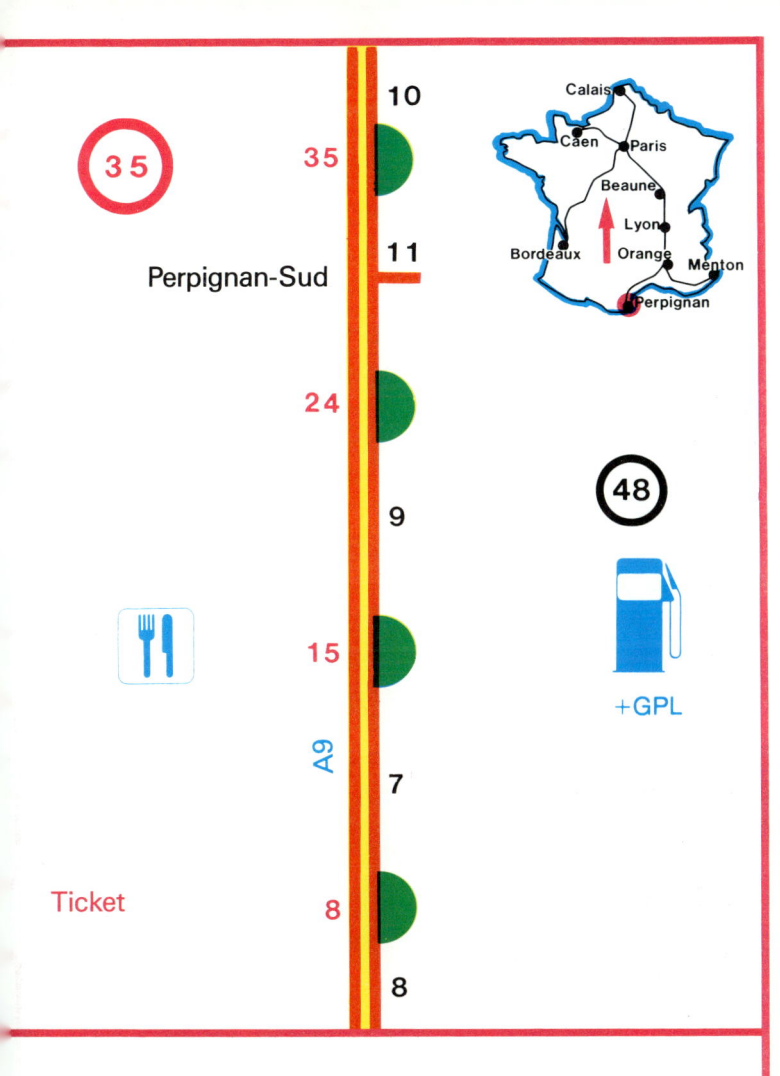

SPAIN

153

Aire de Lespignan
WC ☎

Tables and benches, lit at night, some trees.
SOS — at side.

Aire de Narbonne-Vinessan
🚻 ☎ ♿ 🎁 ☕ ⛽ 💱 🏪 ℹ️

Pique — nique jeux d'enfants, located on a raised ground. Tables and benches, a lot of trees, very large. Recommended.

Aire de Bages
WC ☎

Grassy, tables and benches, lit at night. Very spacious and pretty.
SOS — by the exit of the Area.

Aire de Sigean
WC

A picnic area incorporated also, tables and benches among trees. Lit at night. Very nice.
SOS — at the side.

Aire de Lapalme
WC

Open space type of area, yet with some trees. Tables and benches.
SOS — at side.

Aire de Fitou-Est
WC

Open space type of area, some trees, spacious.
SOS — at the side.

Aire de Château de Salses
WC ☎

Forested, connected with the other side of Motorway's Rest Area serwices by a tunnel.
SOS — at the side.

(74)

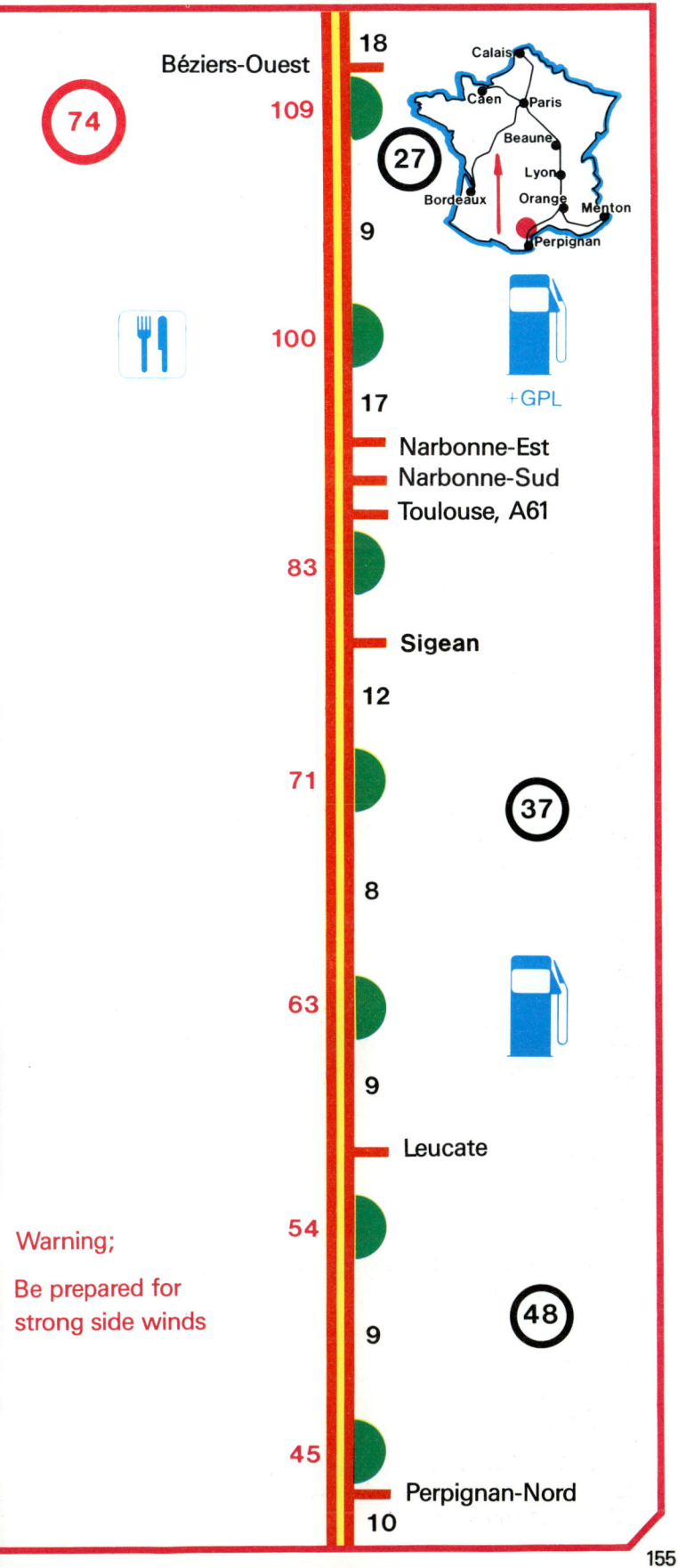

Béziers-Ouest

18
109

9

(27)

100

17

Narbonne-Est
Narbonne-Sud
Toulouse, A61

83

Sigean

12

71

(37)

8

63

+GPL

9

Leucate

54

(48)

9

45

Perpignan-Nord
10

Warning;
Be prepared for
strong side winds

155

Aire de Saint Aunes-Sud

[WC] [📞]

Stone made tables and benches, few trees. Small and pretty.
SOS — at side.

Aire de Barrière de péage

[WC] [📞] [♿]

Just parking spaces.

Aire de Montpellier-Fabreques

[🚻] [📞] [♿] [🎁] [☕] [🧴] [💱] [🛍️] [ℹ️] [✉️]

Very spacious, forested, mainly parking spaces. Footbridge to the other side of motorway Rest Area. Info-Route.

Aire de Gigean

[WC] [📞]

Lit at night, mainly car spaces, few tables and benches.
SOS — at side.

Aire de Loupian

[WC] [📞]

Open space type of area with some trees and picnic area. Lit at night, tables and benches. Spacious.
SOS — at the entry.

Aire de Florensac

[WC] [📞]

Just parking spaces, but pleasant.
SOS — close to the entry.

Aire de Béziers-Montblanc

[🚻] [📞] [♿] [🎁]

Very spacious in parking facilities, some benches.
SOS — close to the entry.

156

7 8

Vendergues

187

Montpellier-Est

61 Frcs

175

12

Montpellier-Sud

33

3

Montpellier-Ouest

Open 24 hrs
L'ARCHE

172

8

164

Gend 900 m

9

Sète

155

45

16

139

Agde, Pézenas

12

127

Béziers-Est

18

+GPL

+GPL

27

157

Aire de Ledenon-Sud

[WC] [📞]

Open space type, stone made tables and benches, small. Nice.
SOS — at side.

Aire de Nimes-Marguerittes

[👥] [📞] [♿] [🎁] [☕] [💱]

Ample parking facilities, cafeteria, grill, boutique.
SOS — at the exit. Info-Route.

Aire de Milhaud-Sud

[WC] [📞]

Small with few tables and benches.
SOS — by the exit.

Aire de Vergeze-Sud

[WC] [📞]

Forested, picnic area with a lot of tables and benches.
SOS — actually on the Rest area.

Aire de Barrière de péage

Seems to offer no facilities of any kind.

Aire de Vidourle

[👥] [📞] [♿] [🎁] [☕] [🍼] [💱] [ℹ️]

Mainly car parking spaces. Cafeteria.
SOS — at side.

Aire de Mas du Roux

[WC] [📞] [🎡]

Pique-nique jeux d'enfants, tables and benches among trees and in the open. Very pretty and recommended.
SOS — at side.

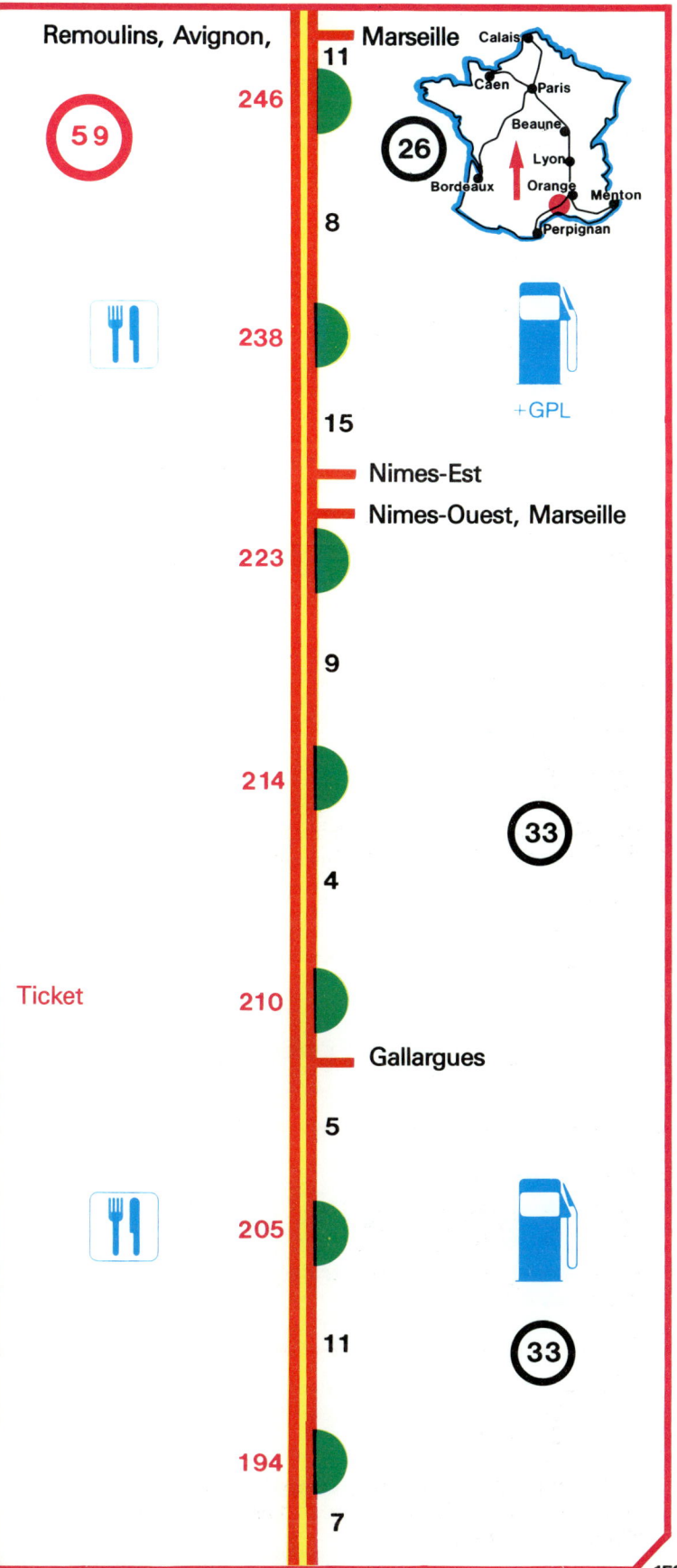

Remoulins, Avignon,	246	Marseille
(59)		11
		8
🍴	238	(26)
		15
		Nimes-Est
		Nimes-Ouest, Marseille
	223	
		9
	214	
		4
Ticket	210	
		Gallargues
		5
🍴	205	
		11
	194	(33)
		7

+GPL

159

ALTEA HOTEL ✶✶✶
Route de Caderousse,
84100 — Orange
Tel.9034-2410, Telex:431550

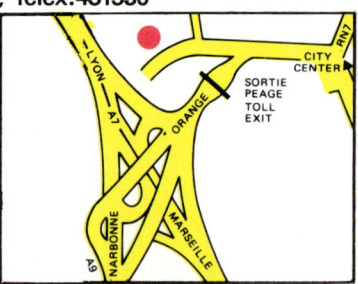

99 rooms with fully equipped bathroom ● radio ● colour TV on request ● direct telephone ● restaurant and barbecue ● bar ● swimming pool ● table-tennis ● american billiard ● parking ● few min. drive to the famous Roman Amphitheatre and the Arc de Triumph ● located in a garden at the intersection of motorway A7 and A9.

Aire de Mormas

This Rest Area's name is for your reference only, when you turn over to page 169 to continue the journey.

Aire de Roquemaure-Est

Open space area, yet with tables and benches among trees. Small and pretty.
SOS — at the exit.

Aire de Tavel-Sud

Incorporated a picnic area facilities. Restaurant, bar and boutique. Info-Route.

Aire de Estezergues-Sud

Very spacious with some bushy trees, tables and benches.
SOS — at side.

HOTEL FORMULE 1

Lyon Nord Dardilly, Autoroute A6
Porte de Lyon
69570 — Dardilly   Tel. 7835-8080

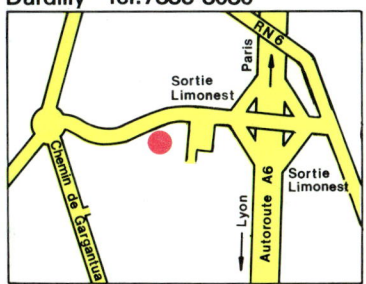

64 rooms with lavobo (basin), cold/hot water ● video ● alarm clock ● radio ● showers and toilets sheared ● 1, 2 or 3 persons in room - same price (99 FF in 1987) ● rooms for disabled people ● parking free ● very competative price petrol station and well stocked shop next door.

To continue for Porte de Lyon and Paris
turn over to page 169

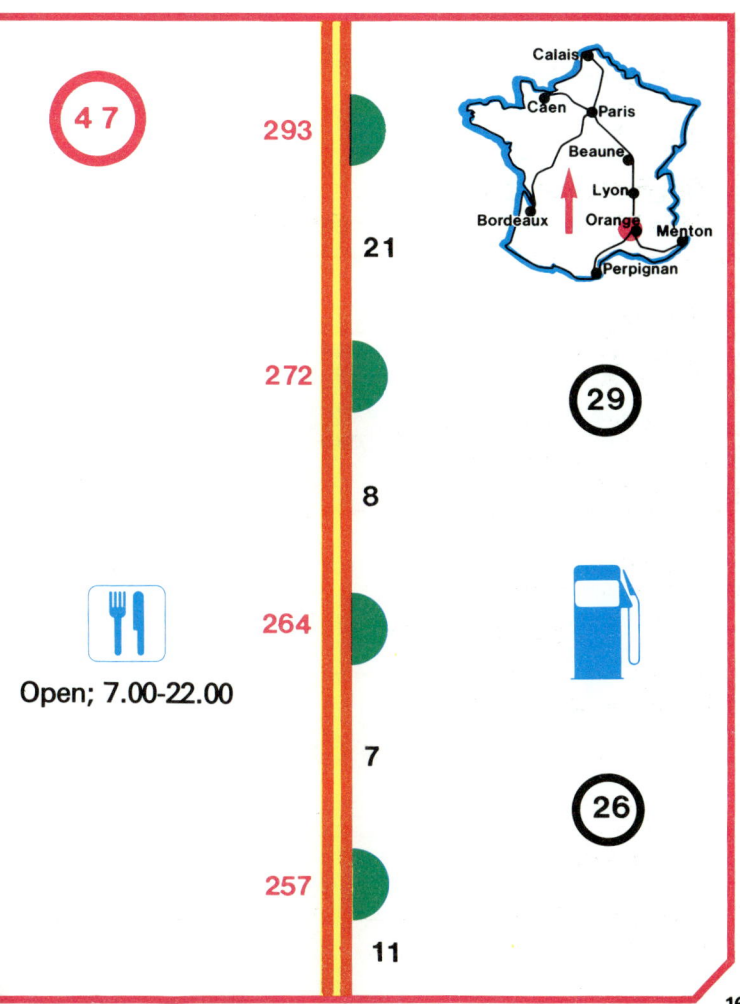

(4 7)

293

21

272

8

(29)

264

Open; 7.00-22.00

7

(26)

257

11

161

Aire de **Bréguirès**

Very spacious which is not apparent at first. Tables and benches, nice area. There is a Musee de L'Automobiliste.

Aire de **Barrière de péage**

As below.

Aire de **Barrière de péage**

As below.

Aire de **Barrière de péage**

Small with parking facilities.
SOS — 400 metres past the area.

Aire de la **Scoperta**

Open space type of area but with a lot of small trees. Tables and benches, very elegant place. Bar, buffet.
SOS — at the side.

	Cannes, Grasse	37	
(56)	56		
		4	
12 Frcs	52		
		18	Antibes, Juan Les Pins
Cagnes-sur-Mer			Grasse
			St. Laurent du Var
			Nice Aeroport,
5 Frcs	34		St. Augustin
		18	
Digne			Nice, St. Isidore
			Nice Nord
			Nice-Est
7.50 Frcs	16		
		2	
	14		
Roquebrune, Monaco		14	

(37)

(42)

+GPL

+GPL

MENTON

163

Aire de Rousset

Very open, just car parking spaces. Bar, cafeteria.
SOS — at the side.

Aire de St. Hilaire

Open type of area with some trees. There are tables and benches.
SOS — by the entry.

Aire Nord de Cambarette

Open space type, few tables and benches. Restaurant, bar.
SOS — at the side.

Aire de Candumy

Forested, tables and benches, rather large area sited on a hill. Nice.
SOS — by the entry.

Aire de Vidauban-Nord

Just parking facilities.
SOS — by the exit.

Aire de Canaver

Spacious area, tables and benches, some trees. Very nice.
Bar — restaurant.

Aire de Barrière de péage

Small, couple of sets of tables and benches.
SOS — close to the entry.

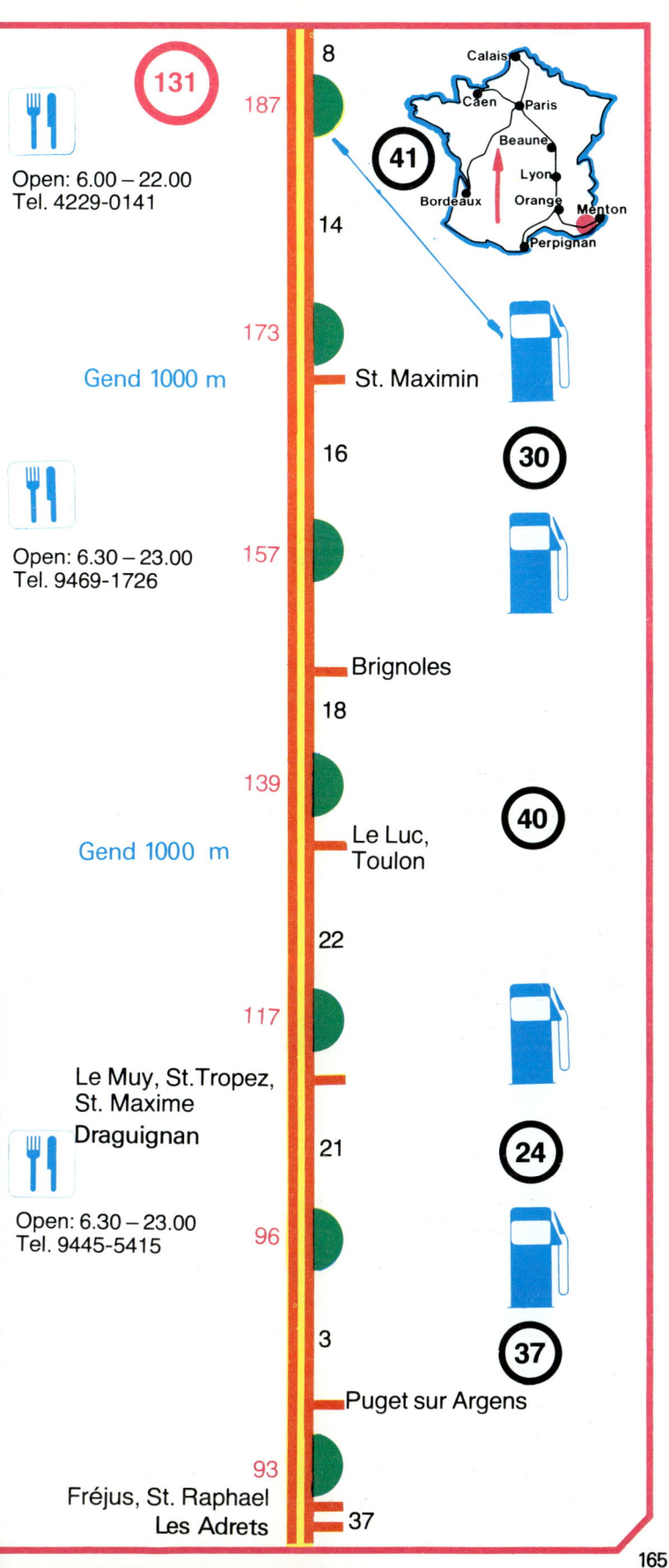

🍴 Open: 6.00 – 22.00 Tel. 4229-0141	(131)	187	8
			14
Gend 1000 m		173	St. Maximin
🍴 Open: 6.30 – 23.00 Tel. 9469-1726		157	16
			Brignoles
			18
Gend 1000 m		139	Le Luc, Toulon
			22
Le Muy, St. Tropez, St. Maxime Draguignan 🍴 Open: 6.30 – 23.00 Tel. 9445-5415		117	21
		96	3
			Puget sur Argens
Fréjus, St. Raphael Les Adrets		93	37

(41)

(30)

(40)

(24)

(37)

165

Aire de **Sénas**

| WC | ☎ |

No tables, just benches. Very small, tidy and interesting.
SOS — by the entry.

Aire de **Barrière de péage**

No facilities. Very limited.

Aire de **Lamanon**

| WC | ☎ | 🚶 |

Forested, jungle like type, spacious, plenty of tables and benches. Pique-nique jeux d'enfants.

Aire de **Barrière de péage**

In a stage of development.

Aire de **Lançon de Provence**

🚻 ☎ ♿ 🎁 ☕ 🧴 💱 🚶 ℹ️

It is an open type of area, yet with tables and benches among trees. Very pleasant. Footbridge to the other side of the motorway.
SOS — at the side.

Aire de **Ventabren-Nord**

| WC | ☎ | ♿ | 🚶 |

Open type of area with some shady spots. Pique-nique jeux d'enfants. Recommended.

Aire de **Barrière de péage**

| WC | ☎ |

Very small. Gendarmerie Station.

Mandelieu, La Napoule
Gend 400 m

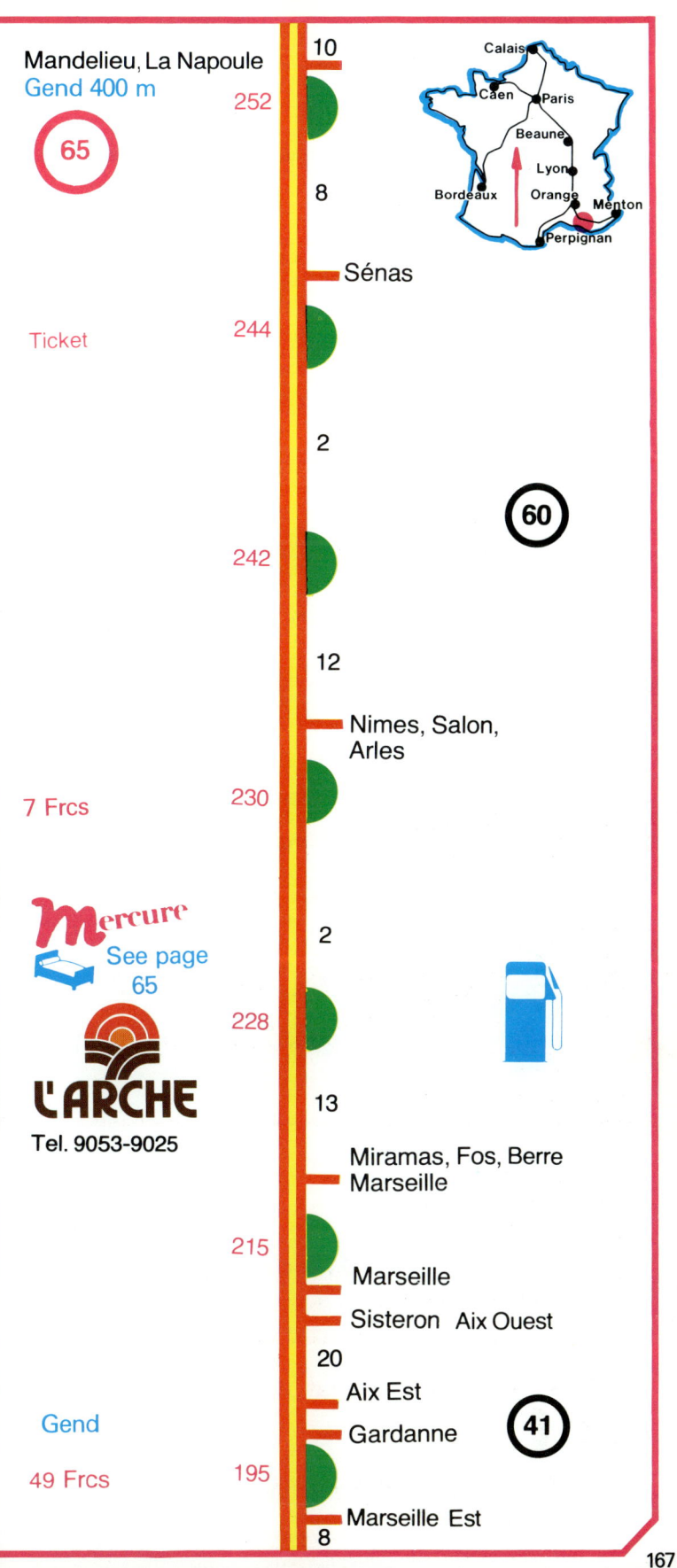

(65)

10

252

8

Sénas

Ticket

244

2

242

(60)

12

Nimes, Salon, Arles

7 Frcs

230

2

Mercure
See page 65

228

L'ARCHE
Tel. 9053-9025

13

Miramas, Fos, Berre
Marseille

215

Marseille

Sisteron   Aix Ouest

20

Aix Est

Gend

Gardanne

(41)

49 Frcs

195

Marseille Est

8

167

Aire de Donzère

WC

Completely open type of area, with tables and benches, very elegant. Small.
SOS — at the side.

Aire de Tricastin

WC ☎

Very small and elegant place with tables and benches. Recommended.

Aire de Mornas

🚻 ☎ ♿ ⛽

Spacious, just parking facilities.
SOS — at the side.

Aire d' Orange

WC ☎ ♿

Pique-nique jeux d'enfants. Large and elegant.

Aire de Sorgues

🚻 ☎ ♿ ⛽ ☕ 🧴 🛒 🏪

Pique-nique jeux d'enfants. Spacious and nice. Restaurant, bar, boutique.
SOS — at the side.

Aire de Noves

WC

Open type with tables and benches, very elegant.
SOS — by the entry.

Aire de Cavaillon

WC ☎

Open type of area, sited on a hill by a water reservoir, sort of a lake. Small and nice.

(92) **Montélimar Sud**
Gend 700 m 344

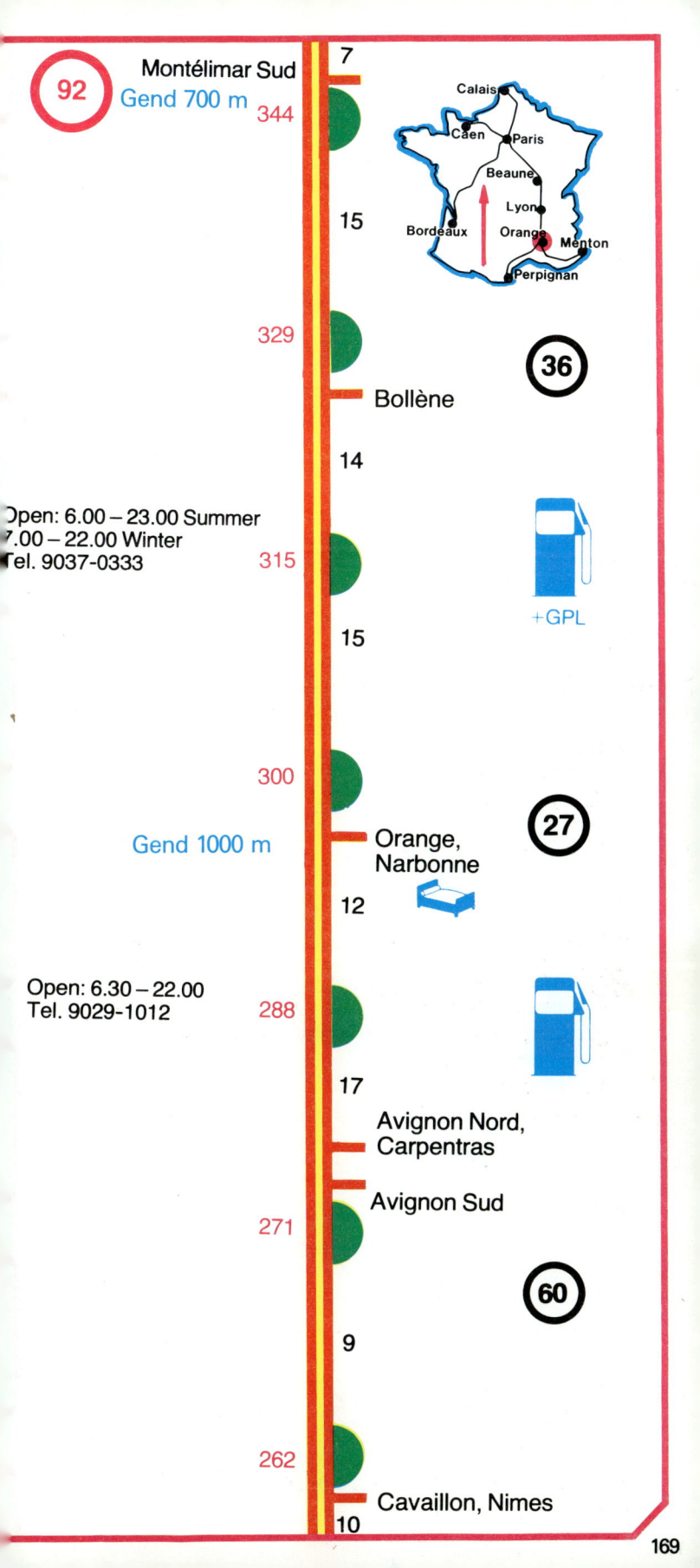

7

15

329

Bollène

14

Open: 6.00 – 23.00 Summer
7.00 – 22.00 Winter
Tel. 9037-0333

315

(36)

15

300

Gend 1000 m

Orange, Narbonne

12

(27)

Open: 6.30 – 22.00
Tel. 9029-1012

288

17

Avignon Nord, Carpentras

Avignon Sud

271

9

(60)

262

Cavaillon, Nimes

10

169

Aire de Latitude 45

WC ☎

Very open, yet some trees. Tables and benches. Very nice.
SOS — at the side.

Aire de Portes-Lès-Valence

Pique-nique jeux d'enfants, small and open type of area.

Aire de Livron

WC ☎

Very small with some tables and benches.
SOS — at the entry.

Aire de Saulce

WC ☎

Pique-nique jeux d'enfants. Very small but pretty and recommended.

Aire du Logis Neuf

WC

Pique-nique jeux d'enfants. Large, very nice. Recommended.
SOS — by the entry.

Aire du Roubion

WC

Pique-nique jeux d'enfants. Very small, open type and nice.
SOS — at side.

Aire de Montélimar

Pique-nique jeux d'enfants. Large with nests of tables and benches in the open and among trees. Nice.
SOS — at the side.

(68)

412 Valence Nord
Gend

(50)

🍴
Open: 6.30 – 23.30
Tel. 7557-3620

18

394 Valence Sud, Grenoble

⛽

9

385

9

Loriol, Privas
376

9

Montélimar Nord, Crest
367

(43)

6

361

Open: 24 hrs Summer
5.00 – 23.00 Winter

Tel. 7546-6000

🍴

10

351

⛽

(36)

7

171

Aire de **Barrière de péage**

Very small and limited.

Aire de la **Grande Borne**

Pique-nique jeux d'enfants. Plenty of nests of tables and stools. Very nice. Recommended.

Aire de **Chanas**

No facilities. Very small but pleasant.

Aire de **St. Rambert d'Albon**

Pique-nique jeux d'enfants. Recommended.

Aire de la **Combe Tourmente**

Pique-nique jeux d'enfants. Recommended.
SOS — at the side.

Aire de la **Galaure**

Pique-nique jeux d'enfants. Nests of tables and benches among trees. Nice.
SOS — at the side.

Aire de la **Bouterne**

Open type of area, tables and benches, very small.
SOS — at the end of the area, by the exit.

71 Frcs (56)

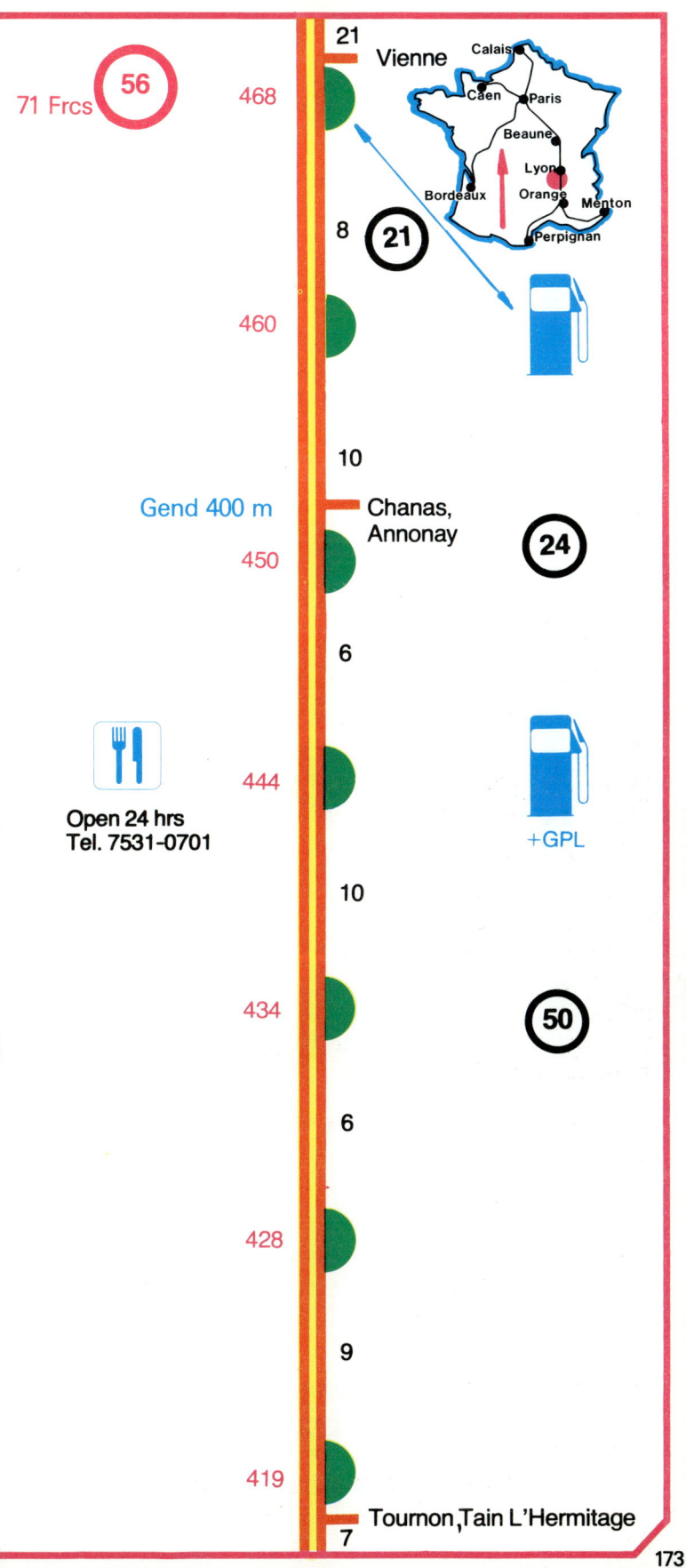

468
21 — Vienne

8 (21)

460

10

Gend 400 m
450 — Chanas, Annonay

(24)

6

🍴
Open 24 hrs
Tel. 7531-0701

444

+GPL

10

434

(50)

6

428

9

419

7 — Tournon, Tain L'Hermitage

173

Aire de **Taponas**

Tables and benches.
SOS — at the side.

Aire de **Boitray**

Newly built 1986. Very spacious, by the water reservoir. Tables and benches. Lit at night. Very attractive. Coffee bar. Recommended.

Aire de **Barrière de péage**

Limited.

Aire de **Chères**

There are tables and benches.
SOS — at the side by the exit.

Aire de **Paisy**

As below.

Aire de **Piérre Benite**

There are tables and benches.

Aire de **Sérézin sur Rhône**

Just parking facilities. Grill and sandwich bar.

(82)

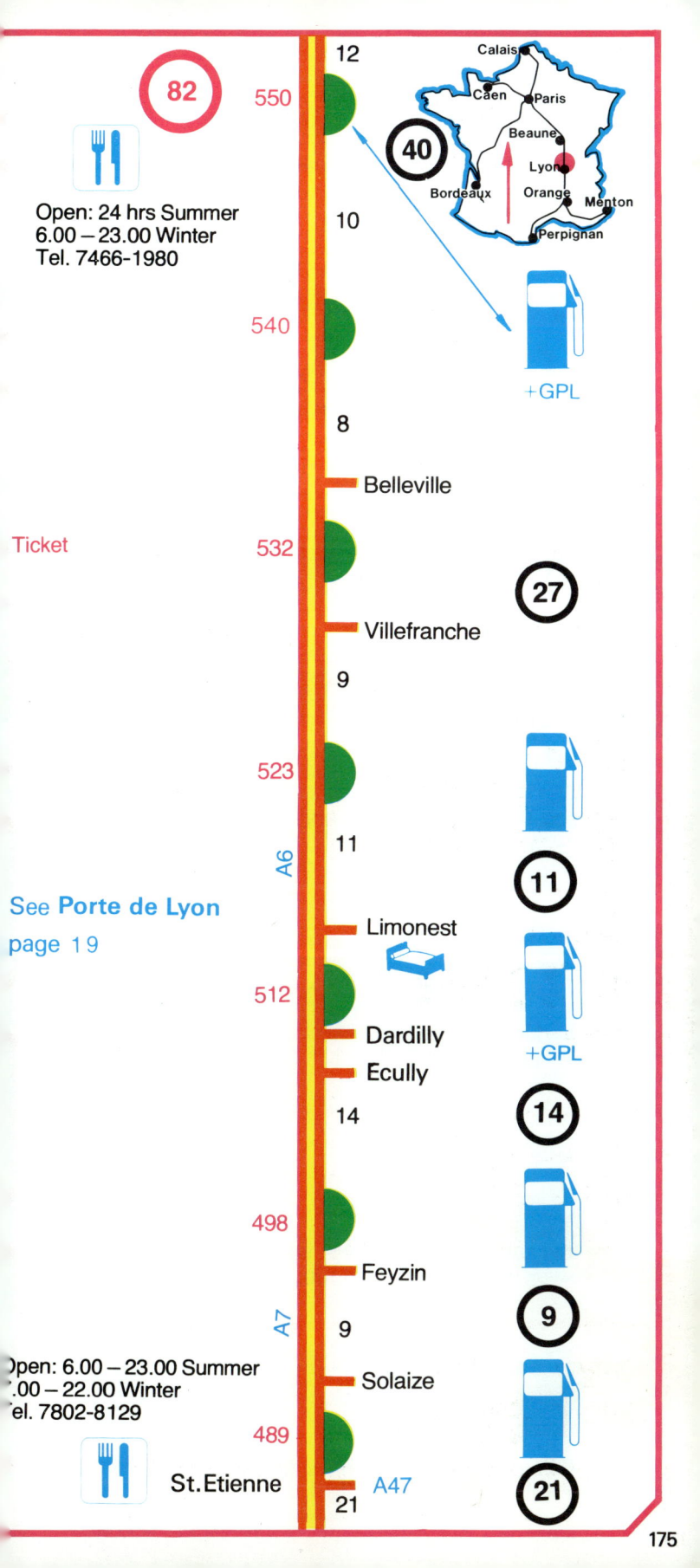

🍴
Open: 24 hrs Summer
6.00 – 23.00 Winter
Tel. 7466-1980

Ticket

See **Porte de Lyon**
page 19

Open: 6.00 – 23.00 Summer
.00 – 22.00 Winter
el. 7802-8129

🍴

12
550

10

540

8
— Belleville

532

— Villefranche
9

523

11
A6

— Limonest 🛏
512
— Dardilly
— Ecully
14

498

— Feyzin
A7
9
— Solaize

489
St.Etienne — A47
21

(40)

+GPL

(27)

(11)

+GPL

(14)

(9)

(21)

175

Aire de la Loyère

There are tables and benches, very small but smart enough to be recommended.
SOS — at the side.

Aire de St. Ambreuil

Just parking spaces. Restaurant, bar.

Aire de Boyer

Very small and grassy.
SOS — at the side.

Aire d' Uchizy

Very small and nice. Tables and benches.
SOS — at the side.

Aire de Mâcon-la-Salle

Just parking spaces
SOS — by the exit.

Aire de la Grisière

Very few tables and benches, small but nice.
SOS — at the side of the Area.

Aire de Sablons

It is very unusual in its form, newly built, interesting origination. Recommended.
SOS — at the side.

(87)

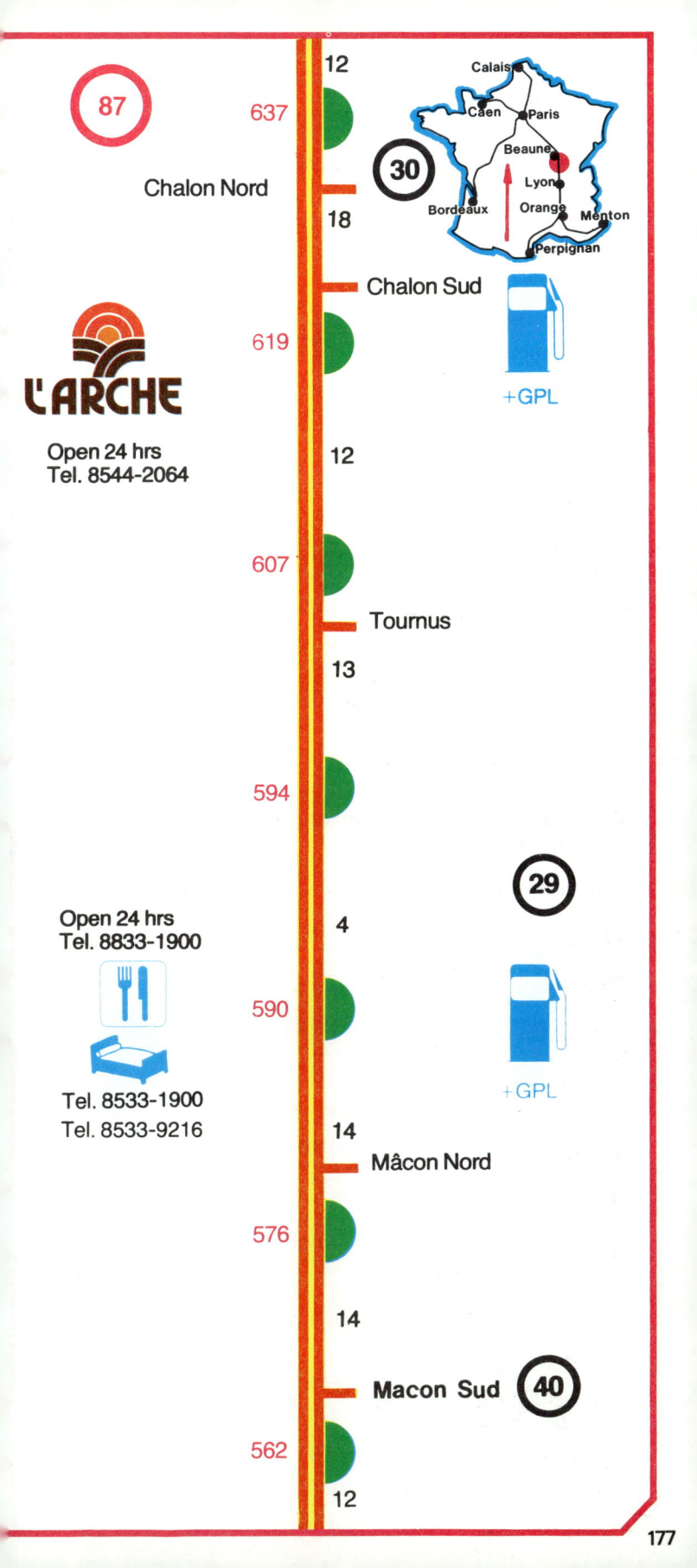

637
Chalon Nord

L'ARCHE

Open 24 hrs
Tel. 8544-2064

12

18

Chalon Sud

619

(30)

12

607

Tournus

13

594

Open 24 hrs
Tel. 8833-1900

4

590

Tel. 8533-1900
Tel. 8533-9216

(29)

+GPL

14

Mâcon Nord

576

14

Macon Sud (40)

562

12

177

Aire de Marcigny

WC 🏞️

Forested, tables and benches, pretty.
SOS — at the side.

Aire de Lochères

🚻 ☎️ ♿ 🗑️ 🍼 💱 🏞️

Small, few tables and benches.
SOS — just past the exit.

Aire de Rèpotte

WC 🏞️

Small and nice, tables and benches.
SOS — by the entry.

Aire de Creux More

🚻 ☎️ ♿ 🗑️ 🏞️

Elegant place with some tables and benches.
SOS — at the side.

Aire de Bois des Carbeaux

WC 🏞️

In two parts; forested and open space, tables and benches, nice.
SOS — at the side.

Aire de Savigny les Beaune

WC

Very open type, tables and benches, nice place.
SOS — at the side.

Aire de Beaune-Merceuil

🚻 ☎️ ♿ 🗑️ ☕ 🍼 ℹ️

Ample parking area in every way.
SOS — at the side.

Bierre Lès Semur

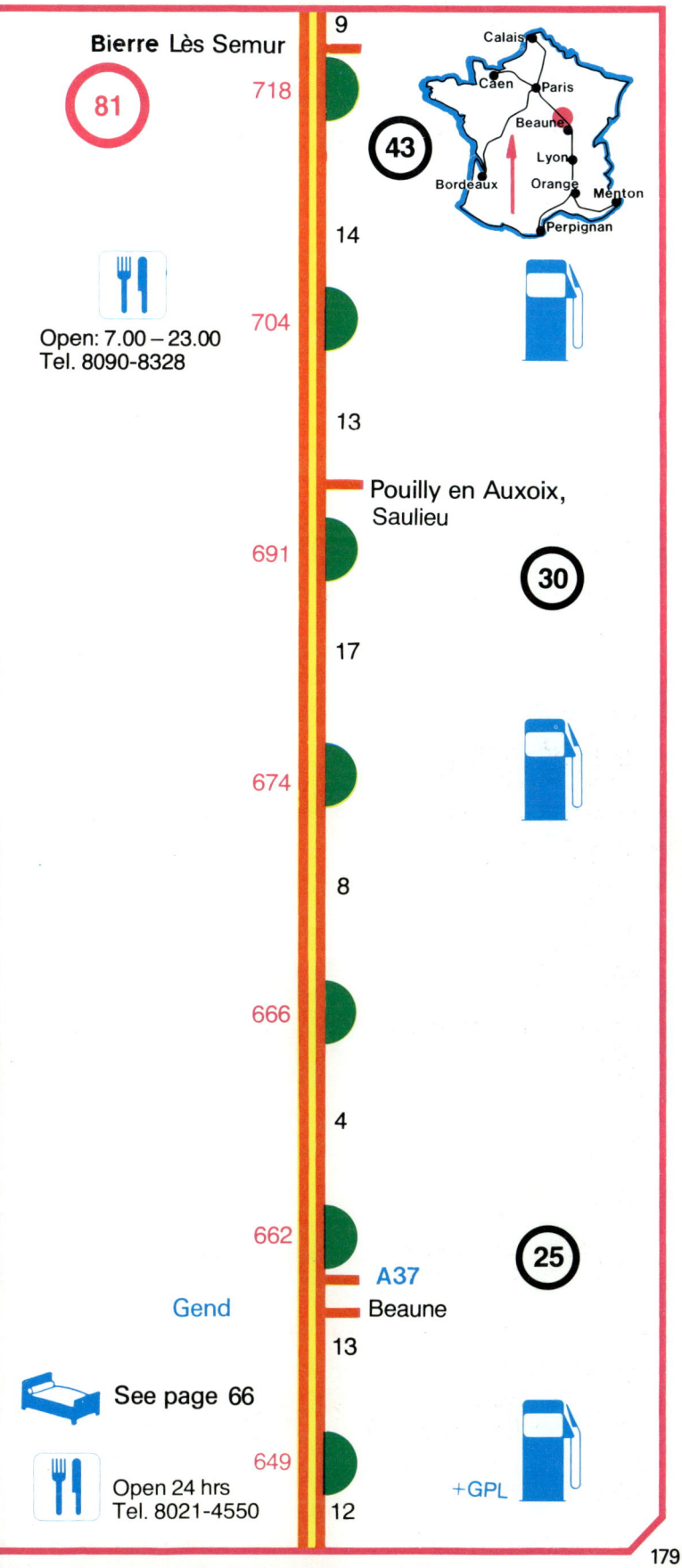

(81)

🍴 Open: 7.00 – 23.00
Tel. 8090-8328

9
718
14
704
13

Pouilly en Auxoix, Saulieu

691
17
674
8
666
4
662

A37
Beaune

Gend
13

🛏 See page 66

649

🍴 Open 24 hrs
Tel. 8021-4550

12

(43)

(30)

(25)

+GPL

179

Aire de Venoy Soleil Levant

Just parking spaces. A footbridge to the other side of motorway.

Aire du Buisson Rond

Again, as below, very nice.
SOS — by the entry.

Aire du Cherveuil

Again, jungle like type, recommended.
SOS — at the side.

Aire d' Hervaux

Very nice, jungle like type of area, spacious with tables and benches.
SOS — at the side.

Aire de Maison-Dieu

Just parking spaces.
SOS — at the side.

Aire du Genetoy

No tables or benches, completely open.
SOS — at the side.

Aire de Côme

Just one lane parking area with no other services provided.
SOS — at the side of the Area.

Open: 6.15 – 23.45
Tel. 8652-3552

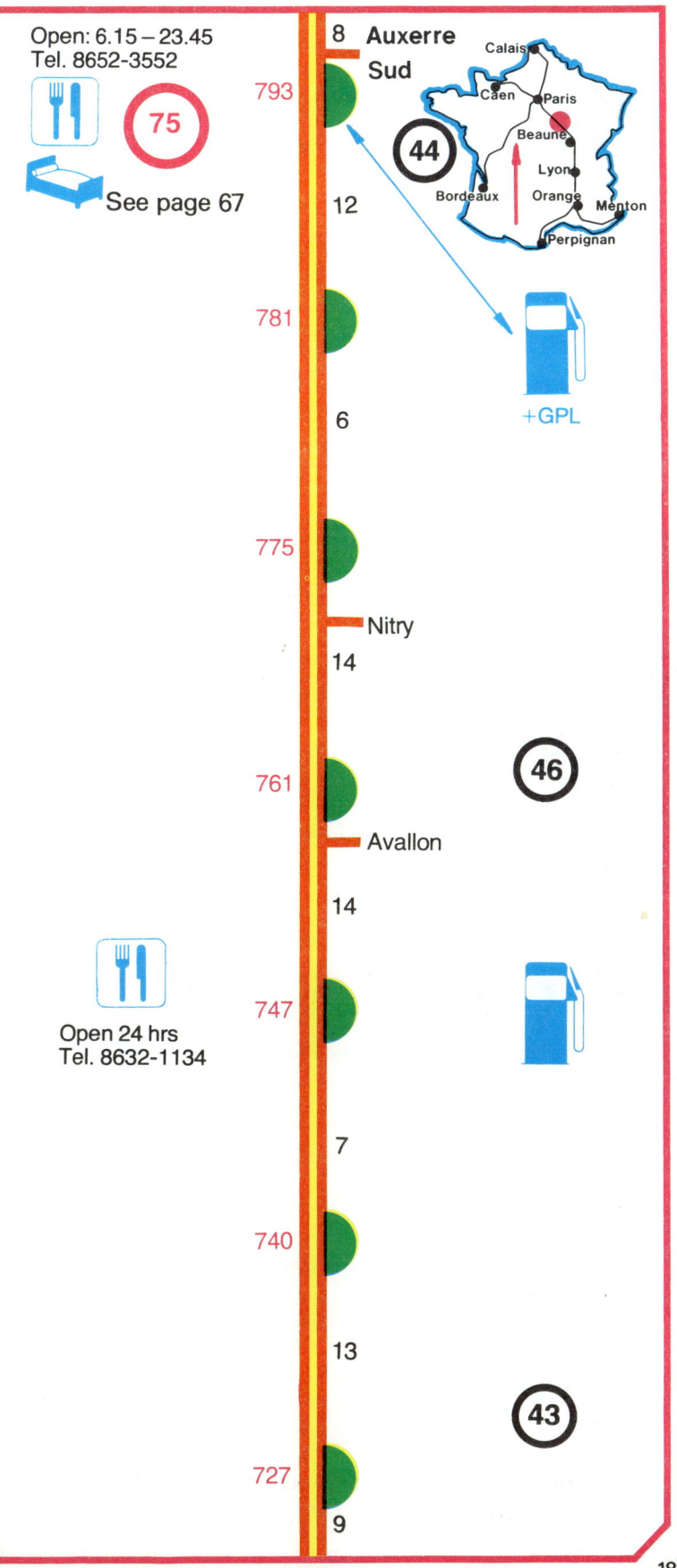

🍴
🛏
(75)
See page 67

8 **Auxerre Sud**

793

(44)

Calais
Caen — Paris
Beaune
Bordeaux — Lyon
Orange — Menton
Perpignan

+GPL

12

781

6

775

Nitry
14

761

(46)

Avallon
14

🍴
Open 24 hrs
Tel. 8632-1134

747

7

740

13

(43)

727

9

181

Aire d' Egreville

WC 🚻

Open space type of area, partly forested. There are tables and benches.
SOS.

Aire de la Roche

WC

As below.
SOS.

Aire des Chênes

WC

Forested area with tables and benches.
SOS.

Aire de la Couline

WC

Basically, just parking spaces.
SOS.

Aire de la Loupière

🚻 📞 ♿ 🧴 ☕ 🍼 🎰 🚻

Tables and benches among trees.
SOS.

Aire des Pâtures

WC ♿ 🚻

Partly open area, partly forested. Tables and benches.
SOS — by the entry.

Aire du Thureau

WC

Tables and benches among trees. See-saws, swings, rocking things.
SOS — at the side.

(76)

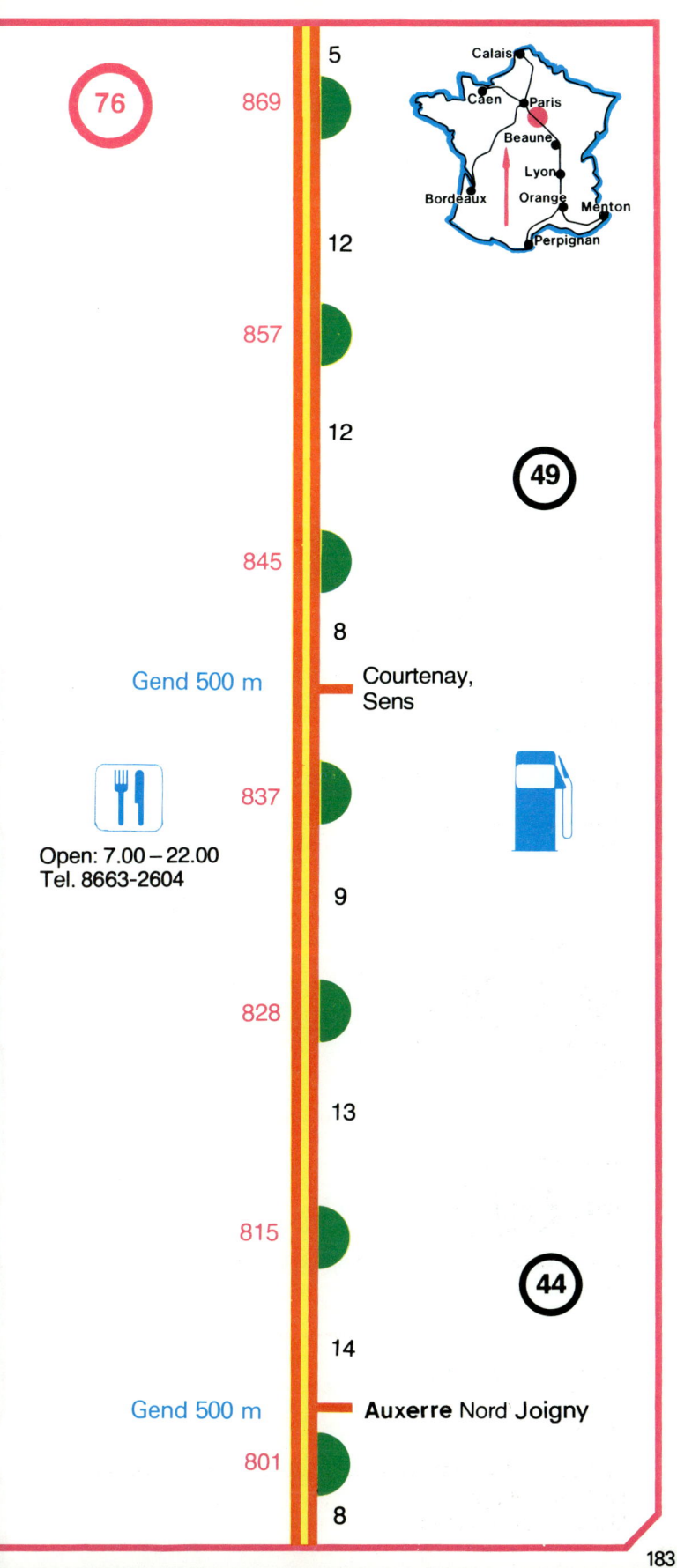

869
5

12
857

12

845
(49)

8
Gend 500 m — Courtenay, Sens

🍴
837
Open: 7.00 – 22.00
Tel. 8663-2604

9

828

13

815
(44)

14
Gend 500 m — **Auxerre** Nord Joigny

801
8

183

Aire de **Villabè**

Just spaces for parking.
SOS — at the side.

Aire de **St. Sauveur**

SOS at the side of the parking area.

Aire de **Barrière de péage**

Just parking spaces. Gendarmerie Station.

Aire d' **Arbonne**

Few tables and benches among trees.
SOS — at the side of the Area.

Aire d' **Achères**

Small and simple.
SOS — at the side.

Aire de **Darvault (Nemours)**

Ample range of quality services. Interconnected with the other side Rest Area.

Aire de **Floée**

Small, few tables and benches.
SOS — at the side.

(Police) Évry Centre,
929.5

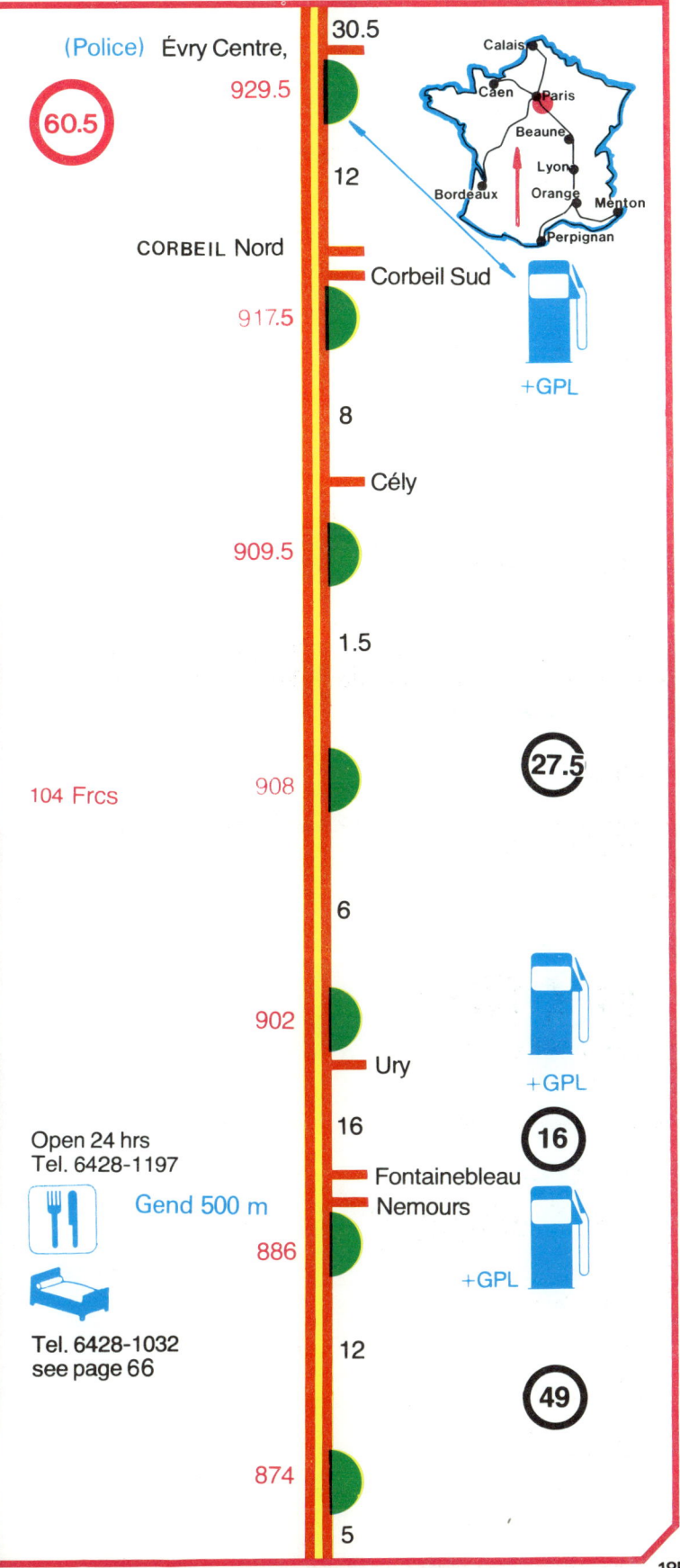

(60.5)

30.5

12

CORBEIL Nord

Corbeil Sud
917.5

8

Cély

909.5

1.5

(27.5)

908

104 Frcs

6

902

Ury

+GPL

Open 24 hrs
Tel. 6428-1197

16

Gend 500 m

Fontainebleau
Nemours

(16)

886

+GPL

Tel. 6428-1032
see page 66

12

(49)

874

5

185

Aire de **Roberval-Est**

WC

Open space type of area, tables and benches, very nice. SOS — by the entry.

Aire de **Barrière de péage**

WC ☎ ♿

Spacious.

Aire de **Vemars**

🚻 ☎ ♿ 🎁 ☕ 🍼

Just parking spaces provided.

Aire de **Villeron**

WC

Sited on the side of a hill, tables and benches. Grassy area. Nice.

Petrol Station Services

🚻 ☎ ♿ 🎁

Just parking spaces.

(54)

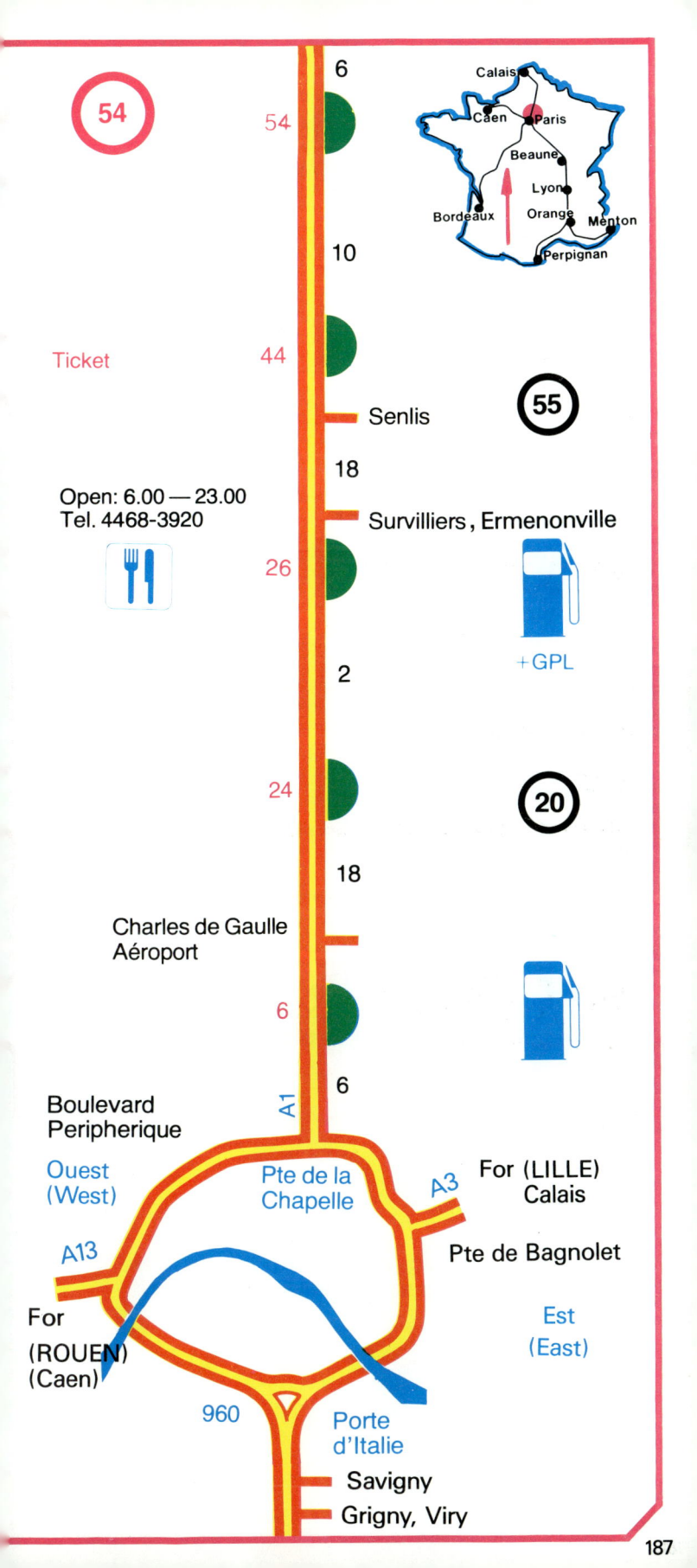

54

6

10

Ticket

44

Senlis

18

(55)

Open: 6.00 — 23.00
Tel. 4468-3920

Survilliers, Ermenonville

26

2

+GPL

24

(20)

18

Charles de Gaulle
Aéroport

6

6

Boulevard
Peripherique

A1

Ouest
(West)

Pte de la
Chapelle

A3

For (LILLE)
Calais

A13

Pte de Bagnolet

For
(ROUEN)
(Caen)

Est
(East)

960

Porte
d'Italie

Savigny

Grigny, Viry

187

Aire d' **Assevillers**

Just parking facilities, grassy area. There are; boutique, cafeteria, self-service.
SOS — at the entry.

Aire de **Fonches**

Open space type of area with no tables or benches. Nice.
SOS — at the side.

Aire de **Goyencourt-Est**

Small, tidy and very nice.
SOS — at the side.

Aire de **Tilloloy-Est**

Plenty of tables and benches among trees. Nice.
SOS — at the side

Aire de **Ressons-Est**

Just spaces for parking. Very pleasant. Bar buffet.
SOS — by the entry.

Aire de **Remy**

Generally open space type of area but there are lots of tables and benches among trees. Very nice. Lit.

Aire de **Chevrières**

Nice, in the stage of development.
SOS — 200 m from the exit.

(68) Tel. 2284-1276 see page 48

L'ARCHE
Tel. 2285-2608

(35)

7
122

13

Peronne
St.Quentin

109

5

104

(41)

12

Gend

Amiens, Roye

92

11

Open: 6.15 – 23.00
Tel. 4442-5576

81

Montidier,
Ressons

+GPL

13

68

8

(55)

60

Noyon, Clermont
Compiégne

6

189

Aire de la Grande Bucaille

WC

Tables and benches in the open and among trees, small. Recommended.
SOS — at the side.

Aire d' Angres

Spacious, grassy, no tables nor benches.
SOS — at the side.

Aire de la Cressonniere

WC

Open space type, nice
SOS — at the side.

Aire de Wancourt-Est

It is partly newly-built, open space type of area and very attractive.
SOS — at the side.

Aire de Croisilles

Few tables and benches.
SOS — at the side.

Aire de Beaulencourt

WC

As below.
SOS — at the side.

Aire de Feuilleres

WC

Small, grassy with tables and benches.
SOS — at the side.

88
Gend

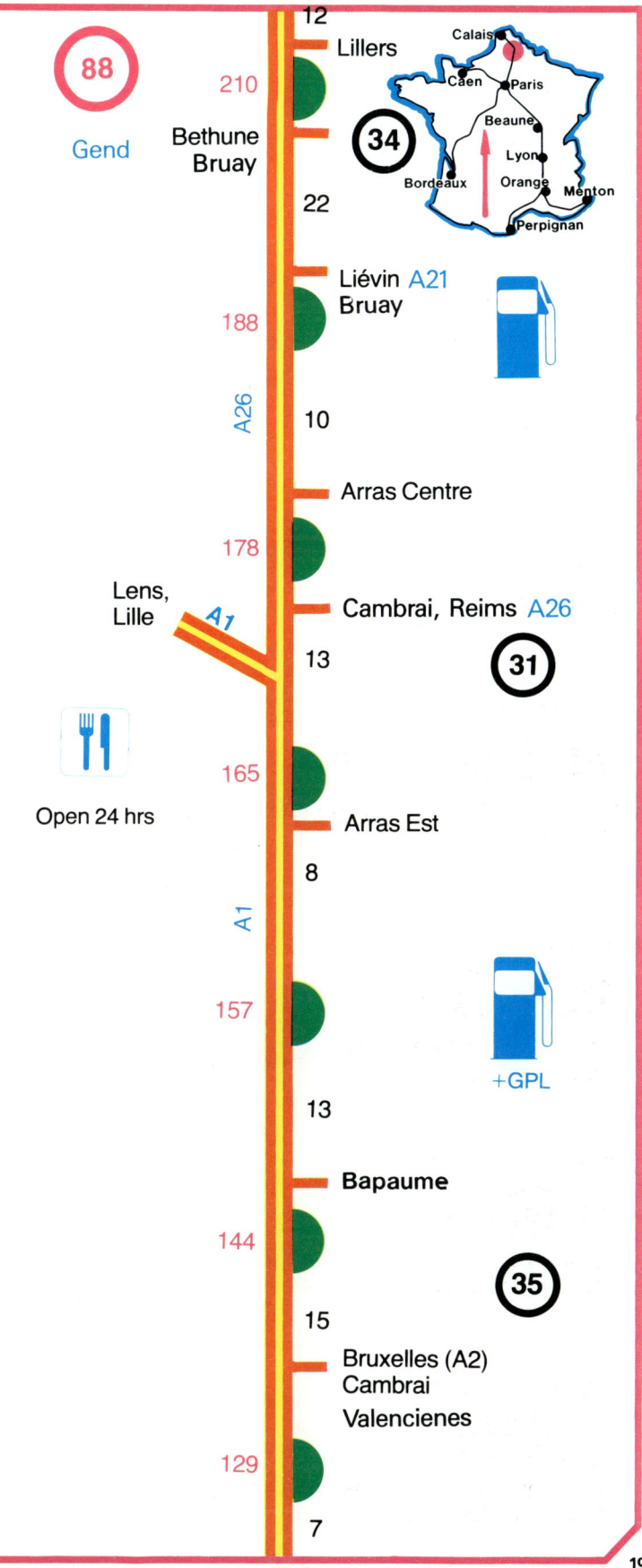

34

	12	Lillers
210		
		Bethune Bruay
	22	
		Liévin A21 Bruay
188		
A26	10	
		Arras Centre
178		
Lens, Lille A1		Cambrai, Reims A26
	13	

31

165		
		Arras Est
	8	
A1		
157		

+GPL

	13	
		Bapaume
144		
	15	

35

		Bruxelles (A2) Cambrai Valencienes
129		
	7	

Open 24 hrs

191

PORT

According to the French Police records, about 50% of all accidents involving British cars, takes place within 80 km of the Channel. Do not rush, take care.

Aire de **Barrière de péage**

|WC| ☎ | ♿ | ℹ |

Just parking spaces. Gendarmerie Station.

Aire de **Villefleur**

|WC| ♿ | ⛺ |

Open space type, small with tables and benches. Nice.
SOS — at the side.

Aire de **St. Hilaire Cottes**

| 🚻 | ☎ | ♿ |

Spacious and grassy.
SOS — at the side.

CALAIS

(73)

See page 67

17

Ardres

6

15

Gend

Frcs 69 Frcs

245

St. Omer, Dunkerque
Boulogne

14

231

9

222

12

(34)

193

Aire de Boisredon

| WC | 📞 | 🎠 |

Open type of Area, tables and benches. Swings, very pleasant. Recommended.
SOS — at the side of Area.

Aire de Saugon

| 🚻 | 📞 | ♿ | 🛒 | 🎠 |

Tables and benches, very spacious Area. Very nice indeed. Recommended.
SOS — at the side.

Aire de Cézac

| WC | 📞 | 🎠 |

Forested, lit at night. Suitable for picnicking, with tables and benches, spacious. Very nice. Recommended.
SOS — at the side.

Aire de Barrière de péage

| WC | 📞 | ♿ | 🎠 |

Small, few benches, no tables. Very pleasant Area.

Petrol Station Services

| 🚻 | 📞 | 🛒 |

Well stocked shop with full range of goods.
SOS — 200 m past the Station Area.

ALTEA HOTEL ★★★
Rue de la Reine Blanche
45160 — Olivet (Orléans)
Tel. 3866-4051, Telex: 760926

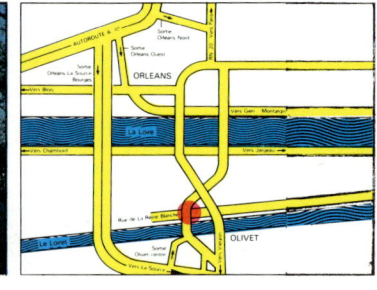

Mirambeau,

(63)

14 Royan
63

15 (48)

Gend 900 m

Montendre,
St.Ciers-s/G
48

+GPL

14

34

10

(43)

Ticket

24

Blaye
St.André-de-Cubzac Nord
19

5

+GPL

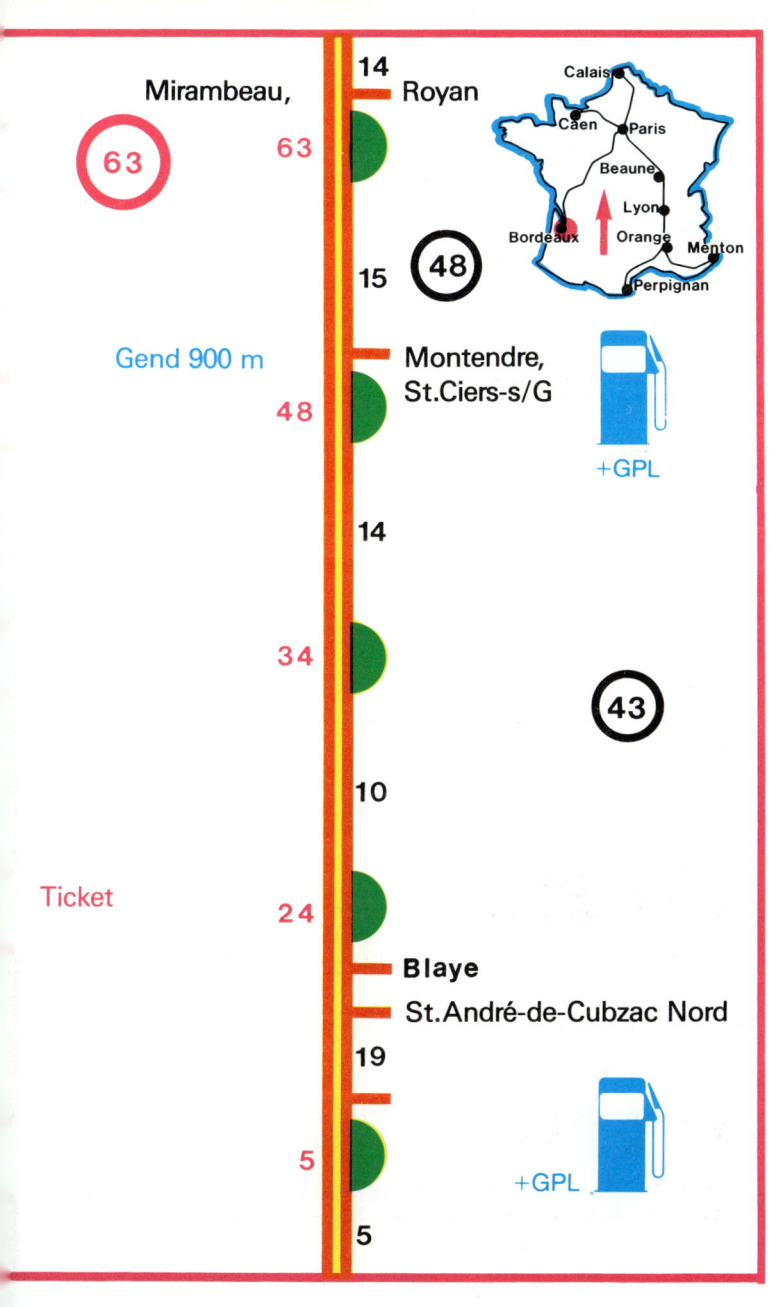

5

BORDEAUX

65 rooms • details page 14 • restaurant • bar • parking • situated 4 km from Orléans, in a country setting on the banks of the Loiret.

195

Aire de la Benâte

WC | ☎ | 🛣

Bigger than average in size. Tables and benches in the open and among trees, swings, rocking things. Lit at night. Very nice.
SOS — at the entry.

Aire de Fenioux

🚻 | ☎ | ♿ | 🗑 | 🛣

Open type of area, located just past the petrol station. Climbing frames, swings.
SOS — at the side.

Aire de Port d'Envaux

WC | ☎ | 🛣

Tables and benches in the open and among trees. Climbing things, swings, small and pretty. Recommended.
SOS — by the entry.

Aire de Chermignac

WC | ☎ | 🛣

Tables and benches, swings, small trees, bushes. Pretty and attractive enough to be recommended.
SOS — at the side.

Aire de Saint-Léger

🚻 | ☎ | ♿ | 🗑 | 💱 | 🛣 | ℹ

Tables and benches. Interconnected by a Tunnel. Very nice. Slides, swings, see-saws. Strongly recommended.
SOS — at the exit of Area.

Aire de St. Palais

WC | ☎ | ♿ | 🛣

Tables and benches in the open and among trees. Suitable for picnicking. Very pleasant. Recommended.
SOS — at the side.

Aire de St. Ciers

WC | ☎ | 🛣

Partly forested, partly open space. Tables and benches, very pretty. Recommended.
SOS — at the entry.

80

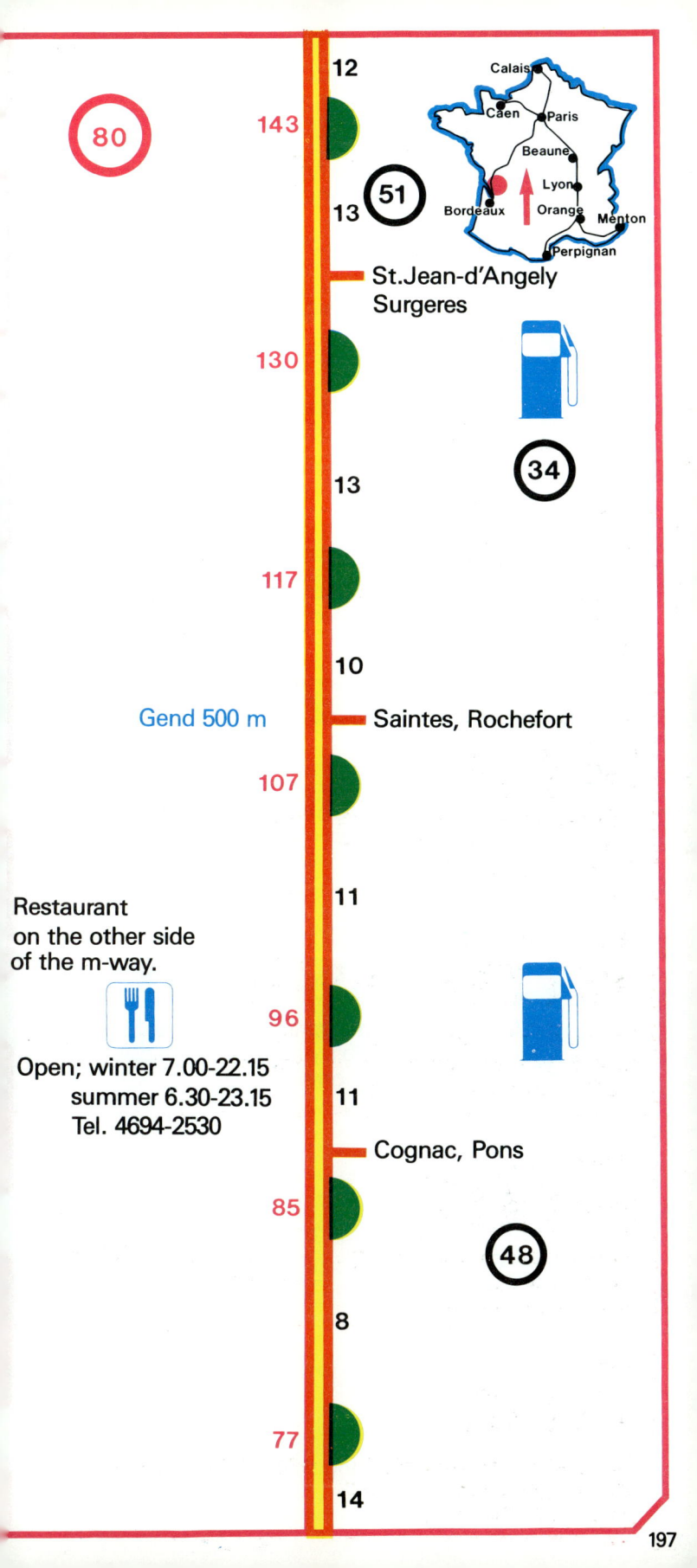

143
12

51
13

St. Jean-d'Angely
Surgeres

130

13

117

10

Gend 500 m

Saintes, Rochefort

107

11

Restaurant
on the other side
of the m-way.

🍴

Open; winter 7.00-22.15
summer 6.30-23.15
Tel. 4694-2530

96

11

Cognac, Pons

85

34

48

8

77

14

197

Aire de Coulombiers-Sud

[WC] [📞] [🚪]

Tables and benches. Open type of area, lit at night. Swings, lot of grass. Recommended.
SOS — at the side of Area.

Aire de Rouillé-Pamproux

[👫] [📞] [♿] [🗑]

Tables and benches in the open and in shady spots. Swings, lot of grass, good picnicking facilities.

Aire de Ste.Eanne-Sud

[WC] [📞] [🚪]

Tables and benches. Lit at night. Swings, climbing things, some shady spots. Recommended.
SOS — at the side.

Aire de Ste.Néomaye-Sud

[WC] [📞]

Tables and benches. Spacious pleasant and recommended.
SOS — close to the entry.

Aire des Les Ruralies

[👫] [📞] [♿] [🗑] [☕] [⛽] [💱] [🚪] [ℹ] [✉]

Tables and benches, shady spots. The other side of the m-way's services accessible by a tunnel (cars go). Very complex Area. Strongly recommended.

Aire de Gript-Sud

[WC] [📞] [🚪]

Small, open type, tables and benches. Slides, swings, climbing things. Nice.
SOS — at the exit.

Aire de Doeuil s/le Mignon

[WC] [📞] [🚪]

Tables and benches, climbing things. Shady spots.
SOS — at the exit

Poitier-Sud

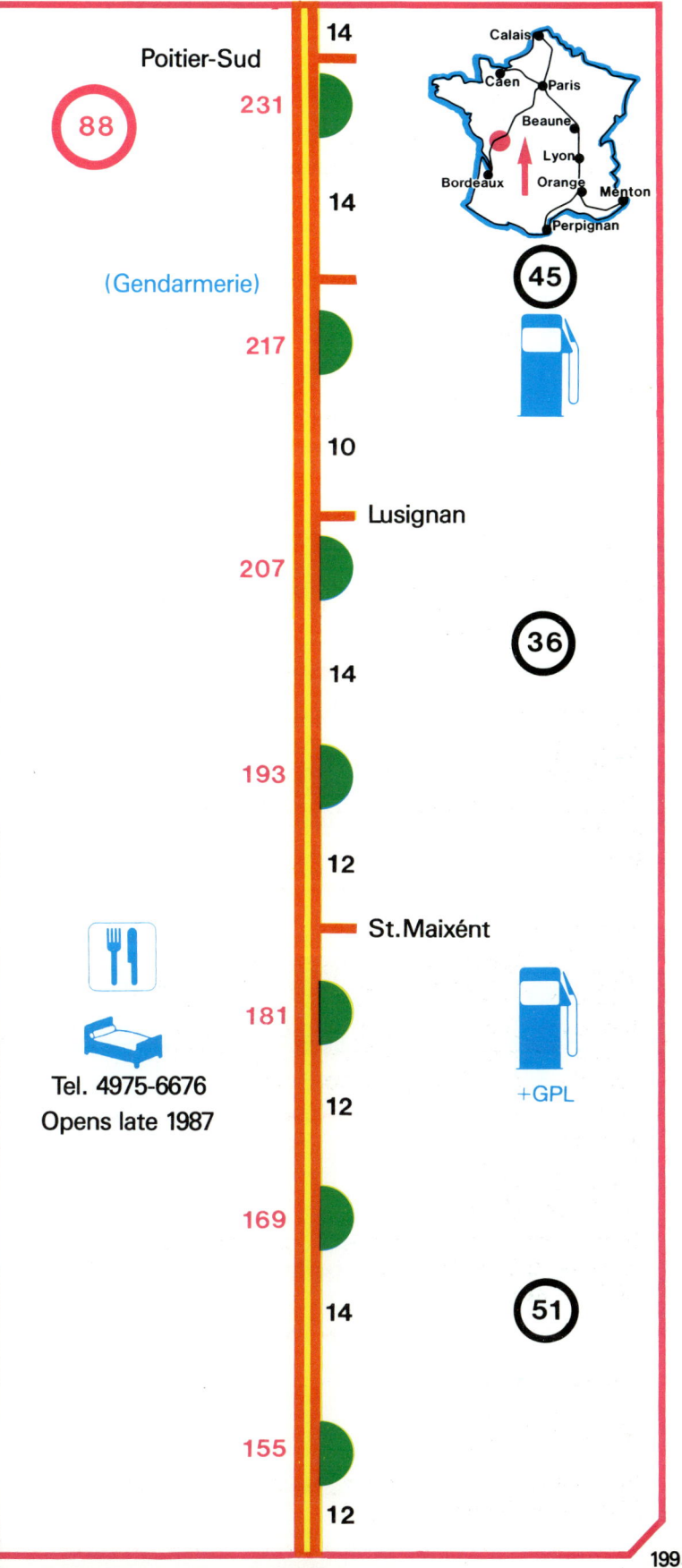

(88)

231

14

(Gendarmerie)

14

217

10

Lusignan

207

14

(45)

193

12

St. Maixént

36

181

Tel. 4975-6676
Opens late 1987

12

+GPL

169

14

51

155

12

199

Aire de **Barrière de péage**

`WC` `☎` `♿`

Few tables and benches

Aire de **Fontaine-Colette**

`🚻` `☎` `♿` `🗑`

Basically, just parking facilities.
SOS — at the side of Area.

Aire de **Nouâtre**

`WC`

Few tables and benches among trees.
SOS — at the side.

Aire de **Châtellerault Usseau**

`🚻` `☎` `♿` `🗑` `☕` `🍼` `💱` `🛍`

Extensive car parking facilities, bar, buffet, cafeteria, self-service.
SOS — at the side.

Aire des **Chagnac**

`WC`

Quite a few benches among trees, very small and pleasant.
SOS — at the side of Area.

Aire de **Poitiers Chince**

`🚻` `☎` `♿` `🗑`

Just parking facilities. Bar, buffet.
SOS — at the side of Area.

Aire des **Quatre Vents**

`WC` `☎`

Few tables and benches. Rather nice.
SOS — at the side of Area.

98
107 Frcs

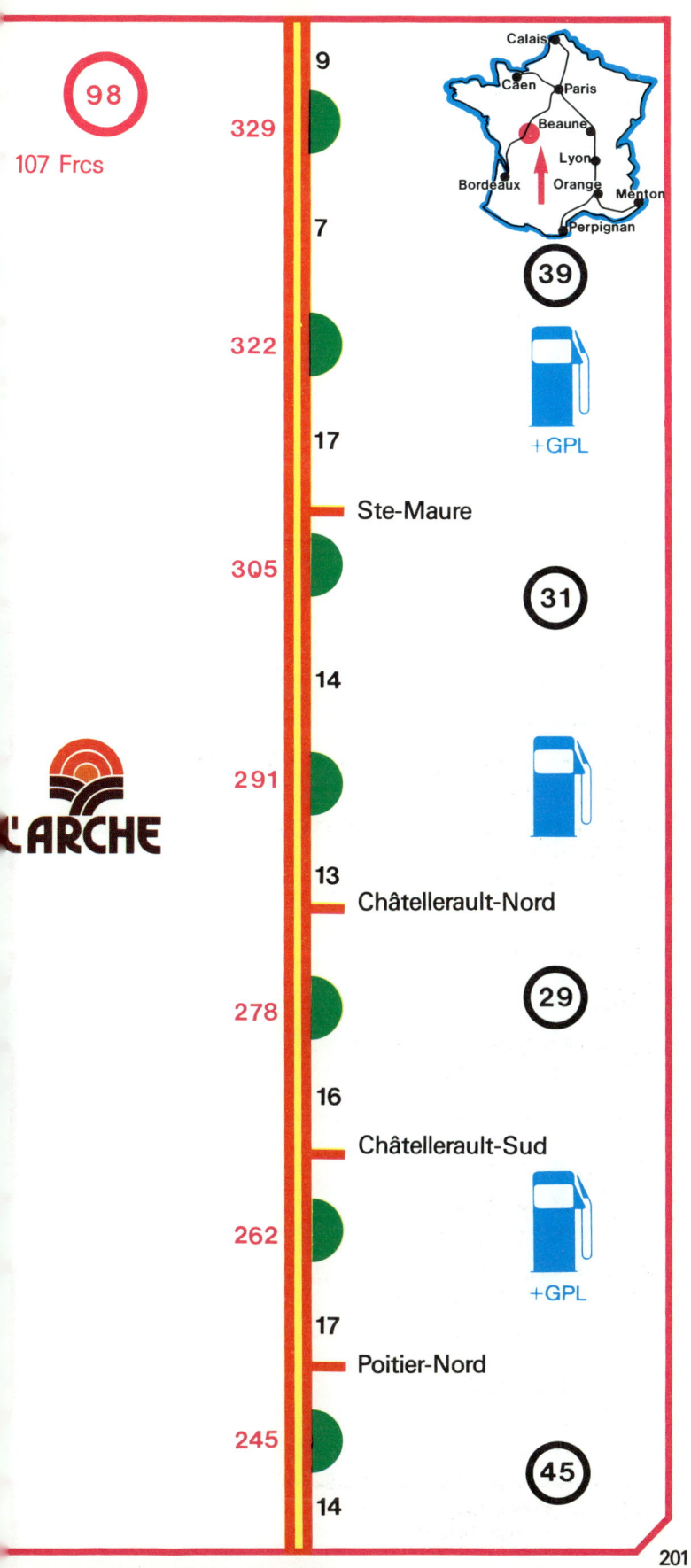

329
9

7
322

17
Ste-Maure
305

14

291

13
Châtellerault-Nord

278

16
Châtellerault-Sud

262

17
Poitier-Nord

245

14

39

+GPL

31

29

+GPL

45

L'ARCHE

Aire de **Brusolle**

WC

Tables and benches. Pretty.
SOS — close to the entry.

Aire de **Blois-Nemars**

Just parking spaces. Cafeteria with slides for children at the side.

Aire des **Bruères**

WC

Open type of Area with tables and benches. Very small and pleasant.
SOS — few hundred m before entry.

Aire de la **Picardière**

WC

A lot of tables and benches among trees, area located in a little forest.

Aire de **Barrière de péage**

WC

Just parking facilities.
SOS — 400 m past the Area.

Aire de **Tours-Val-de-Loire**

Footbridge to the other side of the motorway's Rest Area.
Bar, buffet, boutique.
SOS — at the side by the entry.

Aire du **Moulin Rouge**

WC

Forested, with tables and benches among trees. Lot of grassy area, yet a good hiding place during hot weather days. Interesting.
SOS — at the side of Area.

(101)

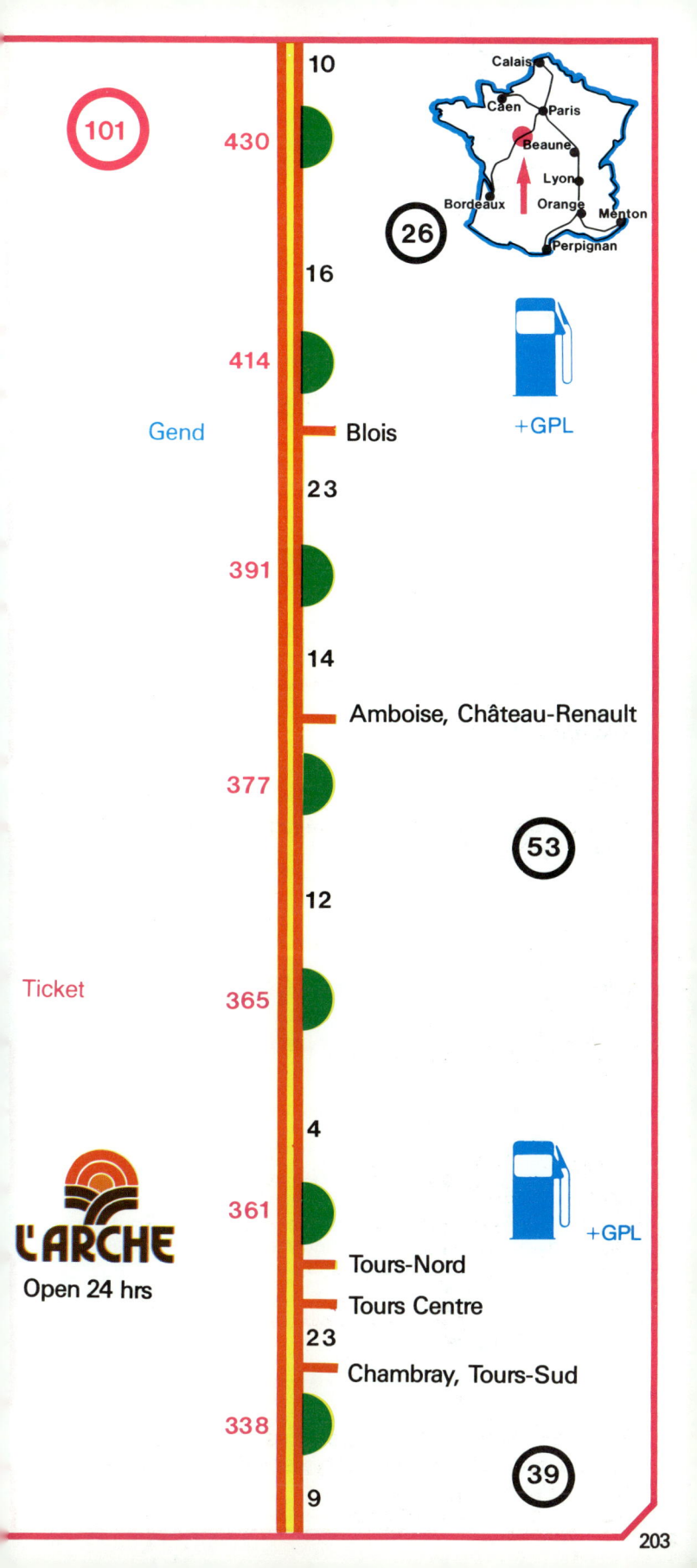

430

(26)

10

+GPL

16

414

Gend

Blois

23

391

14

Amboise, Château-Renault

377

(53)

12

Ticket

365

4

361

+GPL

L'ARCHE
Open 24 hrs

Tours-Nord
Tours Centre
23
Chambray, Tours-Sud

338

(39)

9

203

Aire de Barrière de péage

[WC] [📞] [♿]

Just parking spaces.

Aire des Marnieres

[WC]

Small with a few tables and benches.

Aire du Val-Neuveval

[🚻] [📞] [♿] [🎁] [☕]

Just parking facilities. Bar, buffet.

Aire de la Dauneuse

[WC]

Dense forest with tables and benches amongst.
SOS — at the side of Area.

Aire de Orléans-Gidy

[🚻] [📞] [♿] [🎁] [☕] [⛽] [💱] [🛍️] [✉️]

Cafeteria, grill, boutique. Just parking facilities.
SOS — at the side.

Aire de Chauvry

[WC]

Tables and benches, some shady spots. Very small and nice.
SOS — at the entry.

Aire de Beaugency-Messas

[🚻] [📞] [♿] [🎁]

Just parking facilities.
SOS — 300 m past the Area.

(103) 70 Frcs

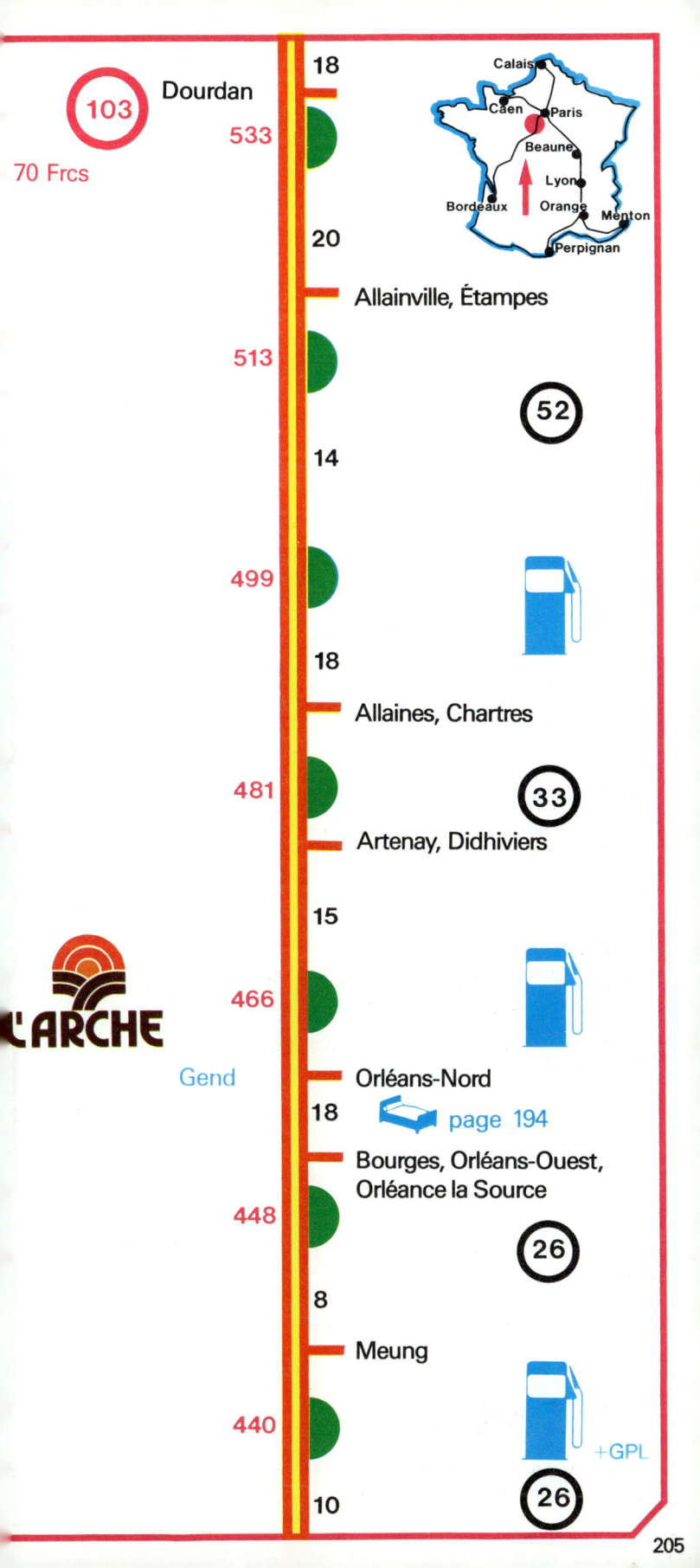

Dourdan
18
533
20
Allainville, Étampes
513
14
499
18
Allaines, Chartres
481
Artenay, Didhiviers
15
466
Gend
Orléans-Nord
page 194
18
Bourges, Orléans-Ouest, Orléance la Source
448
8
Meung
440
10

(52)
(33)
(26)
(26) +GPL

L'ARCHE

Approaching the Boulevard Periphérique from the direction of the Autoroute A6, (which is applicable to both; coming from Bordeaux and from the Riviera) and depending on your destination, you continue your journey using the following information accordingly;-

At the first opportunity you select "Paris — Sud" and follow "Paris" all the way.

Next, you have a choice; "Paris — Ouest" and "Paris — Est". In case you missed it, there will be another choice of the same, but this time the alternatives are more specific; "Paris Ouest, Pte. Orléans" and "Paris — Est, Pte. d'Italie". The same option will be offered to you once again soon after that, before you enter the Boulevard round Paris. The above information and the diagrammatically shown Boulevard on the next page are complementary and together will help you through; nicely.

And finally; for CAEN you follow the sign "ROUEN", and for CALAIS you follow the sign "LILLE" while on the Boulevard Periphérique.

Needless to say that for Caen you should always select "Paris-Ouest" to begin with (much shorter).

Aire de Limours Bris s/s Forges

Just parking spaces. Buffet, bar.
SOS — at the side.

47

To continue your journey, turn over to page;-

208 — for Caen,
187 — for Calais

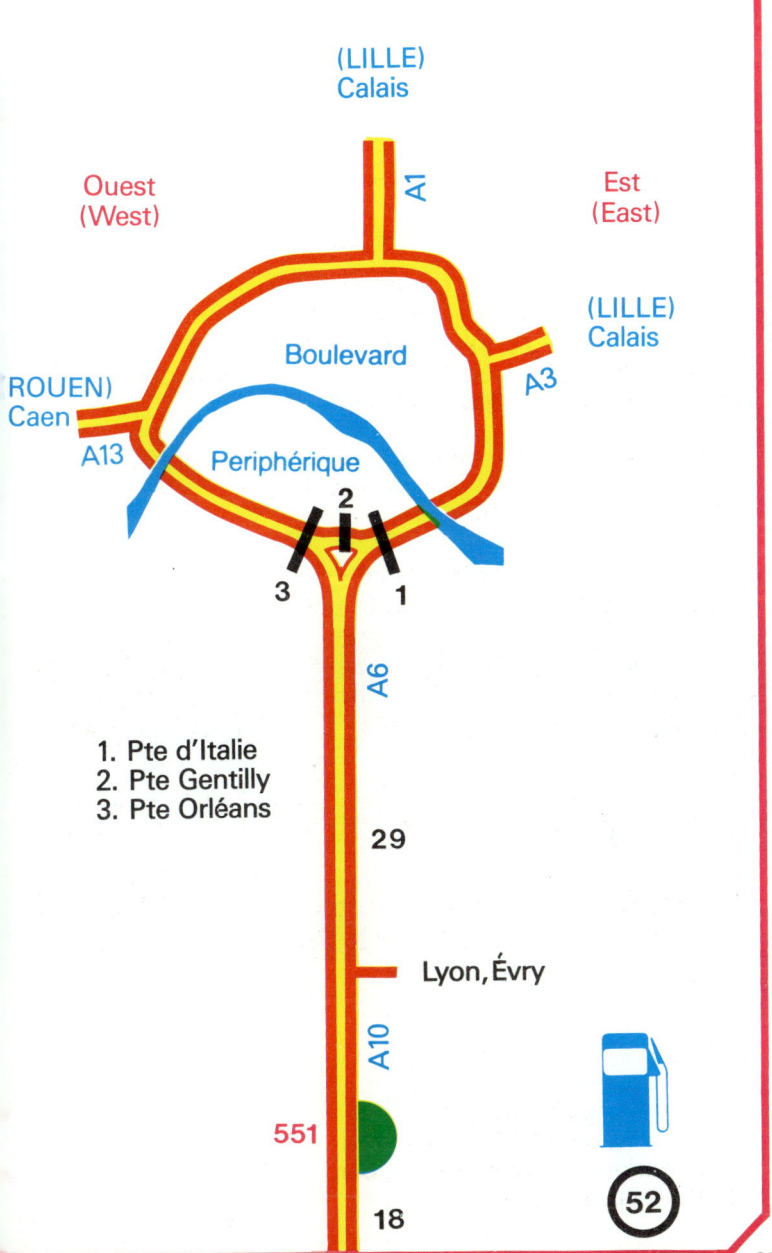

Ouest (West) — **Est (East)**

(LILLE) Calais
A1

Boulevard

(LILLE) Calais
A3

ROUEN) Caen
A13

Periphérique

2
3   1

1. Pte d'Italie
2. Pte Gentilly
3. Pte Orléans

A6

29

Lyon, Évry

A10

551

18

52

207

NO NAME

No facilities.

Few parking spaces.
SOS — close to the entry.

NO NAME

WC — very basic

Very small and limited. Few parking spaces.
SOS — close to the exit.

Aire de Morainvilliers

Interconnected with the other side of the m-way service area by a footbridge.
SOS — located close to the entry.

ALTEA VAL-DE-REUIL * * *
Lieu — dit "Les Clouets" (Rouen)
Tel. 3259-0909, Telex: 180540

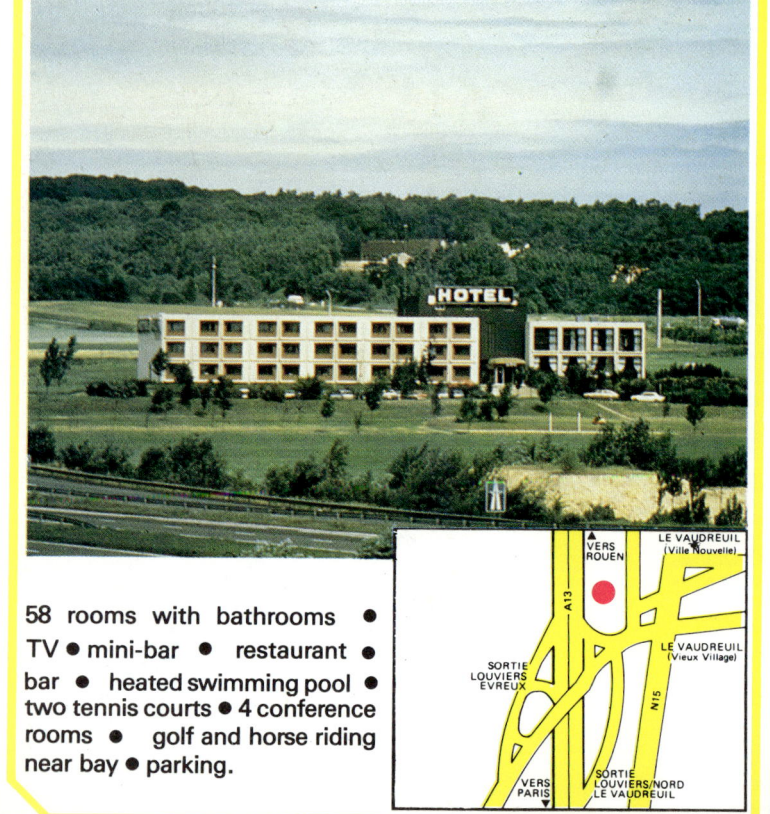

58 rooms with bathrooms • TV • mini-bar • restaurant • bar • heated swimming pool • two tennis courts • 4 conference rooms • golf and horse riding near bay • parking.

Mantes-Est

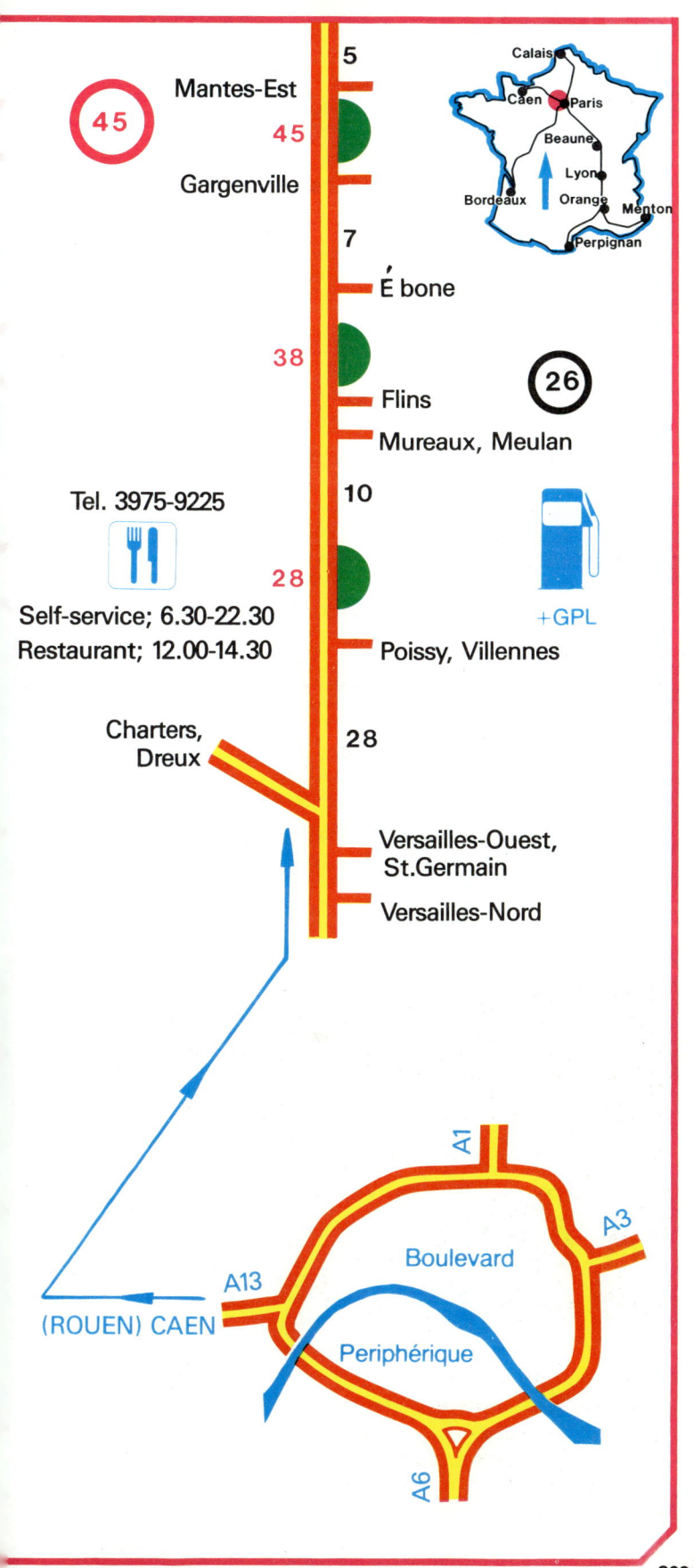

(45)

5
45
Gargenville

7
É bone

38
Flins
Mureaux, Meulan

Tel. 3975-9225
🍴
Self-service; 6.30-22.30
Restaurant; 12.00-14.30

10
28
Poissy, Villennes

Charters, Dreux

28
Versailles-Ouest, St.Germain
Versailles-Nord

(26)

⛽ +GPL

A1 A3
Boulevard
A13
(ROUEN) CAEN
Périphérique
A6

Aire de Vironvay

Interconnected with the other side of the Motorway's Services. Cafeteria, self-service.
SOS — close to the entry.

Aire de Barrière de péage

Just parking spaces. Simple.

Aire de Bauchene

Small, forested with few tables and benches.
SOS — by the entry.

Aire Nord de Douains

Few benches among trees. Very small, rather pleasant.
SOS — at the side of Area.

Aire Nord de la Villeneuve en Chevrie.

Open space, grassy, some trees. Tables and benches. Small, best so far.
SOS — at the side of Area.

Aire de Rosny/Seine

SOS — at the side of the area.

Aire de Barrière de péage

Just parking facilities.

(51)

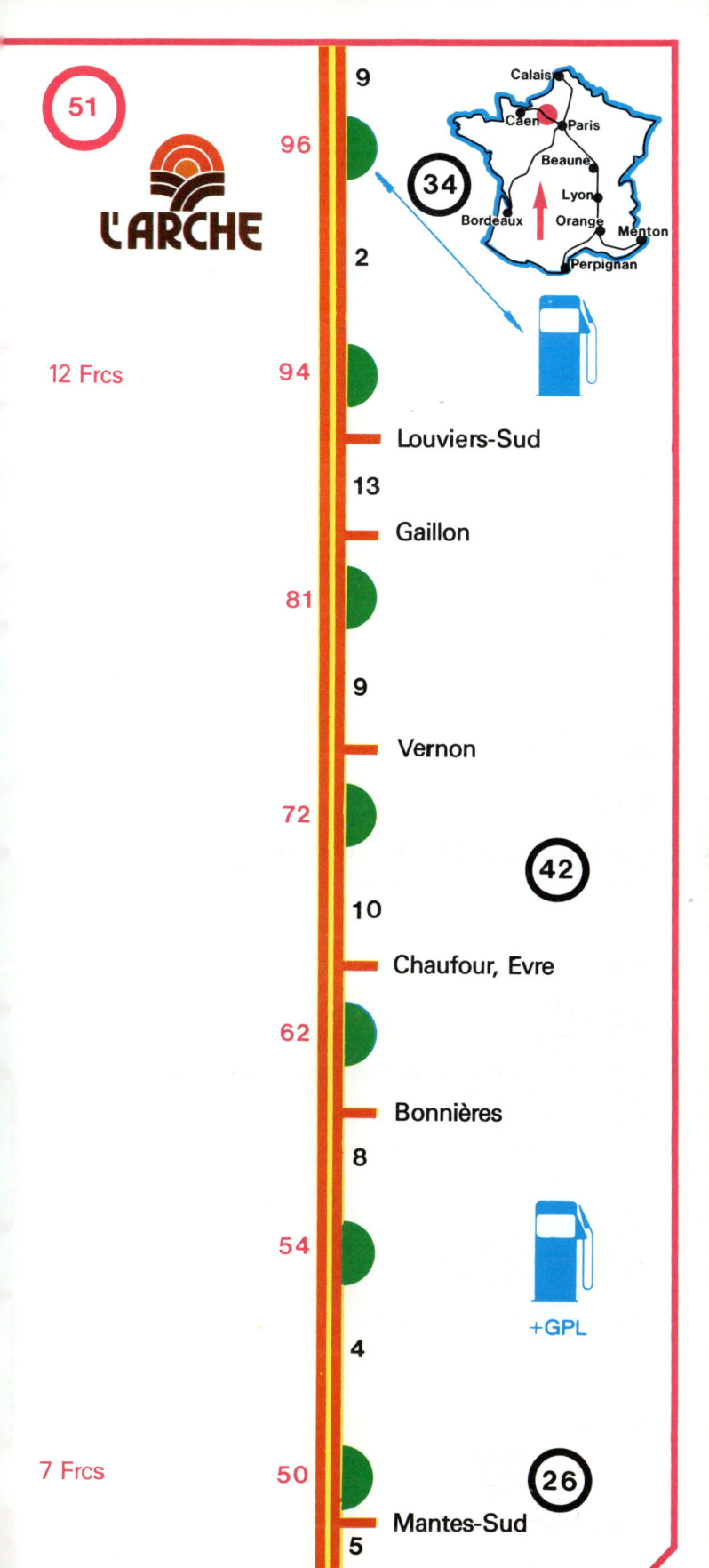

L'ARCHE

12 Frcs

96
9

2

94

(34)

Louviers-Sud
13
Gaillon

81

9

Vernon

72

(42)

10

Chaufour, Evre

62

Bonnières
8

54

4

7 Frcs

50

(26)

Mantes-Sud
5

+GPL

211

Aire d' **Anne Bault**

| WC | 🚪 |

Open type space, grassy, some trees. Tables and benches. Small, isolated from the Motorway by a wall of trees. Very pleasant.
SOS — 100 m from the entry.

Aire Nord de **Beuzeville**

| 🚻 | 📞 | ♿ | 🎁 |

Exstensive parking facilities, grassy. Some trees, tables and benches, spacious and attractive.
SOS — at the side.

Aire de **Barrière de péage**

| 📞 | ♿ |

Just parking spaces.

Aire de **Josapha**

| WC | 🚪 |

Open space type of area. Few tables and benches. Very pleasant.
SOS — 200 m from the entry.

Aire de **Bosgouet**

| 🚻 | 📞 | ♿ | 🎁 | ☕ | ⛽ | 💱 | 🚪 |

Cafeteria, snack bar. Interconnected with the other side Rest Area.
SOS — located close to the entry of the Rest Area.

Aire Nord de **Robert-le-Diable**

| WC |

Open space type of area, very small.
SOS — located by the exit.

Aire de **Bord**

| WC |

Small, grassy, tables and benches. Nice.
SOS — at the side of Area.

(99)

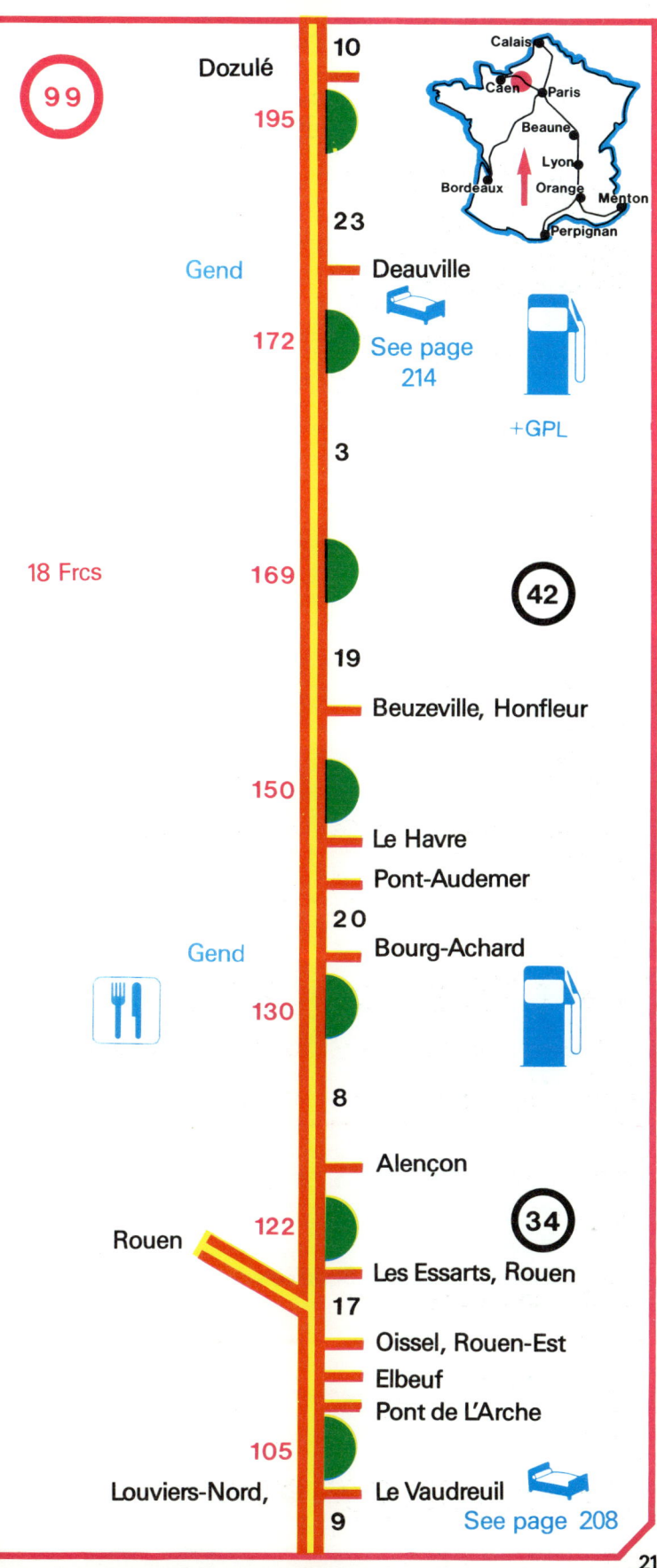

Dozulé
195
10

23
Gend
Deauville
172
🛏 See page 214

⛽ +GPL

3

18 Frcs
169
(42)

19
Beuzeville, Honfleur

150
Le Havre
Pont-Audemer

20
Gend
Bourg-Achard
🍴
130
⛽

8

Alençon
122
(34)
Rouen
Les Essarts, Rouen

17
Oissel, Rouen-Est
Elbeuf
Pont de L'Arche

105
Louviers-Nord,
Le Vaudreuil
🛏 See page 208
9

213

ALTEA PORT — DEAUVILLE ★★★

Boulevard Cornuche
14800 — Deauville
Tel.3188-6262, Telex:170364

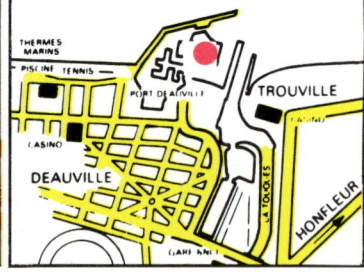

70 rooms ● bathroom ● telephone ● TV ● mini-bar ● numerous sport facilities ● close to the beach.

Aire Nord de **Kiberville**

Few tables and benches. Spacious.
SOS — at the side.

Aire de **Barrière de péage**

Just sort of a bay, no parking facilities.

HOTEL METROPOLE ★★

16 Place de la Gare
14300 — Caen
Tel. 3182-2676, Telex: 170165

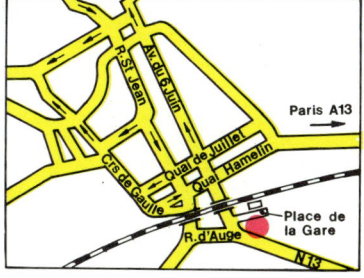

71 rooms with bathrooms or shower, WC ● colour TV on request ● lift ● direct line telephone ● television room ● parking facilities ● restaurants nearby.

According to the French Police records, about 50% of all accidents involving British cars, takes place within 80 km of the Channel. Do not rush, take care.

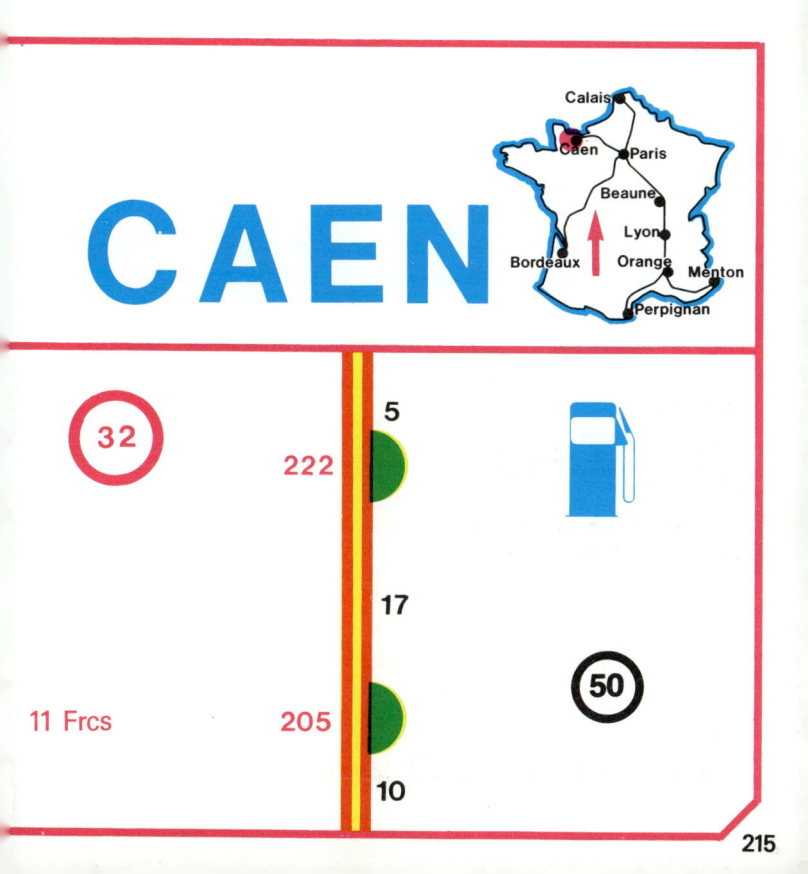

CAEN

32

222

5

17

205

10

11 Frcs

50

215

Errata

Please note the following changes to the printed text.

page

19 Opposite Aire de **Nemours**, *add*
    Altea Hotel
    See page 66

22 Item 3, reference 'see page 9' *change to*
    See facing page

25 4th paragraph, 1st line 'on page 6' *change to*
    on page 7

    5th paragraph, last line 'renders these' *change to*
    resolves those

34 Under heading **Speed limits**
    add above first column Normal driving conditions
    and above second column Wet weather

59 Last paragraph, 2nd line, 'mail' *change to*
    male